Florida Statutory Interpretation

Florida Statutory Interpretation

Christopher J. Roederer
Professor of Law
Florida Coastal School of Law

Vandeplas Publishing

United States of America

Florida Statutory Interpretation

Roederer, Christopher J.

Published by:

Vandeplas Publishing - December 2010

801 International Parkway, 5th Floor
Lake Mary, FL. 32746
USA

www.vandeplaspublishing.com

ISBN: 978-1-60042-127-3

For
Ericka, Sebastian and Oliver

Preface

Florida Statutory Interpretation is a text designed for either a short stand alone course on Florida statutory interpretation or as a supplement for those wishing to integrate Florida specific materials into a course on statutory interpretation or on legislation more generally. It follows the conventional treatment of statutory interpretation found in standard textbooks on the subject.

This book captures the doctrine on Florida statutory interpretation through recent leading cases and includes introductory materials, notes and questions in order to further explain and probe the doctrinal issues.

The cases in this book are edited, but the edits are moderate compared to many textbooks. Many of the footnotes in the cases have been deleted. These deletions have not been indicated. Other edits to the text are indicated by: ellipses (...) in the case of deletions and bracketed text ([xxx]), in the case of additions.

Acknowledgments

This book would not be possible if not for the summer research grants provided by Florida Coastal School of Law and the dedicated work of several research students, including: Heather Gurglio, Jennifer Boston, Rachel Vulpitta, and Kathryn Davis and my faculty assistants, Patricia Maroney and Christie Smith.

Table of Contents

INTRODUCTION

Florida Statutory Interpretation is concerned with the techniques and tools used to interpret legislation in the state of Florida. Ideally there would be no need for a whole course on how to interpret legislation. Rather, all we would need is command of the English language. If we can all read English then shouldn't we all be able to agree on what a particular piece of legislation says and means? If this were true, there would be little need for lawyers. Unfortunately, there is a great need for lawyers and that need often drives, or gives birth to, inventive interpretations. Statutory interpretation is as much, if not more, about convincing others of an interpretation as it is about figuring out the meaning of a statute. While there are many situations when most everyone agrees on what a statute says and what it means, no-one likes to hear that a given reading or interpretation means that she or he has broken the law (be it civil or criminal), or failed to meet a legal standard that they needed to meet in order to get something they want (e.g. execute a will, form a corporation, or obtain a green card).

Thus, disputes over the meaning of legislation rarely start with an abstract reading of the text, but rather begin with one or more people being unhappy with the way that a particular interpretation and application impacts their lives. Criminal defendants do not like interpretations that make it more likely that they will be found guilty of one or more crimes and it is probably safe to say that prosecutors do not like interpretations that are more likely to lead to acquittals. Corporations often favor interpretations of regulatory statutes that give them more freedom to do what they wish, while corporate counsel has a duty to warn them of the potential pitfalls of ambiguous legislation. Whether statutes are ambiguous on their own, or whether the ambiguity is created by those who favor one interpretive result over another, the fact that there is enough room for a dispute to arise, means that the words do not have an inexorable, fixed and permanent meaning.

Well before America's founding, lawyers and judges began to grapple with this problem.[1] The attempted solution was to create a set of maxims or rules, often called canons of construction, in order to arrive at a suitably well justified meaning for legislative text. Over the years, countless authors have proposed ways of settling the meaning of legislative text. While some judges claim that they would be pleased if there was a settled approach to statutory interpretation (something like a clear rule to govern how to use the other rules, maxims or canons -- a recipe of sorts),[2] most lawyers have little to gain from a fixed, or wooden approach to statutory interpretation.[3]

---

[1] See, e.g. the decision of Lord Coke in Heydon's Case, 3 Co. Rep. 7a, 76 Eng. Rep. 637 [King's Bench 1584]) (discussing the mischief rule).

[2] Eg. Judge Peter D. Webster of the Florida First District Court of Appeal in Peter D. Webster, Sylvia H. Walbolt, and Christine R. Davis, Statutory Construction in Florida: In Search of a Principled Approach, 9 FLA. COASTAL L. REV. 435, 523 (2008), whose recipe is:

> "First, always start with the words. Second, assume a reasonable legislature. Third, search for the legislative purpose. Fourth, shun substantive canons of statutory construction. Fifth, respect the legislature's coequal status."

[3] Those who favor a settled approach often claim that this leads to efficiency, predictability, respect for the separation of powers and rule of law. See, e.g. Webster supra note 2 at 514-515. See ANTONIN SCALIA, A MATTER OF INTERPRETATION: FEDERAL COURTS AND THE LAW (1997).

These maxims or canons are an important set of tools, and their use in combination with the particular facts of the case, the context, and the legislation in question, are what separate the lawyer as a creative chef, from the lawyer who can follow a simple recipe. The "following a recipe" approach does not always work very well in the context of statutory interpretation, in part, because the ingredients, their strength, and proportions, are often beyond the lawyer's control. Sometimes a client's or party's facts are very strong, and sometimes very weak; sometimes they fall within the clear core meaning of a statute's provisions and sometimes they are closer to the edge, or what is sometimes called the penumbra or shadow of a statute's meaning. Sometimes they are members of a sympathetic class and sometimes they are associated with an unsympathetic class. Sometimes the application of given canons of construction result in very persuasive arguments and sometimes they do not. Sometimes the canons all work to support the same result but sometimes they outright conflict and often they are in tension. Many judges have their own favored recipe for combining these elements, but they too will often change their recipe when one element is just too overpowering to stomach, or when a judge needs to persuade a majority of the court to join her or his opinion.[4] Often the various judges on the bench have different approaches to statutory interpretation, and you will need to find a way to satisfy at least a majority of them with the arguments you dish up for them.

Although there is no settled single correct formula or recipe in Florida for interpreting or for persuading others of the correct meaning of statutes, a few things are settled, at least in form if not substance. In the state of Florida, it is well settled that "legislative intent" is the so called "polestar" of statutory interpretation.[5] It is, however, a "polestar" that provides little to no guidance. The idea behind a polestar, e.g. the northern star, is that it is fixed in the sky and thus it can be used for navigation, to guide us to where we need to go. However, the practice in Florida is not to look to the "polestar" of legislative intent in order to navigate the meaning of statutory text. Rather, the general rule is that one is to look to the text, or in some cases, to the various maxims or tools of interpretation, in order to tell us what the legislature intended.

There are several reasons for this. The first reason is that while the concept of legislative intent sounds attractive as a guiding principle, it is, in fact, a myth. There really is no such thing as the intent of the legislature. It is not possible to know what the legislature as a whole intended when they enacted a piece of legislation. What any

---

[4] See, e.g. Justice Scalia's use of legislative history in FCC v. Fox Television Stations, Inc., 129 S. Ct. 1800, 1815 (2009), reversing 489 F.3d 444 (2d Cir. 2007). It is more common for Justice Scalia to concur in the result of the majority while arguing that it was improper for them to rely on legislative history. See, e.g. Carr v. U.S. 560 U. S., 130 S. Ct. 2229, 2242 (2010) ("I join the Court's opinion except for Part III–C. I do not join that part because only the text Congress voted on, and not unapproved statements made or comments written during its drafting and enactment process, is an authoritative indicator of the law.") See also Samantar v. Yousuf 560 U. S., 130 S. Ct. 2278, 2293 (2010) ("The Court's introduction of legislative history serves no purpose except needlessly to inject into the opinion a mode of analysis that not all of the Justices consider valid. And it does so, to boot, in a fashion that does not isolate the superfluous legislative history in a section that those of us who disagree categorically with its use, or at least disagree with its superfluous use, can decline to join. I therefore do not join the opinion, and concur only in the result.")

[5] McLean v. State, 934 So. 2d 1248, 1258 (Fla. 2006); Rivera v. Torfino Enter., Inc., 914 So. 2d 1087, 1088 (Fla. Dist. Ct. App. 4th Dist. 2005); Bruner v. GC-GW, Inc., 880 So. 2d 1244, 1246 (Fla. Dist. Ct. App. 1st Dist. 2004); Bryan v. State, 865 So. 2d 677, 679 (Fla. Dist. Ct. App. 4th Dist. 2004).

individual legislator intended may, in part, be gleamed from the legislative debates, but even this can be very misleading, given that legislators sometimes put things into the record for strategic purposes, and often a legislator's true intent is left a mystery. Even if we knew what any given legislator intended, it is very unlikely that all, or even a majority of the legislators, intended the same thing. In many cases, the majority of legislators did not even read the entire bill before voting it into law, but relied on colleagues or committee reports.

What the legislature intended when it passed a law is also different from the various purposes that a given law may serve. Although courts are not always careful to distinguish intent from purpose, it is important to try to keep these ideas separate. Legislation can serve many purposes, some of which may have been intended and some not. There are perpetual debates over whether it is more important and legitimate to interpret legislation in light of its spirit or purposes, in light of what the particular drafters intended, or simply in light of the plain and ordinary meaning of the text as written. It may, however, be impossible to discern a plain or ordinary meaning without attributing, implicitly or explicitly a purpose or set of purposes for a given provision.[6]

So why do we even talk about legislative intent, much less refer to it as a "polestar"? It is likely due to the fact that by pretending that the court's guidance comes from what the legislature intended, the court appears to act with restraint and to respect the separation of powers between it and the legislative branch. It is merely applying the law as the legislature "intended" it. Thus, legislative intent is a polestar, not in the sense that it guides the practice of interpretation, but in the sense that it justifies the practice.

The real polestar, in most cases, is the text, or some version of what is called the "plain meaning" of the statute. In many cases it is easier to treat the text as a fixed polestar for determining what the legislature intended than the other way around. The idea is that the legislature is presumed to have expressed its intent through the use of words put into the statute.[7]

If the "plain meaning" of statutes settled the question, there would be little need for the rather long list of what are generally referred to as maxims, canons or tools for construing statutes. One person's plain meaning is often not another's. Meaning is often rendered plain or fixed in relation to the context the text is perceived to come from, or the context the text is currently within, and the purpose or purposes that one imagines the text to serve. Again, for purposes of legitimacy, some prefer to fix the meaning of a text by confining it to the context in which it was originally adopted and as serving the purposes that it would appear to have served at the time of original adoption.[8] As can be imagined, this may lead to a very different plain meaning than a meaning derived by

---

[6] It is questionable whether one can understand any given part without some understanding of the whole that the part fits into. A statutory term fits into a provision, which fits into a section, which fits into a piece of legislation adopted against the backdrop of the existing code and common law. All of this is part of a human endeavor to change, and hopefully improve, some aspect of the world in which we live, by making some things easier, or harder to achieve.

[7] Atlantis at Perdido Ass'n, Inc. v. Warner, 932 So. 2d 1206, 1213 (Fla. Dist. Ct. App. 1st Dist. 2006); State, Dep't of Revenue v. Lockheed Martin Corp., 905 So. 2d 1017, 1020 (Fla. Dist. Ct. App. 1st Dist. 2005).

[8] See, e.g., State v. City of Jacksonville, 50 So. 2d 532 (Fla. 1951).

reading the text in light of its current context and in light of a range of purposes the text might serve today.[9]

These two broad approaches to "the plain meaning" (or just, plain "meaning") are sometimes referred to originalism and non-originalism or purposivist. While originalists tend to ground the justification for their approach in what the legislator originally intended, the non-originalists tend to ground their justification in the idea that that the overall purpose of legislation is to serve human needs, and thus it should be interpreted flexibly in order to keep up with changing contexts and needs. Originalists see this as illegitimate judicial activism or legislating. Of course, for the originalist to be correct using its own reasoning, one would need to show that the original legislators intended to have their text interpreted in light of the context in which it was written, only, and as serving the purpose or purposes that they had intended only. This is anything but clear. Legislators are often open to the idea that certain types of legislation be interpreted in light of changing circumstances and needs.[10]

Statutes sometimes provide their own rules for construction, and in such cases a "plain" reading of the enacted rule should be applied for the construction of the statute in question.[11]

For the most part, the canons of construction or tools for interpretation are judge made. Although some of the maxims have solidified into something akin to legal rules, once one leaves the "safe" confines of "plain meaning,"[12] the courts are not confined to a single tool or limited set of tools for construction, but can use the whole array of interpretive tools.[13] As the cases throughout this book will demonstrate, the various tools explored below will often pull in different directions. The most persuasive argument for any given interpretation is one that not only proceeds from a plain meaning reading of the text, but one that is also consistent with, and supported by, a range of interpretive tools.

---

[9] As the court in State v. Jacksonville Terminal Co., 90 Fla. 721, 744, 106 So. 576, 584 (1925), stated, "the rules of the common law, as well as the statutes, are designed for application to new conditions and circumstances, as they may be developed by enlightened commercial and business intercourse, that are within the scope and remedial intent of existing provisions and principles of law. The provisions and principles of law are intended to be vitalized by practical utility, subject to organic limitations."

[10] Florida courts, in fact presume that this is what the Legislature intends with regards to remedial statutes. The Florida Supreme Court has held that where a statute is remedial in nature, it should be liberally construed to "preserve and promote access to the remedy intended by the Legislature." Joshua v. City of Gainesville, 768 So. 2d 432, 435 (Fla. 2000) (holding that chapter 760, Florida Statutes, relating to employment discrimination, is remedial and requires a liberal construction to preserve and promote access to the remedy intended by Legislature). Note that in these cases, when the Court is talking about what the legislature "intended," it is really talking about the remedial purpose of the statute.

[11] State v. Burr, 79 Fla. 290, 332; 84 So. 61, 74 (1920).

[12] The word "safe" is put in quotes because often advocates and judges will argue that their interpretations are faithful to the plain meaning of the text as a way of silencing or closing the debate over the text's meaning. It is not uncommon for opposing counsel or the dissent to point to other "equally" plain meanings. Note further that there are many cases in which Florida Courts have held that judges must give effect to the purpose of the law, in addition to, and sometimes, in favor of, the plain meaning. See, e.g. Cason v. Florida Dep't of Mgmt. Servs., 944 So. 2d 306 (Fla. 2006) below.

[13] See State v. Webb, 398 So. 2d 820 (Fla. 1981); Wakulla County v. Davis, 395 So. 2d 540 (Fla. 1981); State, Dep't of Revenue v. Kemper Investors Life Ins. Co., 660 So. 2d 1124 (Fla. Dist. Ct. App. 1st Dist. 1995)

Although the rule is that the tools of statutory interpretation should not be used to create doubt or ambiguity as to the meaning of a statute,[14] as a practical matter, people, judges included, will be more likely to have doubts or see ambiguity if the various tools point towards doubt or ambiguity. The law reports are full of split decision cases on the question of whether a piece of legislation is clear or ambiguous.[15]

Further, the "polestar" of legislative intent may at times influence a decision as to whether a statute is ambiguous. Although it is relatively well settled that the courts do not look to the other tools of statutory construction if the statute is unambiguous,[16] if those tools bring into doubt the "legislature's intent" the legitimizing polestar is undermined.[17] This may incline a judge to more closely scrutinize the text for ambiguity.[18]

It should also be noted that the Florida courts sometimes state the rule in practical terms and at other times as an obligatory rule. In other words, sometimes the rule is articulated as "there is no need to resort to statutory construction"[19] or "the court has no further reason to apply the rules of statutory construction"[20] as opposed to holding that the court is forbidden or prohibited from turning to these rules, or tools. Some justices hold the view that the court may look to what are called the "intrinsic textual tools" in order to arrive at the plain meaning of statute, but that if these produce a clear plain meaning then other tools of construction should not be pursued.[21]

---

[14] Fajardo v. State, 805 So. 2d 961, 964 (Fla. Dist. Ct. App. 2d Dist. 2001)

[15] Often the consequences of a given interpretation give rise to doubt or ambiguity for any given party. We are more likely to question the meaning of something if we do not like the result.

[16] Miller v. Anheuser Busch, Inc., 591 F. Supp. 2d 1377, 1383 (S.D. Fla. 2008); City of Parker v. State, 992 So. 2d 171, 176 (Fla. 2008); Kasischke v. State, 991 So. 2d 803, 807 (Fla. 2008); Blanton v. City of Pinellas Park, 887 So. 2d 1224 (Fla. 2004); State v. Menuto, 912 So. 2d 603 (Fla. Dist. Ct. App. 2d Dist. 2005), review denied, 935 So. 2d 1220 (Fla. 2006); State, Dep't of Revenue v. Lockheed Martin Corp., 905 So. 2d 1017, 1020 (Fla. Dist. Ct. App. 1st Dist. 2005); Bruner v. GC-GW, Inc., 880 So. 2d 1244, 1246 (Fla. Dist. Ct. App. 1st Dist. 2004). There are, however, many cases in which the Court notes that it is not merely the literal meaning that must be adhered to. As the Florid Supreme Court noted in Cason v. Florida Dep't of Mgmt. Servs. 944 So.2d 306, 313 (Fla. 2006), "in construing statutory language we must give consideration not only to the literal and usual meaning of the words, but also to their meaning and effect on the objectives and purpose of the statute's enactment." Florida Birth-Related Neurological Injury Comp. Ass'n v. Florida Div. of Admin. Hearings, 686 So.2d 1349, 1354 (Fla.1997)."

[17] If the plain meaning of the language is clear and unambiguous, then the court need not delve into principles of statutory construction unless that meaning leads to a result that is either unreasonable or clearly contrary to legislative intent. Polite v. State, 973 So. 2d 1107, 1111 (Fla. 2007), as clarified, (Jan. 24, 2008).

[18] One might be puzzled as to how the Court is influenced by these other tools if they do not "look" to them. The simple answer is that lawyers present them, judges look at them, and sometimes they are influenced by them and use them to justify the decision they make.

[19] Florida Dep't of Envtl. Prot. v. ContractPoint Fla. Parks, LLC, 986 So. 2d 1260, 1265 (Fla. 2008).

[20] Arnold, Matheny and Eagan, P.A. v. First Am. Holdings, Inc., 982 So. 2d 628, 633; 65 U.C.C. Rep. Serv. 2d 645 (Fla. 2008).

[21] As Justice Lewis stated in his dissent in Kasischke v. State 991 So.2d 803, 822 (Fla. 2008):

> The majority "explores legislative history" before applying the doctrines of statutory interpretation and canons of construction that may aid us in interpreting the text of the relevant statute. See majority op. at 808-813. However, we generally examine the statutory text, which may include the application of canons of construction and interpretive doctrines (such as our adherence to the established rules of grammar), and then consult relevant legislative history if

The tools of statutory interpretation can be broken down into two broad categories of tool or maxims, and those categories can be further broken down. On the one hand, there are a set of tools that are internal to, or intrinsic in, the text itself. These tools include textual tools relating to word association, grammar, reading particular parts of a statute in light of the whole statute, and avoiding errors and absurd results. There are a number of substantive tools for interpreting text. These tools can either be seen as intrinsic or extrinsic, depending on how they are conceived. The tools include: interpreting public interest and remedial statutes liberally; interpreting criminal statutes narrowly or in favor of the accused (the rule of lenity); and interpreting the text in light of fundamental values, including Constitutional values and respect for state sovereignty/ federalism. One can see these tools as either being inextricably linked to the statutes that one is interpreting, or as external sources that impact one's interpretation of the text. While these tools are external to the text, there is no question that the values and principles that are being referenced here are intrinsic to the legal system. They are foundational aspects of the legal context in which any given statute is written and to be interpreted. They are not external in the same way that recourse to social policy or socio-economic context is external.

There is also a set of tools that more clearly require that one consult extrinsic or external sources for guidance in interpreting the text. Those tools include: interpretation in light of the common law; interpretation in light of the objects, purposes, or policy behind the law; interpretation in light of the legislative history; and giving deference to the interpretation of legislation by administrative agencies. Again, while some of these tools take one outside "the text" most of them are tools that are clearly drawn from within the legal universe. They are extra-textual but not extra-legal.[22]

The chapters that follow will track the above breakdown of interpretive tools.

further clarification is necessary or probative. See, e.g., State v. Sousa, 903 So.2d 923, 928 (Fla.2005) ("The fundamental rule of construction in determining legislative intent is to first give effect to the plain and ordinary meaning of the language used by the Legislature. Courts are not to change the plain meaning of a statute by turning to legislative history if the meaning of the statute can be discerned from the language in the statute.").

[22] There is considerable debate over what is intrinsic or internal and what is external or "alien." The terms are very loaded and are sometimes used as a rhetorical device to privilege one set of tools over another.

SECTION I: INTERNAL/INTRINSIC TEXTUAL TOOLS

A. Plain Meaning

KNOWLES V. BEVERLEY ENTERS.-FLA., INC.

898 So.2d 1 (Fla. 2004)

PER CURIAM.

We have for review Beverly Enterprises-Florida, Inc. v. Knowles, 766 So.2d 335 (Fla. 4th DCA 2000) (en banc). The district court certified the following question as one of great public importance:

> MAY A PERSONAL REPRESENTATIVE BRING A STATUTORY CAUSE OF ACTION UNDER SECTION 400.023(1), FLORIDA STATUTES (1997), ON BEHALF OF A DECEASED RESIDENT OF A NURSING HOME FOR ALLEGED INFRINGEMENT OF THE RESIDENT'S STATUTORY RIGHTS PROVIDED BY SECTION 400.022, FLORIDA STATUTES (1997), WHERE THE INFRINGEMENT HAS NOT CAUSED THE RESIDENT'S DEATH?

Beverly Enterprises-Florida, Inc. v. Knowles, 763 So.2d 1285, 1285 (Fla. 4th DCA 2000). We have jurisdiction. See art. V, § 3(b)(4), Fla. Const. For the reasons set forth in this opinion, we answer the question in the negative and approve the decision of the Fourth District Court of Appeal.

STATEMENT OF THE CASE & FACTS

The personal representative of the estate of Gladstone Knowles, deceased, filed an action against Beverly Enterprises seeking damages under the provisions of section 400.023(1), Florida Statutes (1997), which provides:

> Any resident whose rights as specified in this part are deprived or infringed upon shall have a cause of action against any licensee responsible for the violation. The action may be brought by the resident or his or her guardian, by a person or organization acting on behalf of a resident with the consent of the resident or his or her guardian, or *by the personal representative of the estate of the deceased resident when the cause of death resulted from the deprivation or infringement of the decedent's rights.*

(Emphasis supplied.) The facts that gave rise to the personal representative's action are set out in the Fourth District's opinion:

Gladstone Knowles, an elderly gentleman, was a resident of Washington Manor Nursing Home and Rehabilitation Center for approximately 67 days while he convalesced from hip-replacement surgery. While at Washington Manor, Knowles developed severe bedsores and other serious ailments allegedly because of neglectful and improper treatment and care provided by Washington Manor. Knowles was transferred to a medical hospital where he later died. Maggie Knowles, the personal representative for Gladstone Knowles, sued Washington Manor for violation of the Patient's Bill of Rights under sections 400.022 and 400.023, Florida Statutes (1997). Washington Manor moved for summary judgment because the complaint did not allege that any violation of the statute caused Gladstone's death. Appellee conceded that Gladstone's death did not result from any of the alleged violations of the Patient's Bill of Rights. Interpreting section 400.023(1) to preclude actions by a personal representative when the patient's death is not caused by a deprivation of rights under the statute, the trial court granted appellant's motion for summary judgment. After the trial court disposed of the statutory negligence claims, the case went to trial on a common law negligence theory.

The jury returned a verdict for Washington Manor.

Beverly Enterprises-Florida, Inc. v. Knowles, 766 So.2d 335, 335-36 (Fla. 4th DCA 2000) (en banc). However, after the return of the jury verdict, the trial court concluded that it had erred in granting a summary judgment on the statutory claim and ordered a new trial. The new trial order relied upon a newly rendered decision from the Fourth District.

Prior to its en banc decision in Knowles, the Fourth District had held in Greenfield v. Manor Care, Inc., 705 So.2d 926, 933-34 (Fla. 4th DCA 1997), that section 400.023(1) permitted a personal representative to bring a cause of action for damages arising out of violations of section 400.022 regardless of whether the violations caused the death of the resident. See Knowles, 766 So.2d at 336. When the Fourth District's decision in Greenfield was called to its attention, the trial court granted petitioner's motion for a new trial.

Upon subsequent review, however, the Fourth District receded from its earlier decision in Greenfield and reversed the trial court's order for a new trial. The district court, sitting en banc, held that "the language of section 400.023 unambiguously provides that a personal representative of a deceased, nursing home resident may bring a cause of action against the nursing home for violation of the Patient's Bill of Rights only when the deprivation or infringement of the resident's rights caused the patient's death." Knowles, 766 So.2d at 336. Accordingly, the Fourth District held that the trial court was correct in initially dismissing the statutory negligence claims. See id.

In Greenfield, the personal representative of the estate of a deceased resident who died from causes unrelated to the alleged statutory violations filed suit against the nursing home for its failure to adequately advise residents of the costs of services. See Greenfield, 705 So.2d at 933. The trial court dismissed the action because the personal representative had failed to demonstrate that the decedent died as a result of the statutory violations. Id. On appeal, the Fourth District reversed. It reasoned:

> The trial court dismissed count VII on the basis that appellant did not allege that her husband's death resulted from the deprivation or infringement of his rights under Chapter 400. We do not agree with that interpretation of the statute.
>
> On one level, section 400.023 lends itself to the interpretation espoused by the trial court, that is, that suits by personal representatives on behalf of deceased residents are allowed only when the nursing home's alleged negligence caused the resident's death. On the other hand, we do not think that such an interpretation was intended by the Legislature in light of section 46.021, Florida Statutes (1993), which provides that "no cause of action dies with the person." To construe section 400.023 as foreclosing all causes of actions for nursing home negligence which does not cause the resident's death is to nullify section 46.021. See generally Beverly Enterprises-Florida, Inc. v. Estate of Maggiacomo, 651 So.2d 816 (Fla. 2d DCA), quashed on other grounds, 661 So.2d 1215 (Fla. 1995) (personal representative sued on behalf of deceased resident under section 400.023 for deprivation of nursing home rights for theft of diamond ring which was allegedly forced from finger of resident causing bruises; resident died of unrelated causes); Arthur v. Unicare Facilities, Inc., 602 So.2d 596 (Fla. 2d DCA), rev. denied, 613 So.2d 4 (Fla. 1992) (when death results from complained-of injuries, The Wrongful Death Act applies; when death results from an independent cause, claim is preserved by section 46.021, the survival of actions statute). As such, we hold that section 400.023, Florida Statutes (1993), must be read *in pari materia* with section 46.021, Florida Statutes (1993) in order to reach a logical result. See generally Inciarrano v. State, 447 So.2d 386 (Fla. 4th DCA 1984), quashed on other grounds, 473 So.2d 1272 (Fla. 1985) (the Legislature is presumed to know the state of the law in passing statutes and consequently the legislation is to be construed on the premise that the particular statute in question is to be applied relative to other statutes affecting the same subject matter). We therefore reverse the trial court's dismissal of appellant's statutory cause of action, and remand for further proceedings consistent with this opinion.

Greenfield, 705 So.2d at 933-34.

In the en banc Knowles opinion, the district court relied upon and adopted the reasoning of Judge Warner's partial dissent in Greenfield, which provided:

> The rights protected under section 400.022 are rights that are largely personal to the resident of the facility, such as the right to religious liberty, see § 400.022(1)(a), the right to organize and participate in groups in the facility, see § 400.022(1)(e), and the right to manage one's personal affairs, see § 400.022(1)(h) to name a few. The resident also has the right to adequate medical care and proper treatment, see § 400.022(1)(l) and under section 400.023(1), if the violation of these rights results in a death then, the personal representative of the estate of the deceased resident has a cause of action. However, as to the other personal rights, I can conceive of valid policy reasons why the legislature would not want such actions to survive, as post-death vindication would not bring any personal satisfaction to the resident. Considering the fact that attorney's fees are available for successful suits proving infringements of these statutory rights, it may have been part of the

> legislative bargain in passing the resident's bill of rights to limit actions to the lifetime of the patient, other than those alleging that the violation of the rights resulted in the death of the resident.
>
> Moreover, section 400.023(1) was enacted long after section 46.021 and I do not see how the two can be harmonized.... As a general rule of statutory construction, a special statute controls over a general statute. See McKendry v. State, 641 So.2d 45 (Fla.1994).

Knowles, 766 So.2d at 336-37 (quoting Greenfield, 705 So.2d at 934 (Warner, J., concurring in part and dissenting in part)). In a separate opinion, the Fourth District certified the above-mentioned question as one of great public importance. See Knowles, 763 So.2d at 1285.

ANALYSIS

It is well settled that legislative intent is the polestar that guides a court's statutory construction analysis. See State v. Rife, 789 So.2d 288, 292 (Fla.2001); McLaughlin v. State, 721 So.2d 1170, 1172 (Fla.1998). In determining that intent, we have explained that "we look first to the statute's plain meaning." Moonlit Waters Apartments, Inc. v. Cauley, 666 So.2d 898, 900 (Fla.1996). Normally, "[w]hen the language of the statute is clear and unambiguous and conveys a clear and definite meaning, there is no occasion for resorting to the rules of statutory interpretation and construction; the statute must be given its plain and obvious meaning." Holly v. Auld, 450 So.2d 217, 219 (Fla.1984) (quoting A.R. Douglass, Inc., v. McRainey, 102 Fla. 1141, 137 So. 157, 159 (1931)).

Accordingly, we begin our analysis by first determining the plain meaning of the pertinent language in section 400.023(1), Florida Statutes (1997), which provides:

> Any resident whose rights as specified in this part are deprived or infringed upon shall have a cause of action against any licensee responsible for the violation. The action may be brought by the resident or his or her guardian, by a person or organization acting on behalf of a resident with the consent of the resident or his or her guardian, or *by the personal representative of the estate of the deceased resident when the cause of death resulted from the deprivation or infringement of the decedent's rights.*

(Emphasis added.) The district court, and the trial court in its initial ruling, held that section 400.023(1) unambiguously states that a cause of action may be filed by the personal representative of a deceased resident only when the death resulted from a violation of the rights under chapter 400. Knowles, 766 So.2d at 337. It provides that a personal representative of the estate of a deceased resident may bring a cause of action against a nursing home only *when the death of the resident resulted from the deprivation or infringement of the decedent's rights.* Hence, section 400.023(1), when read by itself, clearly limits the circumstances upon which a personal representative may sue for violation of the decedent's rights.

On its face, the phrase "when the cause of death resulted from the deprivation or infringement of the decedent's rights" puts a limitation on the person who is entitled to sue, in other words, the personal representative of the estate of a deceased resident. The phrase also indicates that the suit may be brought when the death of the deceased resident is caused by the deprivation or infringement of the decedent's rights. Because the Legislature used the term "resulted from," it limited actions by the estate of a deceased resident to those based on violations which caused the decedent's death. Thus, the court below reasonably concluded that the plain meaning of the language used in the statute indicates that only personal representatives of the estate of a deceased resident *whose death resulted from the deprivation or infringement of the decedent's rights* may bring an action for damages under the statutory rights scheme.

Legislative Intent

Notwithstanding the above, petitioner contends that the district court's interpretation of section 400.023 is contrary to the Legislature's intent. She asserts that even when language of a particular statutory provision appears to be clear, "[i]t is a fundamental rule of statutory construction that legislative intent is the polestar by which the court must be guided, and *this intent must be given effect even though it may contradict the strict letter of the statute.*" State v. Webb, 398 So.2d 820, 824 (Fla.1981) (emphasis added).[2] This Court has also noted that "[i]t is axiomatic that all parts of a statute must be read *together* in order to achieve a consistent whole." Forsythe v. Longboat Key Beach Erosion Control Dist., 604 So.2d 452, 455 (Fla.1992). "Where possible, courts must give full effect to all statutory provisions and construe related statutory provisions in harmony with one another." Id. Hence, the petitioner asserts that where the language of a particular statutory provision is clear, but the clear meaning does not comport with the Legislature's intent or it conflicts with other provisions of the statute, the Court should not blindly adopt the plain meaning of the statute without additionally considering if the Legislature's intent is supported by such a reading. "The primary guide to statutory interpretation is to determine the purpose of the legislature." Tyson v. Lanier, 156 So.2d 833, 836 (Fla.1963); see also Byrd v. Richardson-Greenshields Sec., Inc., 552 So.2d 1099, 1102 (Fla.1989) ("As the Court often has noted, our obligation is to honor the obvious legislative intent and policy behind an enactment, even where that intent requires an interpretation that exceeds the literal language of the statute."); Tampa-Hillsborough County Expressway Auth. v. K.E. Morris Alignment Serv., Inc., 444 So.2d 926, 929 (Fla.1983) ("Statutes should be construed in light of the manifest purpose to be achieved by the legislation."); State v. Egan, 287 So.2d 1, 4 (Fla.1973) ("[T]he purpose of all rules relating to the construction of statutes is to discover the true intention of the law.").

Petitioner claims that her interpretation of section 400.023(1) is supported by (1) the remedial nature of section 400.023(1), which should be construed liberally; (2) the effect of section 400.023(1) when viewed in light of section 400.022, Florida Statutes (1997), sections 768.16-768.27, Florida Statutes (1997), and section 46.021, Florida Statutes (1997); and (3) the legislative purpose and history of section 400.023(1). Accordingly, she asserts, even if the "plain meaning" of the specific language in section 400.023(1) appears to prevent petitioner in the instant case from bringing a statutory cause of action, courts should at least question if the plain meaning of section 400.023(1) is what the Legislature intended.

Remedial Statutes Should be Liberally Construed

Petitioner contends that section 400.023(1) is remedial in nature and therefore should be liberally construed. Indeed, we have held that where a statute is remedial in nature, it should be liberally construed to "preserve and promote access to the remedy intended by the Legislature." Joshua v. City of Gainesville, 768 So.2d 432, 435 (Fla.2000) (holding that chapter 760, Florida Statutes, relating to employment discrimination, is remedial and requires a liberal construction to preserve and promote access to the remedy intended by Legislature); see also Golf Channel v. Jenkins, 752 So.2d 561, 566 (Fla.2000) (liberally construing Whistle-Blower Act in favor of granting access to remedy provided by Legislature). As mentioned above, section 400.023(1) provides a remedy to those residents whose rights have been deprived or infringed upon by the nursing home. Under this analysis, petitioner asserts that a liberal interpretation of the statute would permit suit by the personal representative of the estate of a deceased resident whose death did not result from a violation of the act but who was injured by said violation.

However, it is apparent that such an interpretation would alter the clear and unambiguous language of section 400.023(1) by either injecting a different circumstance upon which suit may be brought or by ignoring the language expressly used in the statute. In other words, to give the statute the liberal interpretation urged by petitioner, this Court would have to add words to the statute stating that the cause of death is irrelevant or it would have to ignore the term "when death resulted from." The law is well settled that courts in this state are "without power to construe an unambiguous statute in a way which would extend, modify, or *limit*, its express terms or its *reasonable and obvious implications*." Holly, 450 So.2d at 219 (quoting Am. Bankers Life Assurance Co. of Fla. v. Williams, 212 So.2d 777, 778 (Fla. 1st DCA 1968)). Thus, while petitioner is correct that section 400.023(1) should be liberally construed, such construction does not mean that this Court may rewrite the statute or ignore the words chosen by the Legislature so as to expand its terms. See id.

Consideration of Related Statutes

Petitioner also contends that courts should avoid interpreting a statute in a way that would render related statutes meaningless. She argues that instead of construing the statutory phrase in section 400.023(1) in isolation, the court below should have considered section 400.023(1) with other, related statutes in determining legislative intent. Petitioner points specifically to subsection 400.022(1)(h)(4), which states that the nursing home facility must hold, safeguard, manage and account for the resident's personal funds deposited with the facility and, upon the death of the resident, convey those funds to the decedent's beneficiary or person responsible for administering the decedent's estate within thirty days. Petitioner argues that because this right does not become effective until the death of the resident and because the violation of this right would never lead to death, this right would not be actionable under section 400.023(1) as construed by the court below, thereby rendering it meaningless.

We have stated that "[i]t is axiomatic that all parts of a statute must be read *together* in order to achieve a consistent whole." Forsythe, 604 So.2d at 455. Furthermore, where it is possible, courts must give full effect to *all* statutory provisions and construe related statutory provisions in harmony with one another. Id. However, we disagree here that the lower court's construction of section 400.023(1) would render the right identified in section 400.022(1)(h)(4) meaningless. First, subsection 400.022(1)(h)(4) does not become effective until the resident dies. At that time, the facility has the obligation to return all deposited funds to the administrator of the resident's estate or, if none has been appointed, to the resident's spouse or next of kin. Thus, there is no danger of this right abating upon the resident's death. Second, section 400.162, which deals with the property and personal affairs of the residents, requires the facility to return all deposited funds to the administrator of the decedent's estate. See § 400.162, Fla. Stat. (1997). Specifically, section 400.162(6) states:

> In the event of the death of a resident, a licensee shall return all refunds and funds held in trust to the resident's personal representative, if one has been appointed at the time the nursing home disburses such funds, and if not, to the resident's spouse or adult next of kin named in a beneficiary designation form provided by the nursing home to the resident.

Thus, a personal representative of the resident's estate would not need to invoke the provisions of section 400.023(1) in order to secure the resident's funds. Rather, the personal representative can ensure the return of all funds under section 400.162. Accordingly, we disagree that the statutory provisions in section 400.022 have been rendered meaningless by the lower court's construction of section 400.023(1).

Wrongful Death Act and Survival Statute

Next, petitioner argues that the court below ignored the legislative intent of section 400.023(1) as evidenced by (1) existing law and (2) the legislative history of the statute. First, petitioner argues that the lower court failed to consider the different purposes of two related statutes. See § 46.021, Fla. Stat. (1997) ("Survival Statute"); §§ 768.16-768.27, Fla. Stat. (1997) ("Wrongful Death Act"). The Survival Statute states: "No cause of action dies with the person. All causes of action survive and may be commenced, prosecuted, and defended in the name of the person prescribed by law." § 46.021, Fla. Stat. (1997).

The Wrongful Death Act, on the other hand, permits a cause of action "[w]hen the death of a person is caused by the wrongful act, negligence, default, or breach of contract or warranty of any person." § 768.19, Fla. Stat. (1997). Under the Wrongful Death Act, however, a personal injury claim abates where personal injuries suffered from the negligent or wrongful act result in death. See Martin v. United Sec. Servs., Inc., 314 So.2d 765, 770 (Fla.1975) (holding that no separate statutory action for personal injuries resulting in death can survive the decedent's demise). Damages are limited to the survivor's loss of support and services, companionship, and his or her own pain and suffering. The estate may also recover loss of earnings of the deceased and medical and funeral expenses. See § 768.21, Fla. Stat. (1997).

Petitioner argues that the court below erroneously applied the canon of statutory construction that the specific statute controls over a general statute, when it should have read section 400.023(1) in harmony with section 46.021. It is true that courts must presume that the Legislature passes statutes with the knowledge of prior existing statutes and that "the legislature does not intend to keep contradictory enactments on the books or to effect so important a measure as the repeal of a law without expressing an intention to do so." Woodgate Dev. Corp. v. Hamilton Inv. Trust, 351 So.2d 14, 16 (Fla.1977). We have also noted that "[w]here possible, it is the duty of the courts to adopt that construction of a statutory provision which harmonizes and reconciles it with *other provisions of the same act*." Id. (emphasis added). However, as noted by the Third District, "[t]here must be a hopeless inconsistency before rules of construction are applied to defeat the plain language of one of the statutes." Agency for Health Care Admin. v. Estate of Johnson, 743 So.2d 83, 87 (Fla. 3d DCA 1999).

On the one hand, section 400.023, as written by the Legislature and construed by the court below, might appear to extinguish a statutory cause of action for those claimants in petitioner's position; the district court's interpretation of section 400.023 precludes a personal representative's ability to bring a survival action based on the statutory cause of action where death was not the result of a violation of the act. The effect of this interpretation could be viewed as extinguishing or abating a cause of action the decedent clearly would have had under the statute, had he not died. Such a result appears to conflict with the purpose of section 46.021, which clearly provides that all causes of action survive the death of a person. However, because this is a legislatively created cause of action to be brought by personal representatives only under certain circumstances, we conclude the Legislature had the authority both to determine the extent of the statutory right and to prescribe or limit the remedies available for a violation of the right.

More importantly, section 400.023(1) does not "cut off" a deceased resident's right to bring a cause of action. Section 400.023(1) states that "[t]he remedies provided in this section are in addition to and cumulative with other legal and administrative remedies available to a resident and to the agency." § 400.023(1), Fla. Stat. (1997). Thus, in actuality, section 400.023(1) does not negate or extinguish a cause of action that would otherwise exist as among "other legal and administrative remedies." Rather, such resident (or estate) can bring a common law negligence action as was done in this case. Furthermore, in addition to common law negligence, the facility may be liable depending on the particular facts, under the theories of common law intentional torts, like battery, or abuse of a vulnerable adult under section 415.1111, Florida Statutes (1997). Thus, section 400.023(1) does not necessarily conflict with section 46.021.

Furthermore, we note petitioner was not deprived of or prevented from relying on the violation of Mr. Knowles' chapter 400 rights, because although petitioner proceeded on a common law negligence theory she was permitted to refer to the rights listed in section 400.022 to establish her claim. More importantly, the trial court instructed the jury that residents in nursing homes have rights under section 400.022

and that a violation of those rights constitutes negligence.[3] Thus, while petitioner's statutory claim under section 400.023(1) may have been dismissed, the trial court permitted petitioner to proceed in a manner substantially similar to the statutory cause of action.[4]

Legislative History

Finally, petitioner argues that the district court's interpretation of section 400.023(1) is inconsistent with the legislative purpose and legislative history of the statute. However, the rules of statutory construction are the means by which courts seek to determine legislative intent only when that intent is not plain and obvious enough to be conclusive. See McDonald v. Roland, 65 So.2d 12, 14 (Fla.1953). In that instance, it is well settled that courts will consider the "history of a statute as an aid in determining the Legislature's intent." Id. However, the Fourth District quite properly ruled that it would not consider the legislative history of the statute because it found that "section 400.023(1) is clear and, thus, leaves no room for resort to a consideration of legislative history to determine its meaning." Knowles, 766 So.2d at 337. Because we agree that the language used by the Legislature is unambiguous, it is not necessary to examine the legislative history.

CONCLUSION

Because we too find the language of the statute clear and unambiguous, we agree with the Fourth District's analysis in this case. Accordingly, we answer the certified question in the negative and affirm the Fourth District's decision in this case.

It is so ordered.

WELLS, ANSTEAD, CANTERO, and BELL, JJ., concur.

CANTERO, J., concurs with an opinion, in which WELLS, ANSTEAD, and BELL, JJ., concur.

LEWIS, J., dissents with an opinion, in which QUINCE, J., concurs.

PARIENTE, C.J., recused.

---

[3] ...Violation of this statute is negligence. If you find that a person alleged to have been negligent violated this statute, such person was negligent. You should then determine whether such negligence was the legal cause of the loss, injury or damage complained of.

[4] Petitioner also argues that the court below, in adopting Judge Warner's dissent from Greenfield, improperly holds that the statutory rights provided by section 400.023(1) are "largely personal to the resident of the facility" and thus do not survive the resident's death under section 46.021. Contrary to petitioner's assertion, neither the court below nor Judge Warner in her dissenting opinion in Greenfield stated that personal rights do not survive the death of the resident. Rather, Judge Warner explained that the rights listed in section 400.022 are "largely personal to the resident of the facility." She further explained that she could conceive valid policy reasons why the Legislature would limit the cause of action to violations that caused the resident's death; vindication for violation of several of the rights listed in section 400.022 would not bring any personal satisfaction to the resident after death. Thus, this claim appears to be without merit because the court below did not hold that no personal claims survive the death of the resident.

CANTERO, J., concurring.

I concur in the majority opinion. In my view (and that of the majority, as well as the unanimous en banc district court), the statutory language is clear and unambiguous. I write only to address the dissent's contention that, to justify its conclusion, the majority adds language to the statute.

When interpreting a statute, our first resort is to the words the Legislature chose. "The cardinal rule of statutory construction is 'that a statute should be construed so as to ascertain and give effect to the intention of the Legislature *as expressed in the statute.*' " City of Tampa v. Thatcher Glass Corp., 445 So.2d 578, 579 (Fla.1984) (emphasis added). This Court has stated that

> [i]n making a judicial effort to ascertain the legislative intent implicit in a statute, the courts are bound by the plain and definite language of the statute and are not authorized to engage in semantic niceties or speculations. If the language of the statute is clear and unequivocal, then the legislative intent must be derived from the words used without involving incidental rules of construction or engaging in speculation as to what the judges might think that the legislators intended or should have intended.

Tropical Coach Line, Inc. v. Carter, 121 So.2d 779, 782 (Fla.1960).

The issue here is whether, when a nursing home resident dies, the personal representative may bring an action under the statute *only* when the cause of death resulted from the deprivation or infringement of the decedent's rights. I think the statute clearly answers that question "yes." The statute in question, section 400.023(1), Florida Statutes (1997) (emphasis added), provides as follows:

> Any resident whose rights as specified in this part are deprived or infringed upon shall have a cause of action against any licensee responsible for the violation. The action may be brought by the resident or his or her guardian, by a person or organization acting on behalf of a resident with the consent of the resident or his or her guardian, or by the personal representative of the estate of the deceased resident *when the cause of death resulted from the deprivation or infringement of the decedent's rights.*

The statute allows a personal representative of the estate of the deceased resident to sue "when the cause of death resulted from the deprivation or infringement of the decedent's rights."

The district court, sitting en banc, reading this same language, unanimously concluded that "the language of section 400.023 unambiguously provides that a personal representative of a deceased, nursing home resident may bring an action against the nursing home for violation of the Patient's Bill of Rights only when the deprivation or infringement of the resident's rights caused the patient's death." Beverly Enterprises-Florida, Inc. v. Knowles, 766 So.2d 335, 336 (Fla. 4th DCA 2000); Accord

Estate of Doyle v. Mariner Healthcare of Nashville, Inc., 889 So.2d 829, 830 (Fla. 2d DCA 2004) (agreeing that statute "is unambiguous" and adopting Fourth District's analysis of effect of statute); Contra Estate of Youngblood v. Halifax Convalescent Ctr., Ltd., 874 So.2d 596, 604-05, 606 (Fla. 5th DCA 2004) (holding statute not clear and certifying conflict with Knowles). I agree. In my view, therefore, because the language of the statute is clear and unambiguous, the analysis must end there. While this may seem simplistic, it is nevertheless what is required; we have no prerogative to do otherwise. "[T]he legislature is assumed to have expressed its intent through the words found in a statute." Zuckerman v. Alter, 615 So.2d 661, 663 (Fla.1993). Thus, "[i]f the language of a statute is clear and unambiguous, the legislative intent must be derived from the words used without involving rules of construction or speculating as to what the legislature intended." Id. In other words, not only do we not need to resort to legislative history, as the dissent does, to understand this plain meaning; we cannot do so. See Taylor Woodrow Constr. Corp. v. Burke Co., 606 So.2d 1154, 1155 (Fla. 1992) ("The court should look to legislative history only if the court determines that a statute's language is ambiguous.").

The dissent argues that to interpret the clause "when the cause of death resulted from the deprivation or infringement of the decedent's rights" as limiting the circumstances under which a personal representative can sue would actually add another clause of limitation to the statute. Dissenting op. at 22. This is not the case. Rather, the statute has this effect because of the plain meaning of the limiting clause. By stating that the personal representative may bring suit under the statute "when the cause of death resulted from the deprivation or infringement of the decedent's rights," the Legislature has limited the personal representative's power to bring suit under this statute. The word "when," as used here, means "in the event that" or "in what circumstances," "on condition that," or "if." See Webster's Third New International Dictionary 2602 (1993). Cf. People v. White, 144 Cal. Rptr. 128, 130, 77 Cal. App. 3d Supp. 17 (1978) (stating that in statute commencing with word "whenever," the word means "if" and "at any time when"). In other words, the personal representative may bring suit "when" or "if" the condition of the clause is satisfied.

In context, the word "when" in this case means "*only* when." The words "if" and "when," when used to introduce a condition, are commonly understood to mean "if and only if" or "when and only when." For example, in Kinder v. State, 779 So.2d 512 (Fla. 2d DCA 2000), approved, 830 So.2d 832 (Fla.2002), the Second District considered the meaning of a limiting clause in a statute providing that "[t]he trial may be continued upon the request of either party and a showing of good cause, or by the court on its own motion in the interests of justice, *when the person will not be substantially prejudiced.*" Id. at 514 (emphasis added) (quoting § 394.916(2), Fla. Stat. (1999)). The court concluded that the statute provided that a "continuance may only be granted when the detainee will not be substantially prejudiced." Id. at 515 (emphasis added). In State v. Goode, 830 So.2d 817 (Fla.2002), we reiterated that in this statute "when" meant "only when." Id. at 824 ("As noted above, section 394.916(2) allows for a continuance, upon a showing of good cause by one of the parties or by the court's own motion, *only where the detainee will not be substantially prejudiced.*" (emphasis added).

Other courts also have recognized that, in the context of a statute or rule, "when" must mean "only when." See, e.g., United States v. Anderson, No. 87-00014-1, 1987 WL 7687 (E.D.Pa. Mar.9, 1987) (explaining that a federal pretrial detention statute, 18 U.S.C. § 3142(e), which stated that "if the judicial officer finds no conditions ... will reasonably assure" a person's appearance and community safety, such officer "shall order the detention of the person before trial" meant "pre-trial detention can only be ordered when" those findings are made); Colony-Lobster Pot Corp. v. Director of Revenue, 770 S.W.2d 705, 706-07 (Mo.Ct.App.1989) (interpreting a statute providing that when a party prevails, the court may award litigation expenses "if it finds that the position of the state was vexatious or was not substantially justified," to allow expenses "under certain conditions if, and only if" the state's position was vexatious or not substantially justified); Davis v. State, 99 Nev. 25, 656 P.2d 855, 856 (1983) (stating that an implied consent statute listing conditions as to "when" it applied "bec[ame] operative in only two situations: when a driver [wa]s arrested, or when a driver [wa]s dead, unconscious, or otherwise in a condition rendering him incapable of being arrested").

The majority is mindful that "[w]e are not at liberty to add words to statutes that were not placed there by the Legislature." Hayes v. State, 750 So.2d 1, 4 (Fla.1999). To construe the statute to allow a personal representative to sue regardless of whether "the cause of death resulted from the deprivation or infringement of the decedent's rights" would judicially delete the entire limiting phrase from the statute. But "[w]e are compelled by well-established norms of statutory construction to choose that interpretation of statutes and rules which renders their provisions meaningful. Statutory interpretations that render statutory provisions superfluous are, and should be, disfavored." Hawkins v. Ford Motor Co., 748 So.2d 993, 1000 (Fla.1999) (quoting Johnson v. Feder, 485 So.2d 409, 411 (Fla.1986)); see Burke, 606 So.2d at 1156 ("Where the statutory provision is clear and not unreasonable or illogical in its operation, the court may not go outside the statute to give it a different meaning.").

The dissent contends that this plain language reading of the statute is somehow inconsistent with the First District's opinion in Williams v. Bay Hospital, Inc., 471 So.2d 626 (Fla. 1st DCA 1985), which interpreted the Wrongful Death Act (WDA). I disagree. The WDA provides in part as follows: "*When a personal injury to the decedent results in death*, no action for the personal injury shall survive, and any such action pending at the time of death shall abate." § 768.20, Fla. Stat. (2003) (emphasis added). The conditional "when" clause limits the survival of personal injury actions-i.e., such actions do not survive "[w]hen a personal injury to the decedent results in death." Thus, other personal injury actions-those where personal injury did not result in death-do survive. See Martin v. United Sec. Servs., Inc., 314 So.2d 765 (Fla.1975) ("The only logical construction of the ... sentence is that it expresses the legislative intent that a separate lawsuit for death-resulting personal injuries cannot be brought as a survival action under Section 46.021."). Reading the plain language of the WDA, the First District in Williams correctly recognized that the Act did not eliminate survival claims for pain and suffering or other damages for injuries *not* resulting in death. 471 So.2d at 629. The "when" clauses in the WDA and section 400.023(1) are similarly worded. Both place conditions on causes of action. Both prescribe which actions can be maintained and which cannot. Williams is consistent with the majority's conclusion in this case.

The dissent argues that the case before us represents an "unintended consequence of the specific language chosen for the amending legislation" and thus we must resort to legislative history. Dissenting op. at 18. As noted above, however, the Legislature is presumed to know the meaning of the words it chooses. Thus, where statutory language is unambiguous, we cannot use legislative history to contradict it. Even if we were to do so, however, the dissent's use of legislative history here illustrates its questionable usefulness. For example, the dissent explains that the legislator sponsoring the amendment intended to provide a remedy under the Act where a nursing home resident's death resulted from actions violating the Act. Of course, the majority's holding is that the plain language of the statute provides this remedy. The problem of using a single legislator's comments to "prove" the intent of the Legislature, however, is that the clause at issue was not even included in the amendment the representative offered, which the dissent quotes. Dissenting op. at 21. That clause was inserted into the amendment on the floors of the two houses of the Legislature. See Fla. H.R. Jour. 232 (Reg.Sess.1986); Fla. S. Jour. 258 (Reg.Sess.1986). The limitation was thus an amendment to the amendment. The best way to determine the Legislature's intent remains the language it used in the statute. See Crosby v. National Foreign Trade Council, 530 U.S. 363, 390-91, 120 S.Ct. 2288, 147 L.Ed.2d 352 (2000) (Scalia, J., concurring) ("The *only* reliable indication of that [legislative] intent-the only thing we know for sure can be attributed to all of them-is the words of the bill that they voted to make law.").

WELLS, ANSTEAD, and BELL, JJ., concur.

[LEWIS, J., dissents with an opinion, in which QUINCE, J., concurs. Deleted]

NOTES AND QUESTIONS

1. Does the majority per curium opinion share the view of the concurrence that, "In my view, therefore, because the language of the statute is clear and unambiguous, the analysis must end there. While this may seem simplistic, it is nevertheless what is required; we have no prerogative to do otherwise.' ...In other words, not only do we not need to resort to legislative history, as the dissent does, to understand this plain meaning; we cannot do so."?

2. If it did fully agree with the concurrence, would the opinion have been much shorter?

3. What other approaches to interpretation does the Court address? Why does the Court find that the "plain meaning" of the text trumps these other approaches? Does the Court indicate that the plain meaning would always trump these other approaches?

4. Do the quoted remarks of Justice Scalia at the end of the concurrence adequately explain and justify the use of plain meaning as a means of determining "legislative intent"?

5. The Dissent of Lewis, J with Quince J., concurring was deleted, but in it Lewis argued that:

> ...The majority has today truly created a sad day for Florida's senior citizens. It is particularly troublesome, because it does so in a total vacuum, fails to address the well-established law at the time of statutory amendment, refuses to even consider available legislative history and information, and concludes with the thought that chapter 400 remedies are not that important because common law negligence is available. A court wearing such blinders has, in my view, demonstrated a serious lack of consideration of the applicable law. Based upon the foregoing, I would answer the certified question in the affirmative, and quash the Fourth District's decision below.

Does it matter that the Court's interpretation might make senior citizens in nursing homes more vulnerable to abuse?

6. The dissent also argued that:

> Additionally, both the majority and concurring views fail to acknowledge or even consider that reference to matters extrinsic to the particular words of a statute is not limited to only when the language of a statute is itself ambiguous or unclear. This Court has instructed on two applicable principles:
>
> > When construing a particular part of a statute, it is only when the language being construed in and of itself is of doubtful meaning *or doubt as to its meaning is engendered by apparent inconsistency with other parts of the same or a closely related statute that any matter extrinsic the statute may be considered by the Court in arriving at the meaning of the language employed by the Legislature.* Fla. State Racing Comm'n v. McLaughlin, 102 So.2d 574, 576 (Fla.1958).
>
> We have also instructed:
>
> > A law should be construed together with any other law relating to the same purpose such that they are in harmony. Courts should avoid a construction which places in conflict statutes which cover the same general field. The law favors a rational, sensible construction.
>
> City of Boca Raton v. Gidman, 440 So.2d 1277, 1282 (Fla.1983) (citations omitted).
>
> Florida's survival statute is precisely such a statute that the majority and concurring views simply repeal by implication in the nursing home

context, a result I cannot justify with the applicable law. This conflict in and of itself requires that we explore the parameters of the actions impacted. Relying on decisions from this Court, Judge Ervin wrote in DeBolt v. Department of Health and Rehabilitative Services, 427 So.2d 221 (Fla. 1st DCA 1983):

> Where, as in this case, two statutes are found to be in conflict, rules of statutory construction must be applied to reconcile, if possible, the conflict. We are aided in this task by the maxim that "legislative intent is the pole star by which we must be guided in interpreting the provisions of a law." In our attempt to discern the legislative intent behind the conflicting statutes, we must consider "the history of the Act, the evil to be corrected, the purpose of the enactment, and the law then in existence bearing on the same subject."

Id. at 224 (citation omitted) (quoting Parker v. State, 406 So.2d 1089, 1092 (Fla.1981), and State Board of Accountancy v. Webb, 51 So.2d 296, 299 (Fla.1951)).

More recently, we stated:

> Where ... two statutes are found to be in conflict, rules of statutory construction must be applied to reconcile ... the conflict.

City of Clearwater v. Acker, 755 So.2d 597, 600 (Fla.2000) (quoting DeBolt, 427 So.2d at 224).

NICARRY V. ESLINGER

990 So. 2d 661 (Fla. Dist. Ct. App. 5th Dist. 2008)

Hudson, M., Associate Judge.

Neal E. Nicarry appeals the dismissal of his second amended complaint against Donald Eslinger, Sheriff of Seminole County, Florida, for negligence. The order of dismissal concluded that his complaint was barred by the statute of limitations found in section 95.11(5)(g), Florida Statutes (2004). We affirm.

Nicarry was incarcerated at the John E. Polk Correctional Facility in Sanford, Florida, where he was allegedly exposed to toxic fumes as a result of welding being done on the property. Nicarry alleges that Sheriff Eslinger, the public official in charge of operating the jail, breached his duty to Nicarry by failing to properly ventilate the room where the welding took place. As a direct and proximate cause of Sheriff Eslinger's negligence, Nicarry claims that he suffered bodily injury.

Nicarry filed his original complaint twenty-one months after the incident, and later amended that complaint. Sheriff Eslinger filed motions to dismiss both the original and amended complaints on the ground that they were barred by section 95.11(5)(g). The trial court concluded that Nicarry's claim was barred by the one-year statute of limitations found in that statute and dismissed the amended complaint without prejudice. After Nicarry filed a second amended complaint, which made the same allegations as the original complaint, Sheriff Eslinger filed another motion to dismiss. The trial court granted Sheriff Eslinger's motion and dismissed Nicarry's second amended complaint with prejudice on the ground that it was barred by the one-year statute of limitations found in section 95.11(5)(g). This appeal followed.

. . .

Section 95.11, Florida Statutes, outlines the statute of limitations for all causes of action except for recovery of real property. In relevant part, section 95.11 provides that an action founded on negligence must be commenced within four years of when the action accrued. § 95.11(3)(a) Stat. (2004). The statute also specifies that except for actions relating to disciplinary proceedings, a complaint brought by or on behalf of a prisoner relating to the "conditions of the prisoner's confinement" must be commenced within one year of when the action accrued. § 95.11(5)(g)), Fla. Stat. (2004).[2]

This is a case of first impression in Florida. The integral component of the issue on appeal is the definition of the phrase "conditions of the prisoner's confinement," as contained in section 95.11(5)(g). With no state precedent discussing the meaning of that phrase, this Court must construe the terms of the statute. "Conditions of the prisoner's confinement" is not defined in the statute itself. Therefore, this Court is to give effect to the Legislature's intent. State v. J.M., 824 So.2d 105, 109 (Fla.2002). In order to discern legislative intent, courts should look first to the plain language of the statute. Joshua v. City of Gainesville, 768 So.2d 432, 435 (Fla.2000). Only when the statutory language is unclear or ambiguous should the courts apply rules of statutory construction and explore legislative history to determine legislative intent. Weber v. Dobbins, 616 So.2d 956, 958 (Fla.1993). A statute is "ambiguous" when its language is subject to more than one reasonable interpretation and may permit more than one outcome. Hess v. Walton, 898 So.2d 1046, 1049 (Fla. 2d DCA 2005).

We find that there is no reasonable interpretation for the phrase "conditions of a prisoner's confinement" that would encompass only "ongoing conditions," as urged by Nicarry, especially in light of the statute's clear framework. Sections 95.11(5)(f) and (g) specifically enumerate two exceptions to the one-year statute of limitations for prisoner complaints: extraordinary writs challenging a criminal conviction and actions involving correctional disciplinary proceedings. It is not logical to find that another exception would exist when these specific circumstances were highlighted for exception in the statute. We find that section 95.11(5) encompasses the complaint filed by Nicarry, and limited the time for filing his lawsuit to one year.

As section 95.11(5) is clear and unambiguous, we do not find the need to explore other aids to statutory construction. However, we note that cases issued by the United States Supreme Court interpreting the meaning of "conditions of confinement," albeit not in a statute of limitations context, strongly support this Court's interpretation of section 95.11(5)(g).

In McCarthy v. Bronson, 500 U.S. 136, 111 S.Ct. 1737, 114 L. Ed. 2d 194 (1991), the Supreme Court considered the scope of 28 U.S.C. § 636(b)(1)(B), which authorizes the referral of prisoner petitions "challenging conditions of confinement" to magistrates without the complainant's consent. The prisoner in McCarthy challenged the referral of his complaint of a single episode of excessive force to a magistrate because he was not challenging ongoing prison conditions. The Supreme Court maintained that all prisoner petitions were to be referred to magistrates because "litigation would otherwise arise in trying to identify the precise contour of a petitioner's suggested exception for single episode cases." McCarthy, 500 U.S. at 143, 111 S.Ct. 1737. In reaching this result, the McCarthy Court relied heavily on its previous decision in Preiser v. Rodriguez, 411 U.S. 475, 93 S.Ct. 1827, 36 L. Ed. 2d 439 (1973). In Preiser, the Court differentiated between two distinct types of petitions: petitions challenging the *fact or duration* of confinement and those petitions challenging the *conditions* of confinement. Id. at 498-99, 93 S.Ct. 1827. The Court concluded that challenges to specific instances of conduct were, in fact, challenges to conditions of confinement. Id.

The Supreme Court upheld McCarthy in Porter v. Nussle, 534 U.S. 516, 122 S.Ct. 983, 152 L. Ed. 2d 12 (2002). The prisoner in Porter filed a complaint, alleging that he was harassed and beaten on one occasion. The prisoner did not file an inmate grievance as required by the Prison Litigation Reform Act, 42 U.S.C. § 1997e(a), which bars an action concerning "prison conditions" until the prisoner has exhausted all available administrative remedies. The prisoner argued that the requirement did not apply to single incidents affecting only particular prisoners. The Court, however, found that the requirement to exhaust administrative remedies before filing a suit challenging prison conditions "applies to all inmate suits about prison life, whether they involve general circumstances or particular episodes." Id. at 532, 122 S.Ct. 983.

In light of the clear and unambiguous language of section 95.11(5), Florida Statutes (2004), and mindful of the United States Supreme Court decisions interpreting similar statutory language, we conclude that the one-year statute of limitations applies to both ongoing and isolated conditions of a prisoner's confinement. Since Nicarry did not file his complaint within one year after the alleged incident, the trial court properly dismissed his complaint with prejudice.

AFFIRMED.

LAWSON and COHEN, JJ., concur.

NOTES AND QUESTIONS

1. Would it change the analysis if there was a rule that statutory provisions that modify the common law should be narrowly construed? See Section III. Extrinsic Tools, Part A. Common Law. See also Tillman v. State, 934 So. 2d 1263 (Fla. 2006).

2. Would it change the analysis if there was a rule that statutory provisions that limit common law rights should be narrowly construed? See Section III. Extrinsic Tools, Part A. Common Law. See also Fullerton v. Florida Medical Ass'n, Inc., 938 So. 2d 587 (Fla. Dist. Ct. App. 1st Dist. 2006); Bruner v. GC-GW, Inc., 880 So. 2d 1244 (Fla. Dist. Ct. App. 1st Dist. 2004).

SMALBEIN V. VOLUSIA COUNTY SCH. BD.

801 So.2d 169 (Fla. Dist. Ct. App. 5th Dist. 2002)

PETERSON, J.

John Smalbein appeals a summary judgment granted in favor of the Volusia County School Board (VCSB). Smalbein contends that he has a "valid claim" under section 440.205, Florida Statutes (1995), and the VCSB wrongfully retaliated against him for having filed a claim for workers' compensation benefits. He alleges that the method of retaliation was the removal of his name from a substitute teacher list.

Smalbein suffered injuries in a 1999 traffic accident that he claimed were work related. The Judge of Compensation Claims (JCC) in his workers' compensation case found that Smalbein's injuries were not compensable due to the "going and coming rule," that is, the accident occurred while he was traveling to or from his place of employment and that the travel was not part of his duties. Based on this finding, VCSB moved for summary judgment arguing that the trial court in the instant action was bound by the JCC's factual determinations. VCSB also argued that because the JCC found Smalbein's claim not compensable, the claim was invalid. Smalbein argued that validity was not the equivalent of compensability and that the JCC's determinations were not binding on the trial court in the instant retaliation action. The trial court agreed with VCSB and granted the summary judgment now on appeal.

Smalbein argues that the term "valid claim" under section 440.205 should not be construed as a requirement that the workers' compensation claim be compensable. We agree. Neither section 440.205, nor Chapter 440, defines the term "valid." Where a term is not defined by the Legislature, courts should construe the term to give effect to both the literal and usual meanings of the word as well as the meaning which would give effect to the objectives and purpose of the statute. To give meaning and effect to the purpose of Chapter 440 and especially section 440.205, we construe the words "valid claim" to mean a meritorious claim. Fla. Stat. § 440.02(6). Construing valid as compensable as urged by VCSB would require the successful adjudication of the claim for compensation before the filing and adjudication of the suit for retaliation. In some instances, that construction could result in retaliation against employees with no fear of liability when the four-year statute of limitations for filing a suit under section 440.205 expires before a compensation claim is resolved. See generally Scott v. Otis Elevator, 524 So.2d 642 (Fla.1988) (four-year statute of limitations applies to claims under section 440.205). We find that interpreting "valid" as "compensable" thwarts the purpose and intent of the Legislature to prohibit retaliation whereas construing a valid claim as a meritorious one provides the proper protection to injured employees seeking benefits without over-extending the protection to employees who file frivolous claims.

The administrator of VCSB's educator services department testified that Smalbein was removed from the substitute teacher list because of concerns that working as a teacher would aggravate Smalbein's injuries, not for any disciplinary reasons. Smalbein raised an issue of fact when he testified that the administrator told him that his name was removed because of his worker's compensation claim. This factual issue remains unresolved and if Smalbein's version of the reason for removal from the substitute teacher list is correct, VCSB's action was not a legitimate reason and could be construed as retaliatory in nature.

We reject as meritless VCSB's defense that the trial court was bound under the theory of collateral estoppel to the factual findings of the JCC. Clearly, collateral estoppel would not apply to preclude the trial court from making its own factual determinations for the reason that the JCC lacks jurisdiction over claims under section 440.205. (See, e.g., Smith v. Piezo, 427 So.2d at 185; see also Fla. Stat. § 440.25(1); Fireman's Fund Ins. Co. v. Rich, 220 So.2d 369 (Fla.1969); Belam Florida Corp. v. Dardy, 397 So.2d 756 (Fla. 1st DCA 1981)). Moreover, the issues are not identical. The compensation claim involves compensation for injuries whereas the retaliation claim requires analysis of the employer's actions directed toward the employee as a result of filing the compensation claim.

We vacate the summary judgment and remand for further proceedings.

SUMMARY JUDGMENT VACATED; REMANDED.

SHARP, W., and HARRIS, JJ., concur.

NOTES AND QUESTIONS

1. Was the Court's interpretation of "valid claim" dictated by the plain meaning or was the meaning of the term ambiguous? How much of a role did the Court's interpretation of "the purpose" of Chapter 440 play in interpreting the "plain meaning" of the term?

2. What does it mean to "give effect to both the literal and usual meanings of the word as well as the meaning which would give effect to the objectives and purpose of the statute."? If one is required to do both, then do the objectives and purposes of the statute inform the usual meaning? What if the literal and usual meaning conflict with the objectives and purposes of the statute?

B. THE USE OF DICTIONARIES

CASON V. FLORIDA DEP'T OF MGMT. SERV.
944 So.2d 306 (Fla. 2006)

PARIENTE, J.

In State Department of Management Services v. Cason, 909 So.2d 378 (Fla. 1st DCA 2005), the First District Court of Appeal certified the following as a question of great public importance:

> DO THE JURISDICTIONAL NON-CLAIM PROVISIONS OF SECTION 194.171, FLORIDA STATUTES, APPLY TO BAR A CLAIM OF THE STATE THAT ASSERTS AN ASSESSMENT IS VOID BECAUSE IT WAS MADE ON PROPERTY IMMUNE FROM AD VALOREM TAXATION?

Id. at 382. In ruling on and certifying this question, the First District vested us with jurisdiction. See art. V, § 3(b)(4), Fla. Const. We agree with the First District that because of its sovereign immunity from ad valorem taxation, the State is not a "taxpayer" subject to the sixty-day jurisdictional nonclaim provisions of section 194.171. We therefore approve the First District's decision in this case.

FACTS AND PROCEDURAL HISTORY

This case concerns property in Columbia County, Florida, which, according to the complaint filed in July 2000, is owned by the State and used to operate a 350-bed youthful offender prison, the Lake City Correctional Facility. As a result of nonpayment of ad valorem taxes on the property for the 1996 and 1997 tax years, the tax collector for Columbia County sold two tax certificates for the taxes due. The latter of these certificates, which had a face value of $132,313.84, was issued to Charlie Ottinger, Betty Ottinger, Gina Ottinger, and Valerie Ottinger (collectively referred to as the Ottingers).

The Ottingers applied for a tax deed on the property. After learning of the tax deed application, the Florida Department of Management Services (DMS) filed a complaint in circuit court seeking to enjoin the sale of the property at public auction. The complaint alleged that the State owned the property and was using it for a governmental purpose, rendering the 1996 and 1997 tax year assessments void based on the State's sovereign immunity from taxation. According to the complaint, the sale of the property through a tax deed would cause irreparable harm to the guards and employees of the facility, the youthful offenders housed there, and the juvenile justice system.

The Ottingers moved for summary judgment, asserting that the failure to challenge the tax assessments within sixty days after the assessments were certified for collection as required by section 194.171(2), Florida Statutes (2006), created a jurisdictional bar to the action to enjoin the tax deed sale. DMS argued that section

194.171(2) was inapplicable because the State's immunity from taxation rendered any ad valorem tax assessment on the property void. The trial court granted summary judgment in favor of the Ottingers. The court concluded that it lacked jurisdiction over the suit to enjoin the tax deed sale because the complaint was untimely under section 194.171(2). The trial court did not decide whether the property is immune from ad valorem taxation.

On appeal, the First District reversed and held that the jurisdictional bar in section 194.171 does not apply to a claim by the State contesting a tax assessment based on an assertion of sovereign immunity. See Cason, 909 So.2d at 381-82. In reaching this conclusion, the First District determined that decisions by this Court broadly applying section 194.171 to actions by private property owners contesting assessments should not be extended to property owned by the state and federal governments that is immune from taxation. Id. at 381. The First District also presumed that the Legislature was aware of court decisions recognizing the State's immunity from taxation when it enacted section 194.171, and found no language in the statute reflecting an intent to waive that immunity and classify the State as a taxpayer subject to the same jurisdictional requirements as private property owners. Id. at 381-82. However, because of uncertainty caused by language in this Court's opinions construing the statute, the First District certified the issue to this Court as a question of great public importance. Id.

ANALYSIS

The certified question asks whether the provisions of section 194.171 apply when the State is the owner of property that is immune from taxation. Our review of the First District decision addressing this issue of statutory interpretation is de novo. See B.Y. v. Dep't of Children & Families, 887 So.2d 1253, 1255 (Fla.2004). Because the certified question calls upon us to construe the statute in light of the State's immunity from ad valorem taxation, we first turn to the concept of sovereign immunity in the context of property taxation.

I. Sovereign Immunity from Taxation

It is well settled that the State is immune from taxation. See Fla. Dep't of Revenue v. City of Gainesville, 918 So.2d 250, 255 (Fla.2005); Dickinson v. City of Tallahassee, 325 So.2d 1, 3 (Fla.1975). We have explained that "[p]recedent and logic both dictate that the sovereign's general freedom from taxation derives from an 'immunity,' not from an 'exemption.' " Dickinson, 325 So.2d at 3. Further, we have observed that the immunity of State-owned lands from taxation "is not dependent upon statutory or constitutional provisions but rests upon broad grounds of fundamentals in government." State ex rel. Charlotte County v. Alford, 107 So.2d 27, 29 (Fla.1958). Thus, in Dickinson we cited with approval Orlando Utilities Commission v. Milligan, 229 So.2d 262 (Fla. 4th DCA 1969), in which the Fourth District Court of Appeal clarified the distinction between an exemption and immunity:

> Exemption presupposes the existence of a power to tax whereas immunity connotes the absence of that power. The state and its political subdivisions, like a county, are immune from taxation since there is no power to tax them.

325 So.2d at 3 (quoting Milligan, 229 So.2d at 264); See also City of Gainesville, 918 So.2d at 255.

Despite the State's immunity, "within constitutional limits, the Legislature may provide for the taxation of lands or other property of the State." Alford, 107 So.2d at 29. However, the authority to tax the State cannot be inferred. Such authority must be manifested by "clear and direct expression of the State's intention to subject itself to" the tax. Dickinson, 325 So.2d at 4.

II. Section 194.171, Florida Statutes (2006)

...Section 194.171 is part of a "comprehensive statutory scheme for counties to assess and collect taxes simultaneously with procedures for taxpayer challenges to tax assessments." Ward v. Brown, 894 So.2d 811, 814 (Fla.2004).

Section 194.171 provides:

> (1) The circuit courts have original jurisdiction at law of all matters relating to property taxation. Venue is in the county where the property is located, except that venue shall be in Leon County when the property is assessed pursuant to s. 193.085(4).
>
> (2) No action shall be brought to contest a tax assessment after 60 days from the date the assessment being contested is certified for collection under s. 193.122(2), or after 60 days from the date a decision is rendered concerning such assessment by the value adjustment board if a petition contesting the assessment had not received final action by the value adjustment board prior to extension of the roll under s. 197.323.
>
> (3) Before an action to contest a tax assessment may be brought, the taxpayer shall pay to the collector not less than the amount of the tax which the taxpayer admits in good faith to be owing. The collector shall issue a receipt for the payment, and the receipt shall be filed with the complaint. Notwithstanding the provisions of chapter 197, payment of the taxes the taxpayer admits to be due and owing and the timely filing of an action pursuant to this section shall suspend all procedures for the collection of taxes prior to final disposition of the action.
>
> (4) Payment of a tax shall not be deemed an admission that the tax was due and shall not prejudice the right to bring a timely action as provided in subsection (2) to challenge such tax and seek a refund.
>
> (5) No action to contest a tax assessment may be maintained, and any such action shall be dismissed, unless all taxes on the property assessed in years after

the action is brought, which the taxpayer in good faith admits to be owing, are paid before they become delinquent.

(6) The requirements of subsections (2), (3), and (5) are jurisdictional. No court shall have jurisdiction in such cases until after the requirements of both subsections (2) and (3) have been met. A court shall lose jurisdiction of a case when the taxpayer has failed to comply with the requirements of subsection (5).

. . .

III. Applicability of 194.171 to Challenges by the State

We now consider the effect of sovereign immunity on the application of section 194.171 to actions filed by the State. The crucial inquiry is whether the language of section 194.171 clearly and unambiguously demonstrates legislative intent to apply this section to challenges by the State on State-owned property. Although legislative intent is the "polestar" of statutory interpretation, such intent is derived primarily from the language of the statute. See State v. J.M., 824 So.2d 105, 109 (Fla.2002). We conclude that no such "clear and direct" expression is manifested from the language of this statute. Dickinson, 325 So.2d at 4.

Section 194.171(2) provides that "[n]o action shall be brought" beyond the sixty-day period. It does not identify specific entities or persons to whom this requirement applies. Thus, we look to the other provisions of section 194.171 to determine whether the State is subject to the requirements of subsection (2). See Golf Channel v. Jenkins, 752 So.2d 561, 564 (Fla.2000) ("[R]elated statutory provisions should be read together to determine legislative intent...."); Forsythe v. Longboat Key Beach Erosion Control Dist., 604 So.2d 452, 455 (Fla.1992) ("It is axiomatic that all parts of a statute must be read together in order to achieve a consistent whole.").

Section 194.171(6), which provides that all the requirements of subsections (2), (3), and (5) are jurisdictional, refers to "the taxpayer." Both subsections (3) and (5) also refer to actions "the taxpayer" must take to contest an assessment. Subsection (3) requires "the taxpayer" to pay to the tax collector the amount that he or she "admits in good faith to be owing" for the tax year in which the assessment is levied, while subsection (5) provides that "the taxpayer" cannot maintain a legal challenge to an assessment unless her or she pays taxes admittedly owed for subsequent tax years. We conclude that the Legislature intended subsection (2), like subsections (3), (5), and (6), to apply to "taxpayers." Cf. Ward, 894 So.2d at 812 (stating that the sixty-day time requirement in section 194.171 "applies broadly to *taxpayers*' actions challenging the assessment of taxes against their property regardless of the legal basis of the challenge") (emphasis supplied).

"Taxpayer" is not defined in section 194.171 or elsewhere in chapter 194. We therefore turn to a standard dictionary and to a related statute to derive the common, ordinary meaning of the term. See Nehme v. Smithkline Beecham Clinical Labs., Inc., 863 So.2d 201, 205 (Fla.2003) (stating that where the Legislature has not defined a term, its plain and ordinary meaning can be taken from a dictionary); State v. Mitro,

700 So.2d 643, 645 (Fla.1997) ("In the absence of a statutory definition, resort may be had to case law or related statutory provisions which define the term, and where a statute does not specifically define words of common usage, such words are construed in their plain and ordinary sense."). Chapter 192 supplies a definition of "taxpayer" for purposes of ad valorem taxation that could encompass the State as a property owner, because taxpayer status is tied to assessments and all property, including State property, must be assessed. See § 192.001(13), Fla. Stat. (2006) (" 'Taxpayer' means the person or other legal entity in whose name property is assessed ...."); § 193.085(1), (3)(a)-(b), Fla. Stat. (2006) (requiring all Florida property, including property owned by the State, to be assessed). The dictionary defines "taxpayer" as "one that pays or is liable for a tax." Merriam-Webster's Collegiate Dictionary 1209 (10th ed.1999). Although useful, neither of these definitions is controlling, because in construing statutory language we must give consideration not only to the literal and usual meaning of the words, but also to their meaning and effect on the objectives and purpose of the statute's enactment." Florida Birth-Related Neurological Injury Compensation Ass'n v. Florida Div. of Administrative Hearings, 686 So.2d 1349, 1354 (Fla.1997).

Thus, the term "taxpayer" as used in section 194.171 should be construed in a manner consistent with the statute's purpose, which is to ensure a reliable and predictable method for counties to collect revenue while also providing for taxpayer challenges to tax assessments. See Ward, 894 So.2d at 815. Subsection (2) of the statute serves this purpose by creating a relatively brief window in which legal challenges may be brought. Subsections (3) and (5) serve the statute's purpose by ensuring that the disputed assessment does not disrupt the flow of taxes that are not in dispute. See id. Under these provisions, a "taxpayer" is not merely the entity in whose name the property is assessed, but one whom the county has the power to tax subject to disputes about individual assessments. In short, a "taxpayer" under section 194.171 is a taxable entity. This definition excludes the State and its political subdivisions, which are "immune from taxation since there is no power to tax them." Dickinson, 325 So.2d at 3. Accordingly, where the State files suit challenging ad valorem taxation on grounds of sovereign immunity, the State's assertion that it is not a taxable entity takes it outside the category of "taxpayer" targeted by section 194.171. As suggested by the First District, this is an important distinction from Markham and Ward, in which we focused on the nature of the challenges made by the private property holders rather than on their status as taxpayers. See Cason, 909 So.2d at 381 (expressing doubt that this Court intended the rationale of Markham and Ward to be extended beyond their facts).

The necessity of a clear expression of legislative intent to authorize taxation of the State reinforces our construction of section 194.171. We presume that the Legislature was aware of precedent recognizing both the State's immunity and the necessity of a clear and direct expression of intent to authorize taxation of the State when it enacted the jurisdictional nonclaim provision, section 194.171, in 1983. See Cason, 909 So.2d at 382; see generally Holmes County Sch. Bd. v. Duffell, 651 So.2d 1176, 1179 (Fla.1995) ("The legislature is presumed to know existing law when it enacts a statute."). Thus, the absence of specific language imposing the procedural requirements on the State, rather than on taxpayers generally, is significant.

Language in chapter 196, Florida Statutes (2006), which governs tax exemptions, further demonstrates an absence of legislative intent to subject lawsuits brought by the State to challenge tax assessments on grounds of immunity to the jurisdictional statute of nonclaim. Although it speaks in terms of exemption rather than immunity, section 196.199(1)(b) provides that "[a]ll property of this state which is used for governmental purposes shall be exempt from ad valorem taxation except as otherwise provided by law." As noted by the First District, this provision demonstrates that the Legislature has heeded the dictate that intent to authorize taxes on lands of the State must be expressed in "clear and unmistakable terms." Cason, 909 So.2d at 382. The Legislature has also expressly exempted from ad valorem taxation the leasehold interest in State-owned property when the property is leased to a nongovernmental lessee who "serves or performs a governmental, municipal, or public purpose or function, as defined in s. 196.012(6)"; or is "an organization which uses the property exclusively for literary, scientific, religious, or charitable purposes." § 196.199(2)(a), (2)(c) , Fla. Stat. (2006). Thus, we conclude that the absence of a clear and unmistakable waiver of immunity from taxation and the exemption of State property used for governmental purposes from ad valorem taxation demonstrate that the Legislature does not intend for section 194.171(2) to constitute a jurisdictional bar to lawsuits brought by the State to challenge tax assessments on State property that is either immune or exempt from taxation.

The related provisions of the statutory scheme for counties to assess and collect taxes also supports this conclusion. Even when no exemption applies and a leaseholder of State property is subject to ad valorem taxation, the penalty for nonpayment falls on the leaseholder and not the State. Section 196.199(8)(a) prohibits any taxes on a leasehold by a nongovernmental lessee from becoming a lien on the governmental property itself. Instead, these taxes "constitute a debt due and shall be recoverable by legal action or by the issuance of tax executions that shall become liens upon any other property in any county of this state of the taxpayer who owes said tax." Id. Similarly, section 197.432(9), Florida Statutes (2006), prohibits either the issuance of a tax certificate or the creation of a lien on property owned by a governmental unit that has become subject to taxation due to the lease of the property to a nongovernmental lessee. Delinquent taxes must either be "enforced and collected in the manner provided in s. 196.199(8)" or, in certain circumstances, "the delinquent taxes become a lien on the leasehold." Id.

Under these related statutory provisions, even when the State has leased its property to a nongovernmental entity and the property is used for nongovernmental purposes, the Legislature has specifically prohibited an issuance of a tax certificate or a lien on the property itself. Thus, under no circumstances can the State lose its property when the lessee fails to pay (or challenge) ad valorem taxes. On the other hand, there are no similar provisions prohibiting the issuance of a tax certificate when the State is the owner of property that it is using for a governmental purpose. This omission is significant in that it suggests the Legislature never contemplated that the State would be a taxpayer whose property could be lost through nonpayment of ad valorem taxes. We conclude that the Legislature did not intentionally enact a statutory scheme that precludes the loss of State property for nonpayment of taxes on leased property but allows the loss through a tax deed sale of State property that has not been leased merely because the State failed to file a timely challenge to the assessment.

We also note that the provisions of section 194.171 differ from the civil statute of limitations, which specifically includes the State within its operation. See § 95.011, Fla. Stat. (2006) (providing that limitations period in chapter applies to civil actions including those brought by public entities including "the state"). In the past, we have pointed to language in other statutes to show that the Legislature "knows how to" accomplish what it has omitted in the statute in question. See, e.g., Rollins v. Pizzarelli, 761 So.2d 294, 298 (Fla.2000) (looking to language in different statute to conclude that "[w]hen the Florida Legislature wishes to provide for set-offs for future benefits it well knows how to express itself") (quoting Pizzarelli v. Rollins, 704 So.2d 630, 633 (Fla. 4th DCA 1997)). Section 95.011 shows that had the Legislature chosen to make the State subject to the sixty-day filing requirement in section 194.171(2), it knew how to do so. The omission is especially significant in light of the overriding principle that any waiver of the State's immunity from ad valorem taxation must be clear and direct.

The petitioners actually use the statute of limitations to support their position that because the Legislature clearly intended the State to be subject to the limitations periods set forth in chapter 95, Florida Statutes (2006), the Legislature also intended the State to be bound by section 194.171(2). Section 95.011 provides that

> a civil action or proceeding, ... *including one brought by the state*, a public officer, *a political subdivision of the state*, a municipality, ... or any agency or officer of any of them, or any other governmental authority, *shall be barred unless begun within the time prescribed in this chapter or*, if a different time is prescribed elsewhere in these statutes, *within the time prescribed elsewhere*.

(Emphasis supplied.) The petitioners contend that for lawsuits challenging ad valorem tax assessments, the "time prescribed elsewhere" is the sixty-day period in section 194.171(2). We disagree.

The reference to "the time prescribed elsewhere" in section 95.011 encompasses other provisions that can also be construed as statutes of limitations, but not jurisdictional statutes of nonclaim such as section 194.171. We have previously noted the important distinction between a statute of limitations and a jurisdictional statute of nonclaim:

> An untimely claim filed pursuant to a jurisdictional statute of nonclaim is automatically barred. Miller v. Nolte, 453 So.2d 397 (Fla.1984). However, a claim filed beyond the time set forth in a statute of limitations is only barred if the statute of limitations is raised as an affirmative defense or, if the defense appears on the face of a prior pleading, by way of a motion to dismiss. Fla. R. Civ. P. 1.110(d). Failure to plead that the statute of limitations has expired constitutes waiver.

May v. Illinois Nat'l Ins. Co., 771 So.2d 1143, 1151 (Fla.2000) (quoting Barnett Bank v. Estate of Read, 493 So.2d 447, 448 (Fla.1986)). Conflating the two would muddle the distinction and yield confusion as to whether actions brought outside the sixty-day period in section 194.171(2) are barred automatically or only when the issue is affirmatively pled. In addition, when the State is the party challenging an ad valorem tax assessment on property it owns, treating section 194.171(2) as a statute of limitations would extract a waiver of the State's immunity from less than clear and unambiguous language.

Accordingly, for all these reasons we conclude that the Legislature did not intend that the sixty-day filing requirement of section 194.171(2) be imposed upon a nontaxpaying governmental entity such as the State.

. . .

CONCLUSION

The jurisdictional requirement that a lawsuit challenging an ad valorem tax assessment must be filed within sixty days after the assessment is certified for collection cannot be used to preclude the State from contesting sales of tax deeds on property that the State owns and claims is immune from taxation. We do not find, either within section 194.171 or elsewhere, the clear and unambiguous expression of legislative intent necessary to conclude that the Legislature intended that the State be subject to the harsh provisions of section 194.171 and as a result lose its immunity from taxation.

Therefore, we answer the certified question in the negative and hold that the jurisdictional nonclaim provisions of section 194.171 do not apply to a claim by the State challenging a tax assessment as void on the ground that the property assessed is immune from ad valorem taxation. We emphasize that our holding does not address whether the property at issue in this case is in fact immune from ad valorem taxation. Rather, we simply determine that sections 194.171(2) and 194.171(6) do not deprive the trial court of the jurisdiction necessary to decide the issue. We approve the First District's decision in this case.

It is so ordered.

LEWIS, C.J., and WELLS, ANSTEAD, QUINCE, CANTERO, and BELL, JJ., concur.

NOTES AND QUESTIONS

1. Is the meaning of "taxpayer" unclear in this case?

2. What else besides the literal and plain meaning effects the Court's interpretation of the statute?

3. Does the Court reach to find an unclear meaning because of the consequences for the state if a plain or literal interpretation of the statute is adopted?

4. Is there any legitimate reason for reading "taxpayer" under the statute as simply referring to the person or entity that is challenging an assessment against them?

C. Canons of Word Association: "Noscitur a Sociis" and "Ejusdem Generis"

STRATTON V. SARASOTA COUNTY

983 So. 2d 51 (Fla. Dist. App. Ct. 2nd Dist. 2008)

VILLANTI, Judge.

Nancy Burns Stratton appeals from the final judgment of foreclosure entered in favor of Sarasota County after it filed liens for the cost of demolition against her real property. Because the final judgment includes amounts to which the County is not entitled, we reverse and remand for further proceedings.

In 2001, Stratton purchased a Gulf-front house that had been originally designed by a renowned architect associated with the Sarasota School of Architecture. The house, which was built in 1970, was known as the "Solomon house," and it was well known in Sarasota, particularly in its art community. The house consisted of a residence and an artist's studio, which were separated by an enclosed courtyard but connected by a raised bridge. When Stratton purchased the house, it was subject to an existing condemnation order from the County because the Gulf of Mexico was rapidly eroding the shoreline of the property. Stratton sought to have the house designated as a historic landmark, which would have allowed her to make extensive repairs to the western portion of the house and to construct protective seawalls and berms without running afoul of various County and FEMA regulations. In the absence of the historic landmark designation or certain variances, numerous regulations and code provisions prohibited Stratton from constructing shore protection and repairing the house.

After several hearings, the County denied Stratton's request to have the house designated a historic landmark and denied her requests for variances. Thus, the erosion of the shoreline continued, and the house began literally crumbling into the Gulf of Mexico. At that point, because the house constituted a hazard to beachgoers, the County declared the house to be an imminent threat to public safety. It then obtained an emergency condemnation and demolition order, solicited an emergency bid to demolish the western portion of the house, and proceeded to demolish that portion of the house. This demolition formed the basis of the County's claim of lien for $129,315.23, which was recorded against the house and property on April 29, 2003. Of this total, $18,865.67 represented an amount claimed by the County for the payroll expenses allegedly incurred by its code enforcement employees in supervising the demolition. An additional $2167.87 was for expenses incurred by the Sarasota County Fire Marshal for keeping a fire watch on the house during demolition, and $3465.00 was for expenses incurred by the Sarasota County Sheriff's Office for providing security around the house during demolition. The County filed its initial foreclosure action on this lien on August 18, 2004.

Due to the continued encroachment of the Gulf of Mexico onto Stratton's property, the County subsequently declared the eastern portion of the house unsafe as well, and it obtained two bids for this demolition. The County then demolished the remainder of the house, and this demolition formed the basis of the County's second claim of lien, which was recorded on January 7, 2005. This lien was for $91,072.86, of which $5382.48 was for the payroll expenses allegedly incurred by code enforcement employees in supervising the demolition. The County did not claim any expenses for the fire marshal's or the sheriff's time in this lien. The County then amended its foreclosure action to include both liens.

In the trial court, Stratton stipulated that the County's liens were valid, and she contested only the reasonableness of the amounts claimed by the County. After a nonjury trial, the trial court entered a final judgment of foreclosure and scheduled a foreclosure sale of the property. That sale was stayed pending this appeal.

In this appeal, Stratton raises four grounds for reversing the foreclosure judgment [only one of which the Court addresses in depth] (3) the County was not entitled to include the payroll expenses of its employees in its liens. [W]e agree with Stratton on ground (3) that the County's claim of lien included certain amounts to which it was not entitled, and we reverse and remand for recalculation of the foreclosure judgment on that basis alone.

. . .

In ground (3) of her appeal, Stratton argued that the County was not entitled to include in its claim of lien the payroll expenses incurred by the County for its employees' time in dealing with the demolitions. In response, the County argued that its local ordinances allow for an award of "the entire cost of demolition" and "all administrative costs" and that all of the disputed payroll expenses fall under one of these categories. Neither party's position is entirely correct.

Chapter 162, Florida Statutes (2004), which deals with county or municipal code enforcement, limits the County to imposing fines and collecting the repair costs it actually incurs in correcting code violations. Section 162.09(1), Florida Statutes (2004), permits a local code enforcement board to impose fines against a property owner who fails to correct conditions constituting code violations on his or her property. The County may also "make all reasonable repairs which are required to bring the property into compliance and charge the violator with the reasonable cost of the repairs along with the fine imposed pursuant to this section." § 162.09(1). Section 162.09(2)(a) sets forth the permissible per diem fines and permits those fines to be imposed together with "all costs of repairs pursuant to subsection (1)." Section 162.09(2)(b) sets forth the criteria to be used in determining the amount of the fine. Nothing in these provisions permits the County to directly pass through the payroll expenses for the time spent by its code enforcement employees to an individual property owner in a code enforcement proceeding.

In this appeal, the County argues that it is relying on its local code provisions rather than the provisions of chapter 162 to collect these payroll expenses from Stratton. However, the County has no authority to impose penalties that are not authorized by law. See Art. V, § 1, Fla. Const. (permitting the legislature to create commissions and administrative bodies and grant them quasi-judicial powers); Art. I, § 18, Fla. Const. (forbidding administrative bodies from imposing any penalties except as provided by law); see also Op. Att'y Gen. Fla. 2000-53 (2000). Neither chapter 162 nor any other statute permits the County to directly pass through its payroll expenses for code enforcement employees' time spent on an individual case. Instead, the County is authorized only to impose fines to recoup these costs. Therefore, the County cannot rely on local code provisions to collect these expenses in contravention of the authorized penalties set forth in chapter 162.

In the alternative, the County argues that the payroll expenses for its code enforcement employees were properly included in the lien on Stratton's property as part of the "costs of repair" incurred in correcting the violation. However, this argument fails for three reasons.

First, the plain language of section 162.09(2) makes it clear that "costs of repair" do not include payroll expenses for code enforcement employees' time. Section 162.09(2)(d) permits counties to impose higher fines than those set out in section 162.09(2)(b) under certain circumstances. In addition to those higher fines, section 162.09(2)(d) permits a county to "*impose additional fines to cover all costs incurred by the local government in enforcing its codes* and all costs of repairs pursuant to subsection (1)." (Emphasis added.)

From this statutory language, it is apparent that the legislature did not contemplate that the "costs incurred by the local government in enforcing its codes" could be included as "costs of repairs" because these two items are listed separately. If the phrase "costs of repairs" is interpreted to include the County's payroll expenses for its code enforcement employees, then the language permitting additional fines to cover the costs of enforcing the County's code would be surplusage. This court will not interpret statutes so as to render portions of them meaningless when a reading that gives meaning to all portions is possible. Am. Home Assurance Co. v. Plaza Materials Corp., 908 So.2d 360, 366 (Fla.2005); Unruh v. State, 669 So.2d 242, 245 (Fla.1996). This court can give meaning to both portions of the statute by refusing the County's invitation to use an expansive interpretation of the phrase "costs of repairs" to include payroll expenses for County code enforcement employees and by finding that payroll expenses may be included only as part of the increased fines allowed for the costs of enforcing the County's code.

Second, the term "costs" is not generally construed to include the costs of doing business. Instead, "costs" are generally intended to be "expenses incurred in prosecuting or defending an action." Lee County v. Galaxy Fireworks, Inc., 698 So.2d 1371, 1372 (Fla. 2d DCA 1997). The costs involved in "running the system" are not usually recoverable as part of a specific action against an individual. Cf. Mickler v. State, 682 So.2d 607, 609 (Fla. 2d DCA 1996) (affirming the trial court's denial of an award of juror costs against a defendant because they were "expenditures that must be made in order to maintain and operate the judicial system irrespective of specific violations of the law"); Gibson v. Troxel, 453 So.2d 1160, 1163 (Fla. 4th DCA 1984) (disallowing an award of time for the clerk, judge, and jury after a mistrial because "[t]here is no authority to assess costs to reimburse the system") disapproved of on other grounds by Keene Bros. Trucking, Inc. v. Pennell, 614 So.2d 1083, 1085-86 (Fla.1993).

Here, there is no argument that the payroll expenses for code enforcement employees are not part of the cost of running the code enforcement system. The County incurs payroll expenses for its code enforcement employees regardless of the number of violations or any one specific violation of the building code. In other words, the County's operating costs for its code enforcement department are a constant overhead, and no one particular portion can be considered a separate cost actually incurred by the County in prosecuting a particular code violation.

Third, the language of the County's demolition ordinance militates against an interpretation that would include payroll expenses for code enforcement employees as a recoverable "cost." The County code provision relied upon by the County reads as follows:

> 103.5.9(a) The Building Official shall assess the entire cost of demolition and removal including asbestos abatement, the sodding or seeding of the lot, and rodent extermination against the real property in the form of a lien. This lien upon such property shall be superior to all others except property taxes, and shall include all administrative costs including postal expenses, the cost of newspaper publications, and the like.

Sarasota County Building Code § 22-34.

The County contends that it can recover payroll expenses as part of either the "entire cost of demolition" or as an "administrative cost." However, "[u]nder the doctrine of *noscitur a sociis* (a word is known by the company it keeps), one examines the other words used within a string of concepts to derive the legislature's overall intent." Nehme v. Smithkline Beecham Clinical Labs., Inc., 863 So.2d 201, 205 (Fla.2003). When examining the words used, "general and specific words which are capable of an analogous meaning being associated together take color from each other, so that the general words are restricted to a sense analogous to the less general." Carraway v. Armour & Co., 156 So.2d 494, 495 (Fla.1963) (quoting Ex parte Amos, 93 Fla. 5, 112 So. 289, 293 (1927)). Similarly, the doctrine of *ejusdem generis* states that when a general phrase follows a list of specific items, "the general phrase will be interpreted to include only items of the same type as those listed." State v. Hearns, 961 So.2d 211, 219 (Fla.2007).

Here, the code provision relied upon by the County lists asbestos abatement, resodding or seeding, and rodent extermination as "costs of demolition." None of these types of costs are analogous to the payroll expenses incurred for code enforcement employees. Thus, under the doctrine of *noscitur a sociis*, the term "costs of demolition" would not generally be construed to include payroll expenses, a term not remotely in the same company as the listed items. In addition, the same code provision lists postal expenses and newspaper publication charges and "the like" as "administrative costs." Again, neither of these specific items is analogous to the payroll expenses for code enforcement employees. Because payroll expenses are not the same type of expense as postage and costs of newspaper publications, they would not fall within the general phrase "the like" under the doctrine of *ejusdem generis.* Moreover, it simply does not make sense that the County would specify that costs such as postage and rodent extermination could be recovered but would leave the recovery of payroll expenses to be inferred through principles of statutory construction. For these three reasons, we hold that the County was not entitled to pass through the payroll expenses for its code enforcement employees as part of the "costs of demolition" or "administrative costs" recoverable in this case, and we reverse the judgment of foreclosure to the extent that it includes recovery of these expenses.

As to the amounts claimed for the fire marshal's expenses and the sheriff's expenses incurred as part of the demolition of the western portion of the house, however, the analysis is different. In criminal cases, investigative costs of law enforcement and fire departments are recoverable because, unlike the costs of "running the system," they arise from a specific violation of the law. See, e.g., Mickler, 682 So.2d at 610. The same logic applies here. The expenses incurred by the fire marshal and the sheriff's department in this case were not "expenditures that must be made in order to maintain and operate the [code enforcement] system irrespective of specific violations." Mickler, 682 So.2d at 609. Instead, they were case-specific expenses incurred by separate, autonomous County agencies as a result of the unique nature of the destruction of Stratton's property and its location on a public beach. Both the fire marshal and the sheriff's office have duties wholly unrelated to the supervision of the demolition of Stratton's property. Their expenses are not part of the County's code enforcement overhead and were incurred only in connection with curing this specific code violation, as evidenced by the fact that no such expenses were incurred in the demolition of the eastern portion of the house which was not falling into the Gulf. Accordingly, these expenses were properly recoverable by the County in this case as part of the "cost of demolition," and they were properly included in the final judgment.

In sum, we reverse the final judgment of foreclosure and remand for the trial court to recalculate the amount of the lien without an award for the payroll expenses of the County's code enforcement personnel. This will necessitate recalculating the interest claimed by the County as well. In all other respects, the final judgment is affirmed.

Affirmed in part, reversed in part, and remanded for further proceedings.

WHATLEY and WALLACE, JJ., Concur.

NOTES AND QUESTIONS

1. Why do you think the Court applied the "noscitur a sociis" maxim to "payroll expenses" but not to "firemarshall expenses" and "sheriff's expenses"?

2. If you apply the "noscitur a sociis" maxim to the "firemarshall expenses" and "sheriff's expenses" under "costs of demolition" would this part of the case come out differently? In other words, are these costs like anything else in the list of "costs of demolition", i.e. "asbestos, abatement, resodding, or seeding, and rodent extermination"? Are they any more like the things on this list than "payroll expenses"?

D. Canons of Word Association: "Expressio Unius Est Exclusio Alterius"

YOUNG V. PROGRESSIVE SE. INS. CO.
753 So.2d 80 (Fla. 2000)

PARIENTE, J.

We have for review a decision passing upon the following question certified to be of great public importance:

IS A POLICY PROVISION WHICH EXCLUDES A VEHICLE OWNED OR OPERATED BY A SELF-INSURER FROM THE DEFINITION OF "UNINSURED MOTOR VEHICLE" FOR PURPOSES OF UNINSURED/UNDERINSURED MOTORIST COVERAGE PERMISSIBLE UNDER FLORIDA LAW AND PUBLIC POLICY?

Young v. Progressive Southeastern Ins. Co., 712 So.2d 460, 461 (Fla. 2d DCA 1998). We have jurisdiction. See art. V, § 3(b)(4), Fla. Const. We answer the certified question in the negative because the exclusion, which operates to prevent an insured from seeking either uninsured or underinsured motorist coverage under his or her insurance policy when the tortfeasor elects to be self-insured, is impermissible under Florida's uninsured motorist statutory scheme and the policy underlying that statute.

BACKGROUND

The petitioner, Juan Young, was stopped at a red light when he was struck from behind by a sheriff's vehicle owned by the Hillsborough County Sheriff's Office. Subsequently, Young and his wife sued the Sheriff's Office for damages. The Sheriff's Office was self-insured up to $100,000 per person and $200,000 per occurrence.

The Youngs alleged that their damages exceeded the limits of self-insurance established by the Sheriff's Office. Accordingly, the Youngs also filed suit against the respondent, Progressive Southeastern Insurance Company (Progressive), who had issued them an insurance policy providing uninsured/underinsured motorist coverage in the amount of $25,000.

In its answer, Progressive raised as an affirmative defense that a tortfeasor such as the Sheriff's Office who is self-insured does not qualify as either an uninsured or underinsured motorist. Progressive further asserted that the language of its uninsured motorist policy specifically excluded uninsured or underinsured motorist coverage when the tortfeasor's vehicle was self-insured:

> [A]n *uninsured motor vehicle does not include* any vehicle:
>
> . . .
>
> d. *Owned by or operated by a self-insurer* as contemplated by any financial responsibility law, motor carrier law, or similar law.

(Emphasis supplied.) On this basis, Progressive moved for summary judgment, which the trial court granted.

On appeal, the Second District affirmed the order granting summary judgment on the authority of Amica Mutual Insurance Co. v. Amato, 667 So.2d 802 (Fla. 4th DCA 1995), and its recent decision in Comesanas v. Auto-Owners Ins. Co., 700 So.2d 118, 119 (Fla. 2d DCA 1997). See Young, 712 So.2d at 461. The Second District then certified to this Court the question of the validity of the policy provision excluding self-insurers from the definition of "uninsured motorist" as one of great public importance. See id.

ANALYSIS

At this time, Progressive does not contest the Youngs' allegations that their damages exceed the limit of liability established in the certificate of self-insurance provided by the Sheriff's Office. However, because the tortfeasor chose to self-insure its vehicle rather than purchase a commercial liability policy to cover its tort liabilities, Progressive asserts that the Youngs are not entitled to either uninsured motorist coverage or underinsured motorist coverage under their insurance policy.

The core issue in this case is whether the uninsured motorist statute permits an uninsured motorist carrier to exclude coverage when its insured is injured through the negligence of a self-insured motorist and the damages exceed the limits established in the tortfeasor's certificate of self-insurance. The uninsured motorist statute provides that:

> No motor vehicle liability insurance policy which provides bodily injury liability coverage shall be delivered or issued for delivery in this state ... unless uninsured motor vehicle coverage is provided therein or supplemental thereto for the protection of persons insured thereunder who are legally entitled to recover damages from owners or operators of uninsured motor vehicles...

§ 627.727(1), Fla. Stat. (1995). As we explained in Allstate Insurance Co. v. Boynton, 486 So.2d 552, 557 (Fla.1986):

> The legislature wisely enacted a scheme whereby a motorist may obtain a limited form of insurance coverage for the uninsured motorist, by requiring that every insurer doing business in this state offer and make available to its automobile liability policyholders UM coverage in an amount equal to the policyholder's automobile liability insurance. The policyholder pays an additional premium for such coverage.

The reason insurers are statutorily required to offer uninsured motorist coverage to the insured is

> to protect persons who are injured or damaged by other motorists who in turn are not insured and cannot make whole the injured party. *The statute is designed for the protection of injured persons, not for the benefit of insurance companies or motorists who cause damage to others.*

Brown v. Progressive Mut. Ins. Co., 249 So.2d 429, 430 (Fla.1971) (emphasis supplied).

Because the uninsured motorist statute "was enacted to provide relief to innocent persons who are injured through the negligence of an uninsured motorist; it is not to be 'whittled away' by exclusions and exceptions." Mullis v. State Farm Mut. Auto. Ins. Co., 252 So.2d 229, 238 (Fla.1971). For these reasons, provisions in uninsured motorist policies that provide less coverage than required by the statute are void as contrary to public policy. See, e.g., Salas v. Liberty Mut. Fire Ins. Co., 272 So.2d 1, 5 (Fla.1972); Mullis, 252 So.2d at 233-34. Thus, we must determine whether a policy provision that excludes coverage when an insured is injured by a self-insured motorist is contrary to the uninsured motorist statute and void as against the public policy of the statute.

The uninsured motorist statute never specifically provides a definition of an "uninsured" motor vehicle. However, the uninsured motorist statute sets forth in section 627.727(3) the circumstances under which a vehicle will be considered "uninsured" even when the vehicle is actually insured. For example, an "uninsured motor vehicle" shall

> be deemed to include an *insured motor vehicle* when the *liability insurer* thereof:
>
> ...
>
> (b) Has provided *limits of bodily injury liability* for its insured which are *less than the total damages sustained* by the person legally entitled to recover damages....

§ 627.727(3). (emphasis supplied). This is commonly referred to as an "underinsured" motor vehicle. See also § 627.727(6)(a)-(c) (specifically referring to an "underinsured motorist insurer").

We first address whether a self-insured motorist with a certificate of self-insurance with limits of liability lower than the damages sustained by the injured person should be considered an underinsured motorist as defined in the uninsured motorist statute.

Pursuant to the statutory provisions, a motorist is underinsured when the "liability insurer" provides limits of bodily injury liability less than the total damages sustained. § 627.727(3)(b). In addition, sections 627.727(6)(a) and (b) also refer only to motorists with liability insurers as "underinsured" motorists.

Thus, under sections 627.727(3) and (6), in order to be considered underinsured, the tortfeasor must have a liability insurer. The term "liability insurer" is undefined in the part of the Insurance Code related to uninsured motorists coverage. See generally § 627.727. However, an "insurer" is broadly defined in section 624.03, Florida Statutes (1995), as "every person engaged as indemnitor, surety, or contractor in the business of entering into contracts of insurance or of annuity."

In Diversified Services, Inc. v. Avila, 606 So.2d 364 (Fla.1992), a company that leased automobiles provided its lessees compliance with the Financial Responsibility Law through a program of self-insurance. This Court was asked to consider whether the self-insured company was an "insurer" that was required by section 627.727 to offer uninsured motorist coverage to its lessees. We determined in Avila that because the self-insurer was not an authorized insurance company, it had no obligation to provide uninsured motorist coverage. 606 So.2d at 366. We concluded in Avila that

> providing compliance [with financial responsibility laws] through self-insurance is not the same as issuing a "motor vehicle liability policy"; therefore, section 627.727 is not applicable. *Nor does Budget's status as a self-insurer make it an "insurer" under the Florida Insurance Code.*

Id. (emphasis supplied); see also Lipof v. Florida Power & Light Co., 596 So.2d 1005, 1007-08 (Fla.1992) (determining that an entity complying with the financial responsibility law by posting a surety bond rather than buying commercial insurance should not be considered an "insurer" required to offer uninsured motorist coverage). Accordingly, we agree with Progressive that because a self-insurer is not a liability insurer under the Florida Insurance Code, a self-insured motorist cannot be considered an *underinsured* motorist based on the statutory language of section 627.727(3) that limits the definition of underinsured motorists to those having liability insurers.

Having determined that a motorist possessing a certificate of self-insurance with limits of liability lower than the damages sustained is not "underinsured" because a person or entity who is a "self-insurer" is not a "liability insurer," we must next determine whether a self-insured motorist should be deemed an "uninsured" motorist. As we have previously explained, a basic rule of statutory construction is that:

> It is axiomatic that all parts of a statute must be read *together* in order to achieve a consistent whole. Where possible, courts must give effect to *all* statutory provisions and construe related statutory provisions in harmony with one another.

Forsythe v. Longboat Key Beach Erosion Control Dist., 604 So.2d 452, 455 (Fla.1992) (citations omitted). Because the Legislature defined an underinsured motorist in section 627.727(3) and left the term "uninsured" otherwise undefined in section 627.727(1), we must read these provisions together in order to arrive at a consistent and harmonious interpretation of the uninsured motorist statute. Section 672.727(3) sets forth the circumstances where an insured motor vehicle will be considered "uninsured," such as when the vehicle is underinsured because the "liability insurer" provided limits of liability lower than the damages sustained. See § 627.727(3)(b). Reading section 627.727(3) in pari materia with section 627.727(1) leads to a logical and harmonious statutory interpretation of the term "uninsured" as a motorist without a "liability insurer," who is not considered statutorily "underinsured" pursuant to 627.727(3). Thus, a motorist who is self-insured must be deemed statutorily uninsured.

This statutory construction, which would prohibit a self-insurer exclusion as contrary to the uninsured motorist statute, is also consistent with section 627.727(9). That section provides a list of statutorily permissible policy exclusions to uninsured motorist coverage. Significantly, an exclusion for self-insured motorists is not among this list. See § 627.727(9). "Under the principle of statutory construction, expressio unius est exclusio alterius, the mention of one thing implies the exclusion of another." Moonlit Waters Apartments Inc. v. Cauley, 666 So.2d 898, 900 (Fla.1996). By failing to permit self-insured motorist policy exclusions in the list of authorized exclusions, the Legislature has further indicated its intent in section 627.727 not to permit self-insured motorist policy exclusions.

Finally, this statutory interpretation is a reasonable one considering the purpose of the uninsured motorist statute, which is to protect injured persons from deficiencies in the tortfeasor's insurance. See, e.g., Michigan Millers Mut. Ins. Co. v. Bourke, 607 So.2d 418, 420 (Fla.1992). If the Legislature had considered self-insurance an acceptable substitute for commercial liability insurance in the uninsured/underinsured motorist context, the Legislature would have included self-insurance within the definition of an underinsured motorist in section 672.727(3) in those cases where the damages sustained by the injured party exceed the limit of liability set forth in the certificate of self-insurance. Thus, the Legislature implicitly recognized that, while self-insurance is an acceptable substitute to commercial insurance for certain purposes, it does not provide an equivalent guarantee of payment to the injured person in the uninsured motorist context.

. . .

Pursuant to Florida's uninsured motorist statutory scheme, motorists are considered uninsured when they lack liability insurance or possess liability insurance with limits of liability lower than the damages sustained by the policy-holder. We thus conclude that a self-insured motorist exclusion is contrary to the statutory scheme set forth in the uninsured motorist statute, and that the provision in the Progressive uninsured motorist policy refusing to treat a self-insured motorist as either an underinsured or uninsured motorist is void.[5]

---

[5] We disagree with the dissent's assessment that our decision today calls into question the uninsured motorist carrier's right to subrogation. The uninsured motorist carrier retains a right to subrogation against the self-insured tortfeasor, just as it would entertain a right of subrogation against an uninsured tortfeasor.

We answer the certified question in the negative, quash Young and disapprove of the Fourth District's opinion in Amica Mutual and the Second District's recent decision in Comesanas. We also disapprove of Centennial, Gabriel and Johns to the extent they are inconsistent with this opinion.

It is so ordered.

HARDING, C.J., and SHAW, ANSTEAD, LEWIS and QUINCE, JJ., concur.

WELLS, J., dissents with an opinion.***

WELLS, J., dissenting.

I dissent. I conclude that this issue should be decided by the simple and straightforward recognition that a motor vehicle that is covered by a certificate of self-insurance in accord with section 324.031(4), Florida Statutes (1999), and is thereby a self-*insured* motor vehicle, is, for the purposes of the Financial Responsibility Law, precisely what it is stated to be-an insured motor vehicle, not an uninsured motor vehicle. Pursuant to section 627.727, Florida Statutes (1999), a self-*insured* motor vehicle that meets the requirements of section 324.031(4), is just as much an "insured" motor vehicle as one covered by a motor vehicle liability policy pursuant to section 324.031(1). This straightforward recognition answers the certified question "yes" because it is simply a recognition of the plain meaning of the statute. See Amica Mutual Ins. Co. v. Amato, 667 So.2d 802 (Fla. 4th DCA 1995). It is whether a vehicle meets the requirements of the Financial Responsibility Law which is determinative of whether the vehicle is "uninsured."[6]

This conclusion is also consistent with the policy basis for the landmark case of Mullis v. State Farm Mutual Automobile Insurance Co., 252 So.2d 229 (Fla.1971). In Mullis this Court said:

> In sum, our holding is that uninsured motorist coverage prescribed by Section 627.0851 [now 324.031] is statutorily intended to provide the reciprocal or mutual equivalent of automobile liability coverage prescribed by the Financial Responsibility Law, i.e., to say coverage where an uninsured motorist negligently inflicts bodily injury or death upon a named insured, or any of his family relatives resident in his household, or any lawful occupants of the insured automobile covered in his automobile liability policy. To achieve this purpose, no policy exclusions contrary to the statute of any of the class of family insureds are permissible since uninsured motorist coverage is intended by the statute to be uniform and standard motor vehicle accident liability insurance *for the protection of such insureds thereunder as "if the uninsured motorist had carried the minimum limits" of an automobile liability policy.*

---

[6] See ch. 324, Fla. Stat. (1999) (Financial Responsibility Law).

Id. at 237-38 (emphasis added).

> **Manner of proving financial responsibility.**-The owner or operator of a taxicab, limousine, jitney, or any other for-hire passenger transportation vehicle may prove financial responsibility by providing satisfactory evidence of holding a motor vehicle liability policy as defined in s. 324.021(8) or s. 324.151, which policy is issued by an insurance carrier which is a member of the Florida Insurance Guaranty Association. The operator or owner of any other vehicle may prove his or her financial responsibility by:
>
> (1) Furnishing satisfactory evidence of holding a motor vehicle liability policy as defined in ss. 324.021(8) and 324.151; [or]

...

Moreover, I do not follow the complex knitting together of sections 627.727(1) and 627.727(3), Florida Statutes, which undergirds the majority's opinion to reach the rather startling conclusion that "a motorist who is self-insured must be deemed statutorily uninsured." Majority op. at 85. I do not believe such complexly constructed reasoning can convert self-*insured* into uninsured.

...

Finally, this Court's decisions in Lipof v. Florida Power & Light Co., 596 So.2d 1005 (Fla.1992), and Diversified Services v. Avila, 606 So.2d 364 (Fla.1992), do not support the incongruous result that, while a self-insured motor vehicle qualified under section 324.031(4), Florida Statutes, is not an underinsured motor vehicle, the vehicle is an uninsured motor vehicle. I read Lipof and Avila to be statutory constructions of section 627.727 which limit the application of that statute to "policies of liability insurance." These cases give to the statute its plain meaning, as does the analysis of the majority in this case as to underinsured motorist coverage. This is merely giving effect to the requirement of section 627.727 as those requirements pertain to "policies of insurance." However, those cases in no way make the illogical leap that only motor vehicles covered by "policies of liability insurance" are insured vehicles. Simply because a motor vehicle is not covered by a "policy of liability insurance" does not render the word "insured" a nullity in "self-insured." It merely means that the vehicle is "insured" other than by a policy regulated by the insurance code applicable to commercial insurance policies.

Accordingly, I dissent from the majority's opinion and would approve the district court's decision below.

NOTES AND QUESTIONS

1. Is the dissent's "plain meaning" argument as persuasive as the majority's "whole act" argument (reading the provisions together as part of a consistent and harmonious piece of legislation)?

2. Is the dissent's argument as persuasive as the majority's "expressio unius est exclusio alterius" argument?

3. Does the dissent even address the majority's "expressio unius est exclusion alterius" argument?

4. Why do you think this is a 6-1 decision? Is it because of the canons of statutory interpretation?

E. GRAMMAR AND PUNCTUATION RULES

Introduction

In Wagner v. Botts, 88 So. 2d 611, 613 (Fla. 1956) the Supreme Court stated Florida's modern approach to punctuation:

> We realize that punctuation is considered to be the most fallible and the least reliable indication of the legislative intent in interpreting a statute. Historically, parliamentary enactments originally were not punctuated at all. However, the Legislatures of our country have consistently attempted to follow the rules dictated by the grammar books with the result that statutes now are punctuated prior to enactment.
>
> The better rule now seems to be that the punctuation is a part of the Act and that it may be considered in the interpretation of the Act but it may not be used to create[sic] doubt or to distort or to defeat the intention of the Legislature.

KASISCHKE V. STATE
991 So.2d 803 (Fla. 2008)

CANTERO, J.

We review a statute that requires judges to impose conditions of probation on sexual offenders. At issue is whether the statute prohibits sexual offenders serving probation or community control from possessing any pornographic material at all or only such material relevant to the offender's deviant behavior. In the decision below, Kasischke v. State, 946 So.2d 1155, 1159 (Fla. 3d DCA 2006), the Third District Court of

Appeal held that offenders cannot possess any such material. Its decision expressly and directly conflicts with the Second District Court of Appeal's decision in Taylor v. State, 821 So.2d 404, 405-06 (Fla. 2d DCA 2002), which held that a condition prohibiting the defendant from "viewing, owning, or possessing obscene, pornographic, or sexually explicit material," must relate to the defendant's "particular deviant behavior pattern." We have jurisdiction to resolve the conflict. See art. V, § 3(b)(3), Fla. Const. Because, as the Third District acknowledged, the statute "is undeniably susceptible to multiple and irreconcilable interpretations," 946 So.2d at 1157-58, we apply the rule of lenity. We therefore quash the decision below and approve the Second District's decision in Taylor.

I. FACTS AND PROCEDURAL HISTORY

The facts on which the underlying convictions are based are explained in the district court's opinion. See Kasischke, 946 So.2d at 1156. For our purposes, suffice it to say that the Petitioner, Donald Kasischke, pled guilty to three counts each of lewd or lascivious battery and exhibition on a child under age sixteen. He was sentenced to 364 days in prison, followed by two years of community control and eight years of probation. Section 948.03(5)(a), Florida Statutes (1999), requires that courts impose several conditions on sexual offenders receiving probation or community control. For example, defendants are subject to a curfew; they cannot live within 1000 feet of certain places, such as schools, where children congregate; and they must successfully complete a sexual offender treatment program. Another condition that must be imposed-the one relevant here-is the following:

> Unless otherwise indicated in the treatment plan provided by the sexual offender treatment program, a prohibition on viewing, owning, or possessing any obscene, pornographic, or sexually stimulating visual or auditory material, including telephone, electronic media, computer programs, or computer services that are relevant to the offender's deviant behavior pattern.

§ 948.03(5)(a)(7), Fla. Stat. (1999). The Petitioner's plea agreement included such a condition. After he had been released from prison, and while he was serving his community control, a search of his home revealed allegedly "obscene, pornographic, or sexually stimulating" photographs, as well as a pornographic videotape. His community control was revoked and he was ordered incarcerated.

The parties do not dispute the pornographic nature of the videotape. They disagree, however, about whether the Petitioner's possession of these materials violated his community control. The State argues that his conditions forbid possession of any obscene or pornographic material, while the Petitioner argues that they only prohibit possession of such material relevant to his particular deviant behavior (in his case, paying a fifteen-year-old boy to allow him to perform oral sex on the boy and masturbating in the boy's presence).

On appeal, the Third District concluded that the statute was ambiguous. However, it analyzed the statute's legislative history, including a staff analysis explaining a 1997 amendment, and concluded that the Legislature intended to ban possession of all pornographic materials. Kasischke, 946 So.2d at 1159. In contrast, in a similar case, the Second District interpreted the same condition, albeit superficially, to prohibit only possession of materials relevant to the defendant's "particular deviant behavior pattern." Taylor, 821 So.2d at 405-06. We granted review to resolve the conflict. See Kasischke v. State, 954 So.2d 1156 (Fla.2007) (granting review).

II. ANALYSIS

The issue we consider is whether the statute prohibits possession of all pornographic materials, or only those "relevant to the offender's deviant behavior pattern." Although we quoted the statute above, because its language is central to our analysis, it bears repeating. It requires that any order imposing probation or community control include "a prohibition on viewing, owning, or possessing any obscene, pornographic, or sexually stimulating visual or auditory material, including telephone, electronic media, computer programs, or computer services that are relevant to the offender's deviant behavior pattern." § 948.03(5)(a)(7), Fla. Stat. (1999). The specific question is which part of the sentence is modified by the phrase "relevant to the offender's deviant behavior pattern"? The State argues that the phrase modifies "sexually stimulating visual or auditory material," which would mean that the statute prohibits possession of all obscene and pornographic material, *as well as* "sexually stimulating visual or auditory material ... relevant to the offender's deviant behavior pattern." The Petitioner, on the other hand, argues that the phrase modifies "obscene, pornographic, or sexually stimulating visual or auditory material," so that the statute prohibits possession only of such material that is relevant to his deviant behavior. The dissents take a third view (one not advanced by either party here), suggesting that "relevant to the offender's deviant behavior pattern" relates only to "telephone, electronic media, computer programs, or computer services." Lewis, J., dissenting op. at 817; Bell, J., dissenting op. at 829.

For the reasons explained below, we find section 948.03(5)(a)(7), Florida Statutes (1999), ambiguous. We therefore apply the rule of lenity and hold that the phrase "relevant to the offender's deviant behavior pattern" modifies each of the statutory prohibitions.

A. Plain Language

"The interpretation of a statute is a purely legal matter and therefore subject to the de novo standard of review." Kephart v. Hadi, 932 So.2d 1086, 1089 (Fla.2006), cert. denied, --- U.S. ----, 127 S.Ct. 1268, 167 L.Ed.2d 92 (2007). When construing a statute, we strive to effectuate the Legislature's intent. See, e.g., Borden v. East-European Ins. Co., 921 So.2d 587, 595 (Fla.2006) ("We endeavor to construe statutes to effectuate the intent of the Legislature."). To determine that intent, we look first to the statute's plain language. Id. at 595. "[W]hen the statute is clear and unambiguous, courts will not look behind the statute's plain language for legislative intent or resort to rules of statutory construction to ascertain intent." Id. (quoting Daniels v. Fla. Dep't of Health, 898 So.2d 61, 64 (Fla.2005)).

We agree with the district court that this statute "is undeniably susceptible to multiple and irreconcilable interpretations." Kasischke, 946 So.2d at 1157-58. The plain language of the statute could be construed in at least four ways: (1) as prohibiting all obscene, pornographic, or sexually stimulating material, as well as any telephone, electronic media, computer programs, or computer services that are relevant to the offender's deviant behavior pattern, see Bell, J., dissenting op. at 829; (2) as clarifying that "telephone, electronic media, computer programs, or computer services that are relevant to the offender's deviant behavior pattern" are within the ban on "obscene, pornographic, or sexually stimulating" material, see Lewis, J., dissenting op. at 817; (3) as prohibiting only such material relevant to the offender's deviant behavior pattern; and (4) as prohibiting all obscene and pornographic material, but prohibiting sexually stimulating visual or auditory material only when relevant to the offender's deviant behavior pattern. Therefore, as did the district court, see 946 So.2d at 1158, we find the statute ambiguous. We cannot rely solely on its plain language to discover the legislative intent.

Justice Lewis concludes that the plain language of the statute demonstrates that the Legislature intended the entire clause "including telephone, electronic media, computer programs, or computer services that are relevant to the offender's deviant behavior pattern" as merely illustrating a category of materials within the ban on "any obscene, pornographic, or sexually stimulating material." Lewis, J., dissenting op. at 817. In other words, Justice Lewis argues that the Legislature intended to clarify that "Internet-based and other forms of electronic obscenity and pornography" were within the prohibition. Id. at 821. If this were the case, however, the Legislature could have ended the sentence after the phrase, "including telephone, electronic media, computer programs, or computer services." Under Justice Lewis's interpretation, these materials would be prohibited whether or not relevant to the offender's deviant behavior. But the Legislature did not end there; it added the phrase "that are relevant to the offender's deviant behavior pattern." This phrase must modify something. See, e.g., Martinez v. State, 981 So.2d 449, 452 (Fla.2008) ("It is a basic rule of statutory construction that 'the Legislature does not intend to enact useless provisions, and courts should avoid readings that would render part of a statute meaningless.' " (quoting State v. Bodden, 877 So.2d 680, 686 (Fla.2004))). We cannot construe the plain language of the statute in a manner that renders this language superfluous.

[B. Exploring Legislative History- Omitted][2]

. . .

C . Applying the Canons of Statutory Construction

Where legislative intent is unclear from the plain language of the statute, we look to canons of statutory construction. Joshua v. City of Gainesville, 768 So.2d 432, 435 (Fla.2000) ("[I]f the language of the statute is unclear, then rules of statutory construction control."). One such canon is the doctrine of the last antecedent, under which "relative and qualifying words, phrases and clauses are to be applied to the words or phrase immediately preceding, and are not to be construed as extending to, or

---

[2] See below in the Section on Legislative History.

including, others more remote." City of St. Petersburg v. Nasworthy, 751 So.2d 772, 772 (Fla. 1st DCA 2000). The last antecedent is "the last word, phrase, or clause that can be made an antecedent without impairing the meaning of the sentence." 2A Norman J. Singer & J.D. Shambie Singer, Statutes and Statutory Construction § 47.33 (7th ed.2007).

Commentators have questioned the doctrine's utility. See Terri LeClercq, Doctrine of the Last Antecedent: The Mystifying Morass of Ambiguous Modifiers, 2 J. Legal Writing Inst. 81, 89 (1996) ("[R]ather than becoming 'one more aid' in interpretation as Sutherland hoped, the Doctrine of Last Antecedent has, in its hundred-plus year history, created as much confusion and disagreement as the ambiguous modifiers its drafter set out to clarify."). The very formulation of the doctrine recognizes its application only where "no contrary intention appears." Singer & Singer, supra, § 47:33 ("Referential and qualifying words and phrases, where no contrary intention appears, refer solely to the last antecedent."). As Statutes and Statutory Construction explains, "[t]he rule is another aid to discovery of intent or meaning and is not inflexible and uniformly binding. Where the sense of the entire act requires that a qualifying word or phrase apply to several preceding or even succeeding sections, the word or phrase will not be restricted to its immediate antecedent." Id.; see also Barnhart v. Thomas, 540 U.S. 20, 26, 124 S.Ct. 376, 157 L.Ed.2d 333 (2003) ("While [the doctrine of last antecedent] is not an absolute and can assuredly be overcome by other indicia of meaning, we have said that construing a statute in accord with the rule is 'quite sensible as a matter of grammar.' " (quoting Nobelman v. Am. Savings Bank, 508 U.S. 324, 330, 113 S.Ct. 2106, 124 L.Ed.2d 228 (1993))); Porto Rico Ry., Light & Power Co. v. Mor, 253 U.S. 345, 348, 40 S.Ct. 516, 64 L.Ed. 944 (1920) ("When several words are followed by a clause which is applicable as much to the first and other words as to the last, the natural construction of the language demands that the clause be read as applicable to all."). One commentator has explained that the doctrine itself requires interpretation:

> Sutherland begins with what seems the fall-back rule of statutory interpretation and concludes with his specific point. He begins with a qualifier, that interpreters should use the Doctrine of Last Antecedent "where no contrary intention appears." Appears where? Within the phrase or within the document as a whole? In the notes of the committee that wrote the original rule? If the language offers no "contrary intention," then the meaning is already "plain." If the contrary intent shows up within the sentence itself, then there is no need for the rule. And legislative intent or the drafter's intent is usually in question to begin with, so that search rarely clarifies the sentence in question.... Thus the Sutherland rule is a jumble.

LeClercq, supra, at 92-93 (footnotes omitted).

In any event, applying the doctrine here does not result in the State's suggested construction, which is that the phrase, "that are relevant to the offender's deviant behavior pattern" qualifies "sexually stimulating visual or auditory material." To reach this construction, we would have to insert a comma at the end of the intervening phrase "including telephone, electronic media, computer programs, or computer services." To explain, "commas are used to set off expressions that provide additional but *nonessential* information about a noun or pronoun immediately preceding. Such expressions serve to further identify or explain the word they refer to." William A. Sabin, The Gregg Reference Manual 34 (10th ed.2005). These expressions are parenthetical, meaning that the sentence can stand alone without them. When an expression is *essential* to the sentence, however, it is not separated with commas. Id. at 35; see also State v. Tunney, 77 Wash.App. 929, 895 P.2d 13, 16 (1995) ("Under the rules of punctuation, appositives which serve a nonrestrictive (parenthetic) function are set off by commas; appositives which serve a restrictive (necessary) function are not."), aff'd, 129 Wash.2d 336, 917 P.2d 95 (1996); Xcel Corp. v. Dir., Div. of Taxation, 4 N.J.Tax 85, 89, 1982 WL 628231 ("It is an elementary rule of grammar that commas are used to set off nonrestrictive appositives, which are nouns that immediately follow and provide additional but nonessential information about another noun in the sentence."), aff'd, 5 N.J.Tax 480, 1982 WL 628299 (Super.Ct.App.Div.1982). "Evidence that a qualifying phrase is supposed to apply to all antecedents instead of only to the immediately preceding one may be found in the fact that it is separated from the antecedents by a comma." Singer & Singer, supra, § 47:33. Thus, to reach the State's proffered construction, we would have to read the phrase "including telephone, electronic media, computer programs, or computer services" as an appositive phrase that provides nonessential explanatory information about the immediately preceding phrase-"sexually stimulating visual or auditory material." So construed, removing the phrase would make the sentence read, "or sexually stimulating visual or auditory material ... that are relevant to the offender's deviant behavior pattern."

The problem with such a construction is that the Legislature did *not* isolate with commas the phrase "including telephone, electronic media, computer programs, or computer services." We cannot read it as a parenthetical phrase by inserting a comma ourselves. See Wagner v. Botts, 88 So.2d 611, 613 (Fla.1956) ("We have no authority to insert punctuation marks which are not there in order to engraft upon the Act our notion of what the Legislature intended or should have intended.").[7]

Instead, under the doctrine of last antecedent, the last phrase would qualify the immediately preceding phrase, so that "relevant to the offender's deviant behavior pattern" would modify only "electronic media, computer programs, or computer services." See State ex rel. Owens v. Pearson, 156 So.2d 4, 6 (Fla.1963) ("[F]ollowing an enumeration in a series, a qualifying phrase will be read as limited to the last of the series when it follows that item without a comma or other indication that it relates as well to those items preceding the conjunction."); 48A Fla. Jur.2d Statutes § 133 (2007) (recognizing that under the doctrine of last antecedent, "a qualifying phrase in a statute is read as limited to the last item in a series when the phrase follows that item without a comma"). That interpretation, however, would lead to the absurd result that an

---

[7] We note that even inserting a comma would not necessarily eliminate the ambiguity. The statute would then require "a prohibition on viewing ... any obscene, pornographic, or sexually stimulating ... material, including telephone, electronic media, computer programs, or computer services[,] that are relevant to the offender's deviant behavior." The statute could still be interpreted to prohibit only materials relevant to the offender's deviant behavior. If the Legislature intended to prohibit possession of all obscene or pornographic materials, as well as prohibit sexually stimulating material relevant to the offender's deviant behavior, it could have phrased the statute as follows: "a prohibition on ... possessing any obscene or pornographic material, or any sexually stimulating ... material that are relevant to the offender's deviant behavior, including telephone, electronic media, computer programs, or computer services."

offender would be prohibited from "viewing, owning, or possessing" all "obscene, pornographic, or sexually stimulating visual or auditory material" in print form, but not the same material in "telephone, electronic media, computer programs, or computer services" unless it was "relevant to the offender's deviant behavior pattern." Possession of a "sexually stimulating" photograph would violate the statute, but possession of a computer image of that photograph would not, unless it was relevant to the particular offender's deviant behavior pattern. We cannot apply the doctrine of last antecedent in a manner that leads to such a result. See, e.g., Warner v. City of Boca Raton, 887 So.2d 1023, 1033 n. 9 (Fla.2004) ("[A] statutory provision should not be construed in such a way that it renders the statute meaningless or leads to absurd results."); City of St. Petersburg v. Siebold, 48 So.2d 291, 294 (Fla.1950) ("The courts will not ascribe to the Legislature an intent to create absurd ... consequences, and so an interpretation avoiding absurdity is always preferred."); Haworth v. Chapman, 113 Fla. 591, 152 So. 663, 665 (Fla.1933) ("There is a strong presumption against absurdity in a statutory provision; it being unreasonable to suppose that the Legislature intended their own stultification....").

The final possible interpretation of the last phrase is that it modifies the entire sentence so that defendants are prohibited from possessing any obscene, pornographic, or sexually stimulating material, but only to the extent the material is relevant to the offender's deviant behavior pattern. This interpretation seems at least as faithful an interpretation of the text as the others, if not more so. It has the benefit of prohibiting obscene, pornographic, and sexually stimulating material to the same extent and gives a logical meaning to the last phrase.

Such an interpretation is also supported by another canon of statutory construction: the rule of lenity. In Florida, the rule is not just an interpretive tool, but a statutory directive. See § 775.021(1), Fla. Stat. (2007) ("The provisions of this code and offenses defined by other statutes shall be strictly construed; when the language is susceptible of differing constructions, it shall be construed most favorably to the accused."). The rule requires that "[a]ny ambiguity or situations in which statutory language is susceptible to differing constructions *must* be resolved in favor of the person charged with an offense." State v. Byars, 823 So.2d 740, 742 (Fla.2002) (emphasis added). As we have emphasized before, " '[o]ne of the most fundamental principles of Florida law is that penal statutes must be strictly construed according to their letter.' " Id. (quoting Perkins v. State, 576 So.2d 1310, 1312 (Fla.1991)). "Indeed, our system of jurisprudence is founded on a belief that everyone must be given sufficient notice of those matters that may result in a deprivation of life, liberty, or property." Perkins, 576 So.2d at 1312; see also United States v. Santos, --- U.S. ----, ----, 128 S.Ct. 2020, 2025, 170 L.Ed.2d 912, ---- (2008) (plurality opinion) ("Under a long line of our decisions, the tie must go to the defendant. The rule of lenity requires ambiguous criminal laws to be interpreted in favor of the defendants subjected to them."); State v. Winters, 346 So.2d 991, 993 (Fla.1977) ("Penal statutes must be strictly construed in favor of the accused where there is doubt as to their meaning and must be sufficiently explicit so that men of common intelligence may ascertain whether a contemplated act is within or without the law, and so that the ordinary man may determine what conduct is proscribed by the statute.").

We recognize that the rule of lenity is a canon of last resort. See, e.g., United States v. Shabani, 513 U.S. 10, 17, 115 S.Ct. 382, 130 L.Ed.2d 225 (1994) ("The rule of lenity, however, applies only when, after consulting traditional canons of statutory construction, we are left with an ambiguous statute."); cf. Bautista v. State, 863 So.2d 1180, 1185 n. 4 (Fla.2003) (recognizing that the rule of lenity does not apply where legislative intent to the contrary is clear). As discussed above, however, and as the Third District acknowledged in this case, the statute "is undeniably susceptible to multiple and irreconcilable interpretations." 946 So.2d at 1157. The dissenting justices have presented two of many possible interpretations of the statute. Their lengthy dissents to this opinion only highlight the difficulty in interpreting this hopelessly ambiguous statute. We have been unable otherwise to resolve this ambiguity and cannot simply choose our preferred construction. We therefore apply the rule of lenity and hold that the limiting phrase "relevant to the offender's deviant behavior pattern" must be interpreted as qualifying each of the prohibitions in section 948.03(5)(a)(7). See Clines v. State, 912 So.2d 550, 560 (Fla.2005) (applying the rule of lenity to an ambiguous statute that "generate[d] differing reasonable constructions"). In other words, the Petitioner violated the statute only if the "obscene, pornographic, or sexually stimulating" material recovered from his home was relevant to his "deviant behavior pattern." That issue has not been addressed in this case and is outside the scope of the conflict. See, e.g., McEnderfer v. Keefe, 921 So.2d 597, 597 n. 1 (Fla.2006) (declining to reach issues "that were either not directly addressed by the district court ... or were merely implied or cursory, at best"); Gaines v. Sayne, 764 So.2d 578, 586 (Fla.2000) (declining to address an issue outside the scope of the conflict). We therefore leave it for resolution on remand.

III. CONCLUSION

We hold that the phrase "relevant to the offender's deviant behavior pattern" qualifies each of the prohibitions in section 948.03(5)(a)(7), Florida Statutes (1999). An offender does not violate this condition unless the "obscene, pornographic, or sexually stimulating" material at issue is relevant to the "deviant behavior pattern." We therefore approve the Second District's decision in Taylor and quash the Third District's decision in Kasischke. We remand this case to the district court with instructions that it be returned to the trial court for further proceedings consistent with this opinion.

It is so ordered.

QUINCE, C.J., and WELLS, ANSTEAD, and PARIENTE, JJ., concur.

LEWIS and BELL, JJ., dissent with opinions.

LEWIS, J., dissenting.

This case involves interpretation of section 948.03(5)(a)(7), Florida Statutes (1999), which is a default term of probation and community control for Florida's convicted sexual offenders. This question of statutory interpretation is subject to de novo review. See, e.g., Daniels v. Fla. Dep't of Health, 898 So.2d 61, 64 (Fla.2005). The 1999 version of section 948.03(5)(a)(7),reads as follows:

> *Unless otherwise indicated in the treatment plan provided by the sexual offender treatment program*, a prohibition on viewing, owning, or possessing *any* obscene, pornographic, or sexually stimulating visual or auditory material, *including* telephone, electronic media, computer programs, or computer services that are relevant to the offender's deviant behavior pattern.(Emphasis supplied.) The majority opinion does not adequately address the presence or significance of (1) the adjective *"any,"* (2) the participle *"including,"* (3) the *comma* preceding "including," which further indicates that the entire clause introduced by "including" is illustrative, or (4) a series of *intervening nouns*.

When one reads section 948.03(5)(a)(7) it is apparent that the clause "*including* telephone, electronic media, computer programs, or computer services that are relevant to the offender's deviant behavior pattern," is merely illustrative and indicates that these materials fall within the general ambit of the *total prohibition* against the sexual offender "viewing, owning, or possessing *any* obscene, pornographic, or sexually stimulating visual or auditory material." Cf. Wagner v. Botts, 88 So.2d 611 (Fla.1956). The grammatical structure and phrasing of this default term of sexual-offender probation and community control simply does not admit of any other *reasonable interpretation*; therefore, the rule of lenity does not apply. See, e.g., Clines v. State, 912 So.2d 550, 560 (Fla.2005) ("[T]he rule [of lenity] 'is applicable to sentencing provisions' if they 'create ambiguity or generate differing *reasonable constructions*.' " (quoting Nettles v. State, 850 So.2d 487, 494 (Fla.2003) (emphasis supplied)); Wallace v. State, 860 So.2d 494, 497-98 (Fla. 4th DCA 2003) ("Application of [the] rule [of lenity] means that if there is a *reasonable construction* of a penal statute favorable to the accused, the court must employ that construction."(emphasis supplied)).

I. ANALYSIS

A. The Plain Text of Section 948.03(5)(a)(7)

The plain text of section 948.03(5)(a)(7) clearly conveys the intent of the Legislature. Further, "the statute's plain and ordinary meaning must control, unless this leads to an unreasonable result or a result clearly contrary to legislative intent." Daniels, 898 So.2d at 64. Here, the plain text neither leads to an absurd outcome nor results in the creation or perpetuation of an unintended evil. Therefore, the analysis of the majority should have concluded with the plain text of the statute without applying such doctrines as the rule of lenity.

The Legislature has not in any way indicated an intent to abandon the total prohibition against sexual offenders "viewing, owning, or possessing *any* obscene, pornographic, or sexually stimulating visual or auditory material." § 948.03(5)(a)(7), Fla. Stat. (1999) (emphasis supplied). Rather, the Legislature simply clarified that this broad prohibition "*includ[es]* telephone, electronic media, computer programs, or computer services that are relevant to the offender's deviant behavior pattern." Id. (emphasis supplied). This is an illustrative clause separated by a comma and introduced by the participle "including"; therefore, under the rules of grammar and the rule of the last antecedent, the relative clause "that are relevant to the offender's deviant behavior pattern" modifies the grouping of nouns "including telephone, electronic media, computer programs, or computer services," and does *not* modify the noun "material" contained in the separate, preceding clause "any obscene, pornographic, or sexually stimulating visual or auditory material." Id.; see Owens, 156 So.2d at 6 ("[T]he established rules of grammatical construction [dictate] that, following an enumeration in series, a qualifying phrase will be read as limited to the last of the series when it follows that item without a comma or other indication that it relates as well to those items preceding the conjunction."); Bodden, 877 So.2d at 685 ("[T]he legislature is presumed to know the meaning of words and the rules of grammar[.]"); see also Gaffney v. Riverboat Servs. of Ind., Inc., 451 F.3d 424, 459 (7th Cir.2006) (stating that use of the participle "including" generally implies an illustrative application) (citing Black's Law Dictionary 687 (5th ed.1979)); In re Glunk, 342 B.R. 717, 729 (Bankr.E.D.Pa.2006) (holding that the use of the participle "including" in 11 U.S.C. § 707(a) indicates that "the three enumerated grounds for dismissal [for lack of a good-faith filing] are illustrative and not exhaustive").

In this context, the reliance of Kasischke and the majority upon Porto Rico Railway, Light & Power Co. v. Mor, 253 U.S. 345, 40 S.Ct. 516, 64 L.Ed. 944 (1920), for a contrary rule of construction is misplaced and improper. See Initial Brief of the Petitioner on the Merits at 19-20; majority op. at 811-812. In Mor, the High Court stated that "[w]hen several words are followed by a clause which is applicable as much to the first and other words as to the last, the natural construction of the language demands that the clause be read as applicable to all." 253 U.S. at 348, 40 S.Ct. 516. However, the Court applied this rule of construction to section 41 of the Jones Act of March 2, 1917, to avoid a potentially absurd result: "Congress could not have intended to give the District Court [of Puerto Rico] jurisdiction of any controversy to which a domiciled alien is a party while denying under similar circumstances jurisdiction where a domiciled American is a party." Id. at 349, 40 S.Ct. 516.

However, in contrast to Mor, an absurd result will not occur based upon a plain-text interpretation of section 948.03(5)(a)(7). Further, a "*natural* construction of the language" of section 948.03(5)(a)(7) demonstrates the grammatical incongruity of reading "relevant to the offender's deviant behavior pattern" as modifying a preceding clause *which is separated from the former clause by (1) a comma, (2) an illustrative participle, and (3) a string of several nouns*. Kasischke and the majority contend that a logical, grammatical reading of section 948.03(5)(a)(7)'s plain text (i.e., interpreting the clause "relevant to the offender's deviant behavior pattern" as modifying "telephone, electronic media, computer programs, or computer services") would lead to an absurd or unreasonable result. See Initial Brief of the Petitioner on the Merits at 19-20; majority op. at 808, 813-814. This is entirely incorrect based upon the language and organization of the statute. The Legislature intended to prohibit the "viewing, owning, or possessing" by convicted sexual offenders of "*any* obscene, pornographic, or sexually stimulating visual or auditory material," and simply clarified that this prohibition "*includ[es]* telephone, electronic media, computer programs, or computer services that are relevant to the offender's deviant behavior pattern." § 948.03(5)(a)(7), Fla. Stat. (1999). (emphasis supplied).

The majority is conspicuously silent with regard to much of this plain-text analysis. In my view, this silence represents an example of the "dog that didn't bark." See Sir Arthur Conan Doyle, Silver Blaze, in The Memoirs of Sherlock Holmes (1894). An absurd or unreasonable result does not occur based on the plain text of the statute because the "including" clause is *illustrative* and clarifies the fact that the total-prohibition clause "includes" *otherwise innocuous* electronic, telephonic, and computer-based materials. The modifying language "relevant to the offender's deviant behavior pattern" merely relates these otherwise innocuous materials back to the total-prohibition clause (i.e., it clarifies that the only "telephone, electronic media, computer programs, or computer services" that convicted sexual offenders are prohibited from "viewing, owning, or possessing" are those that are *"obscene, pornographic, or sexually stimulating" as a matter of law)*. § 948.03(5)(a)(7), Fla. Stat. (1999) (emphasis supplied). According to the evident language, punctuation, and syntactic organization of the statute, there is no difference between an offender's possession of a tangible photograph and the same image stored as a file on the offender's computer or, for that matter, presented as an image on the offender's television. If the photograph is "obscene, pornographic, or sexually stimulating" as a matter of law, then Kasischke-and others subject to the same default term of probation and community control-would be prohibited from "viewing, owning, or possessing" the photo *regardless of whether it is in print, electronic, or televisual form*. This is so because the total-prohibition clause, which bans *"any* obscene, pornographic, or sexually stimulating visual or auditory material," *"includ[es]* telephone, electronic media, computer programs, or computer services that are relevant to the offender's deviant behavior pattern." § 948.03(5)(a)(7), Fla. Stat. (1999) (emphasis supplied).[19]

As stated in the statute, the total-prohibition clause applies "[u]nless otherwise indicated in the treatment plan provided by the sexual offender treatment program." § 948.03(5)(a)(7), Fla. Stat. (1999). However, here, the record does not indicate that any qualified decision-maker ever individually tailored Kasischke's treatment plan by altering his default conditions of probation and community control with the approval of the appropriate court. Cf. § 948.03(6), Fla. Stat. (1999) (affording the appropriate court continuing jurisdiction to modify the offender's release conditions in proper circumstances). On the contrary, Kasischke's community-control officers advised him that the default total prohibition applied and that, consequently, he was prohibited from "viewing, owning, or possessing *any* obscene, pornographic, or sexually

[19] A similar cabining of section 948.03(5)(a)(7), Florida Statutes (1999), and sections 948.30(1)(g), and 947.1405(7)(a)(7), Florida Statutes (2007), is possible through selective reference to the definitions contained in section 847.001, Florida Statutes. Such a cabining could be utilized to construe the terms "pornographic material" and "sexually stimulating visual or auditory material" to remove questions with regard to the constitutional requirements of due process. See § 847.001, Fla. Stat. (2007) (this statute contains detailed definitions of "child pornography" and "sexual conduct," which when appropriately redacted provide an equally detailed definition of "pornography"; further, the statute defines "sexually oriented material," which is sufficiently analogous to "sexually stimulating visual or auditory material" because the statutory term includes "any drawing, etching, painting, photograph, motion picture film, or sound recording that depicts sexual activity" (emphasis supplied)).

To avoid any due-process vagueness issues, reference to these statutory definitions could be utilized when construing this default term of sexual-offender probation, community control, and conditional release. I would leave for another day the question of whether these sufficiently definite classifications raise any overbreadth concerns.

stimulating visual or auditory material." § 948.03(5)(a)(7), Fla. Stat. (1999) (emphasis supplied)..

The majority also offers suspect reasoning with regard to its claim that there are at least four acceptable interpretations of the statute. See majority op. at 807-808. The only grammatically acceptable reading of the statute requires that the clause "relevant to the offender's deviant behavior pattern" modify "telephone, electronic media, computer programs, or computer services," which is the same interpretative result reached in the other dissent. The majority's disjunctive listing of my interpretation of the statute and that offered in the other dissent is totally misleading. Both dissents have correctly interpreted the plain text of the statute; we simply arrive at that interpretation through different rationales.

The number of "interpretations" advanced by the majority is overly generous. One proffered interpretation, which was the interpretation adopted by the Third District below, is incorrect as a matter of grammar. The Third District erroneously adopted the State's *alternative*, secondary argument, which applied the clause "relevant to the offender's deviant behavior pattern" to "sexually stimulating ... material," despite the fact that the adjectives "obscene" and "pornographic" also modify "material." See Kasischke, 946 So.2d at 1159-61. As explained above, "relevant to the offender's deviant behavior pattern" cannot modify "material" due to the syntax and punctuation of the statute. Further, even if this language could somehow modify "material," which it cannot, it would necessarily modify "material" in all of its applications (i.e., "obscene material," "pornographic material," *and* "sexually stimulating visual or auditory material"). Hence, the majority is really reduced to *two* of its "acceptable" interpretations of the statute. However, the majority's adopted reading is inconsistent with the statute as written; therefore, it is *not* an "acceptable" interpretation. See, e.g., Fla. Dep't of Revenue v. Fla. Mun. Power Agency, 789 So.2d 320, 324 (Fla.2001) ("Under fundamental principles of separation of powers, courts cannot judicially alter the wording of statutes where the Legislature clearly has not done so."); Hawkins v. Ford Motor Co., 748 So.2d 993, 1000 (Fla.1999) ("[T]his Court may not rewrite statutes contrary to their plain language."). "[R]elevant to the offender's deviant behavior pattern" cannot modify the total-prohibition clause because of (1) the adjective "any," (2) the illustrative participle "including," (3) the comma preceding "including," and (4) a series of intervening nouns. § 948.03(5)(a)(7), Fla. Stat. (1999); see also Bismarck Lumber, 314 U.S. at 100, 62 S.Ct. 1; Bodden, 877 So.2d at 685; Owens, 156 So.2d at 5; Wagner, 88 So.2d at 612-13. In sum, there is only *one* acceptable, grammatically sound interpretation of the statute-the plain-text interpretation outlined in this dissent as intended and written by the Legislature.

The error of Kasischke and the majority exists in their conflation of the purely illustrative "including" clause with the ban created in the primary total-prohibition clause. That the Legislature felt compelled to add this illustrative clause in 1997 makes perfect sense. See ch. 97-308, § 3, at 5520, Laws of Fla. During the mid-to-late 1990s, Internet-based and other forms of electronic obscenity and pornography were steadily increasing. Some commentators viewed these new materials as qualitatively different from traditional print-based or otherwise tangible obscene or pornographic materials. For example, as two commentators have explained:

> The rapid, worldwide growth of the Internet leads to unprecedented opportunities in applications in business, communication, education, and entertainment. Commercial interests act as a driving force behind these applications, but one of the byproducts is sex-lots of it. Sex is one of the most researched words on the Internet. Pornographic web sites have shown tremendous growth in the past few years, increasing by nearly 300 [sites] a day and [generating] $700 million in a year. [As of March 2002,] [t]hey total[ed] approximately 170,000. "Cybersex" or "cyber-porn" came hand-in-glove with global interconnectivity.
>
> Pornography on the Internet is *unique* because sexually explicit materials posted on the Internet *differ from traditional forms of pornographic materials*, such as magazines and videos, in several important ways: (a) it is widely available through Bulletin Board Services (BBS) groups and via the World Wide Web through database accesses, interactive services, e-mail, Internet Relay Chat (IRC), and real-time data feeds; (b) it is *active* and *interactive* through the presentation of materials in multimedia formats such as digitized moving images, animated sequences, sexually explicit texts, hot chats, and interactive sexual games; and (c) consumers also are producers of pornographic materials.... "Pornography in cyberspace is pornography in society-just broader, deeper, worse, and more of it."

Ven-hwei Lo & Ran Wei, Third-Person Effect, Gender, and Pornography on the Internet, 46 J. Broad. & Elec. Media 13, 13-14 (2002) (citations omitted) (quoting Catherine A. MacKinnon, Vindication and Resistance: A Response to the Carnegie Mellon Study of Pornography in Cyberspace, 83 Geo. L.J.1959, 1959 (1995)). Hence, the purely illustrative "including" clause is not surplusage because it clarifies that the total-prohibition clause *includes* (but is not limited to or by) the potentially qualitatively different electronic and telephonic materials contained within the "including" clause. The modifier "relevant to the offender's deviant behavior pattern" merely relates the otherwise innocuous materials outlined in the "including" clause back to the total-prohibition clause's outright ban of "*any* obscene, pornographic, or sexually stimulating visual or auditory material." § 948.03(5)(a)(7), Fla. Stat. (1999) (emphasis supplied).

The construction advanced by Kasischke and the majority is simply unreasonable based upon the plain text of section 948.03(5)(a)(7) because such a construction is inconsistent with the language, punctuation, and syntax of the statute. Moreover, as I explain below, even if we move beyond the plain text of the statute, the relevant legislative history of section 948.03(5)(a)(7) confirms my interpretation of this subsection.[22]

---

[22] The majority "explores legislative history" before applying the doctrines of statutory interpretation and canons of construction that may aid us in interpreting the text of the relevant statute. See majority op. at 808-813. However, we generally examine the statutory text, which may include the application of canons of construction and interpretive doctrines (such as our adherence to the established rules of grammar), and then consult relevant legislative history if further clarification is necessary or probative. See, e.g., State v. Sousa, 903 So.2d 923, 928 (Fla.2005) ("The fundamental rule of construction in determining legislative intent is to first give effect to the plain and ordinary meaning of the language used by the Legislature. Courts are not to change the plain meaning of a statute by turning to legislative history if the meaning of the statute can be discerned from the language in the statute.").

[B. The Relevant Legislative History - Omitted]

***

II. CONCLUSION

I cannot agree with the reading of nonexistent ambiguity into a clearly worded statute. Simply because the Third District and the majority have stated that section 948.03(5)(a)(7) "is undeniably susceptible to multiple and irreconcilable interpretations" does not make it so. Majority op. at 805, 807, 814 (quoting Kasischke, 946 So.2d at 1157). A simple, grammatical, plain-text reading of the statute makes it abundantly clear that the Legislature has maintained the total prohibition against convicted sex offenders "viewing, owning, or possessing *any* obscene, pornographic, or sexually stimulating visual or auditory material" during the term of their probation or community control. § 948.03(5)(a)(7), Fla. Stat. (1999) (emphasis supplied). Further, the Legislature clarified that this prohibition *"includ[es]* telephone, electronic media, computer programs, or computer services that are relevant to the offender's deviant behavior pattern." Id. (emphasis supplied). Any tailoring of this default prohibition to the characteristics of the individual sexual offender occurs *exclusively* through the offender's treatment plan and a corresponding judicial modification of the default prohibition- *not* through the statute itself. See id. (*"Unless otherwise indicated in the treatment plan provided by the sexual offender treatment program,"* the default prohibition applies. (emphasis supplied)). The majority creates ambiguity where none exists and "interprets" the statute contrary to the intent of the Legislature. The Legislature needs to address this statutory provision unless the judicially rewritten statute of the majority truly reflects a heretofore unexpressed legislative intent.

For these reasons, I respectfully dissent.

[BELL, J., dissenting. Omitted]

NOTES AND QUESTIONS

1. Does the majority need to turn to the rule of lenity if the grammar rules lead to an absurd result?

2. Should the grammar rules decide the case?

3. Is the dissent correct that its reading is dictated by the plain meaning of the statute? Do the grammar rules give you the plain meaning?

4. If the meaning is clear then why does the State offer one interpretation, the appellant another, and the dissent yet another interpretation? Are their interpretations based on policy, politics, or external values?

5. Is the majority correct that there are four possible interpretations?

6. We will revisit this case below. See Section III. Extrinsic Tools, Part C. Legislative Background/History. After reading that section, you might ask yourself if the legislative history is a better indication of legislative intent than these grammar rules, or the rule of lenity?

STATE OF FLORIDA V. BODDEN

877 So. 2d 680 (Fla. Dist. Ct. App. 2d Dist. 2002)

PARIENTE, J.

In State v. Bodden, 872 So.2d 916 (Fla. 2d DCA 2002), the Second District Court of Appeal certified the following question of great public importance:

> IN ADMINISTERING FLORIDA'S IMPLIED CONSENT LAW, IS THE FLORIDA DEPARTMENT OF LAW ENFORCEMENT REQUIRED TO ADOPT RULES IN ACCORDANCE WITH THE FLORIDA ADMINISTRATIVE PROCEDURES [SIC] ACT GOVERNING THE COLLECTION, PRESERVATION, AND ANALYSIS OF URINE SAMPLES OBTAINED BY LAW ENFORCEMENT PURSUANT TO SECTION 316.1932(1)(a), FLORIDA STATUTES.

Because we conclude that section 316.1932(1)(a)(1), Florida Statutes (2002), does not require that urine testing procedures be promulgated by rule in accordance with the Florida Administrative Procedure Act (APA), we answer the certified question in the negative.

FACTS AND PROCEDURAL HISTORY

This case arises out of charges that Bodden was driving under the influence in violation of section 316.193(1), Florida Statutes (2002). During a traffic stop the police officer noticed that Bodden had red eyes and slurred speech, swayed while he stood, and smelled of alcohol. The officer read Bodden the implied consent warning, and Bodden agreed to a breath test and a urine test. The breath test results indicated that Bodden's blood-alcohol level was between .060 and .065 percent. The urine test results indicated the presence of a controlled substance.[2]

---

[2] Section 316.193(1), Florida Statutes (2002), provides in relevant part:

(1) A person is guilty of the offense of driving under the influence and is subject to punishment as provided in subsection (2) if the person is driving or in actual physical control of a vehicle within this state and:

(a) The person is under the influence of alcoholic beverages, any chemical substance set forth in s. 877.111, or any substance controlled under chapter 893, when affected to the extent that the person's normal faculties are impaired....

Subsection (2)(a) provides the penalties which apply to a conviction under the section. See § 316.193(2)(a).

The police also searched Bodden and found less than twenty grams of marijuana in his pocket, a marijuana pipe, and rolling papers. Consequently, he was also charged with one count of possession of cannabis in violation of section 893.13(6)(b), Florida Statutes (2002), and one

Bodden filed two motions in limine requesting that the trial court suppress any reference to his urine test results because no regulatory criteria for testing had been promulgated in accordance with chapter 120, Florida Statutes (2002) (the APA). Bodden argued that section 316.1932, part of the implied consent law pertaining to the operation of motor vehicles, requires that any scientific test conducted pursuant to the implied consent law, including a urine test, be an approved test. At the hearing on the motion, the State provided expert testimony regarding the urine testing procedures employed by the Florida Department of Law Enforcement (FDLE) Crime Laboratory in Tallahassee and verified that although FDLE procedures were adapted from published methods, FDLE's specific procedures had not been published or promulgated in accordance with the APA.

The county court judge determined that the implied consent law required that urine testing procedures be promulgated in accordance with the APA, and granted Bodden's motions to suppress. The county judge also certified to the Second District Court of Appeal the same question the Second District subsequently certified to this Court in this case-that is, whether section 316.1932(1)(a)(1) requires that urine testing procedures be approved through formal rule promulgation in accordance with the APA.[5]

The Second District answered the question in the affirmative. See Bodden, 872 So.2d at 917. According to the Second District, the sole question to be answered was whether the term "approved" in section 316.1932(1)(a)(1) refers to urine tests as well as breath and blood tests. See id. The Second District determined that the implied consent statute was an ambiguous criminal statute, and, as such, should be construed in favor of the accused. Id. Interpreting the same statute under similar factual circumstances, the Fifth District Court of Appeal in State v. Pierre, 854 So.2d 231 (Fla. 5th DCA 2003), reached a decision contrary to that of the Second District in Bodden. In Pierre, the Fifth District concluded that section 316.1932, taken as a whole, "evinces an unambiguous intent that urine tests need not be approved." See id. at 233. The Fifth District in Pierre certified conflict with Bodden. See id. at 232.

ANALYSIS

A. Certified Question

The certified question presents the narrow issue of whether section 316.1932 requires that procedures for the collection, preservation, and analysis of urine samples be promulgated and approved by rule in accordance with the APA. As in all cases in which we are called upon to construe a statute, we begin with the language used by the Legislature in the specific statutory provision.

---

count of possession of drug paraphernalia in violation of section 893.147, Florida Statutes (2002). Those charges are not at issue.

5...Florida Rule of Appellate Procedure 9.160 governs the district courts' discretionary proceedings to review county court decisions.

Subsection (1)(a)(1) provides in pertinent part:

> Any person who accepts the privilege extended by the laws of this state of operating a motor vehicle within this state is, by so operating such vehicle, deemed to have given his or her consent to submit *to an approved chemical test or physical test including*, but not limited to, an infrared light test of his or her breath for the purpose of determining the alcohol content of his or her blood or breath, *and to a urine test* for the purpose of detecting the presence of chemical substances as set forth in s. 877.111 or controlled substances....

The key to the resolution of the narrow issue we confront is whether the word "approved" in section 316.1932(1)(a)(1) modifies "urine test." An "approved" test under this provision is one that is adopted through rule promulgation in accordance with the APA. See § 120.54(3), Fla. Stat. (2003); see also State v. Bender, 382 So.2d 697, 699 (Fla.1980) (recognizing that approved testing methods are those which have been adopted in compliance with the implied consent statutory provisions and the administrative rules). We have recognized that one purpose of establishing uniform, approved testing methods is to "ensure reliable scientific evidence for use in future court proceedings and to protect the health of those persons being tested." Bender, 382 So.2d at 699. The results of tests that must be approved "are admissible into evidence [under the implied consent law] only upon compliance with the statutory provisions and the administrative rules enacted by its authority." Id. at 699. In this case, if "approved" modifies "urine test" then FDLE must promulgate uniform rules for urine testing in accordance with the APA, which requires a notice and public hearing. To make the determination as to whether "approved" modifies "urine test," we must engage in statutory construction.

We have explained that as a fundamental principle of statutory construction, "legislative intent is the polestar that guides the Court's inquiry." State v. Rife, 789 So.2d 288, 292 (Fla.2001) (quoting McLaughlin v. State, 721 So.2d 1170, 1172 (Fla.1998)); see also M.W. v. Davis, 756 So.2d 90, 100 (Fla.2000) (same). Legislative intent is derived primarily from the language of the statute. See Rife, 789 So.2d at 292. Thus, "it is axiomatic that in construing a statute courts must first look at the actual language used in the statute." Woodham v. Blue Cross & Blue Shield of Florida, Inc., 829 So.2d 891, 897 (Fla.2002); see also Joshua v. City of Gainesville 768 So.2d 432, 438 (Fla.2000). Applying that principle of statutory construction, we conclude, contrary to the Second District, that the language of the implied consent law provides that the methods for conducting urine tests are not required to be "approved" through APA rule promulgation.

We begin with the actual language used by the Legislature in section 316.1932(1)(a)(1). As we have explained,"[t]he legislature is presumed to know the meaning of words and the rules of grammar, and the only way the court is advised of what the legislature intends is by giving the generally accepted construction, not only to the phraseology of an act, but to the manner in which it is punctuated." Florida State Racing Comm'n v. Bourquardez, 42 So.2d 87, 88 (Fla.1949); see also State v. Hubbard, 751 So.2d 552, 562 (Fla.1999) (relying on Bourquardez for this principle of statutory construction); Beach v. Great Western Bank, 692 So.2d 146, 152 (Fla.1997) (same), aff'd sub nom. Beach v. Ocwen Fed. Bank, 523 U.S. 410, 118 S.Ct. 1408, 140 L.Ed.2d 566 (1998).

The grammatical structure of the first sentence of section 316.1932(1)(a)(1) is such that the implied consent deemed to have been given by an operator of a motor vehicle applies equally to two independent, unrelated tests-the first an "approved chemical test" to determine blood- or breath-alcohol level, and the second a urine test to determine the presence of chemical or controlled substances. The grammatical structure can be illustrated as follows:

> A person who accepts the privilege extended by the laws of this state of operating a motor vehicle within this state is, by so operating such vehicle, deemed to have given his or her consent to submit
>
> > *to an approved chemical test or physical test including, but not limited to, an infrared light test of his or her breath for the purpose of determining the alcoholic content of his or her blood or breath,*
>
> *and*
>
> > *to a urine test for the purpose of detecting the presence of chemical substances as set forth in s. 877.111 or controlled substances,*

As is illustrated, "approved" directly modifies only "chemical test." It does not modify "urine test." In order to accept Bodden's argument that "approved" modifies "urine test," this Court would be required to insert the word "approved" between "a" and "urine," so that the implied consent created by the statute applies "to an approved urine test." This we decline to do. The plain language of this section demonstrates that "approved" does not modify "urine test."

In the alternative, Bodden argues that the Legislature intended for "urine test" to fall within the subset of included approved chemical tests. However, the language of section 316.1932(1)(a)(1) in its entirety "makes a distinction between the two tests in numerous places ..., evincing that urine tests are not merely subsets of 'chemical tests.' " Pierre, 854 So.2d at 233. For example, this section explicitly provides a method for urine testing:

> *The urine test* must be incidental to a lawful arrest and administered at a detention facility or any other facility, mobile or otherwise, which is equipped to administer such tests at the request of a law enforcement officer who has reasonable cause to believe such person was driving or was in actual physical control of a motor vehicle within this state while under the influence of controlled substances. *The urine test* shall be administered at a detention facility or any other facility, mobile or otherwise, which is equipped to administer such tests in a reasonable manner that will ensure the accuracy of the specimen and maintain the privacy of the individual involved.

§ 316.1932(1)(a)(1). As the Fifth District recognized, if a urine test were intended to fall within the subset of chemical tests subject to rule promulgation through the APA, the language that sets forth explicit procedure for urine tests would be unnecessary. See id.

We have stated that words in a statute are not to be construed as superfluous if a reasonable construction exists that gives effect to all words. See Hechtman v. Nations Title Ins. of New York, 840 So.2d 993, 996 (Fla.2003) ("It is an elementary principle of statutory construction that significance and effect must be given to every word, phrase, sentence, and part of the statute if possible, and words in a statute should not be construed as mere surplusage."); State v. Goode, 830 So.2d 817, 824 (Fla.2002) ("[A] basic rule of statutory construction provides that the Legislature does not intend to enact useless provisions, and courts should avoid readings that would render part of a statute meaningless."). Applying that principle here, we reject Bodden's alternative construction and decline to interpret this statute in a way which would render superfluous the separate references to urine tests throughout this section.

Our interpretation that urine tests are distinct from chemical tests is borne out by a review of the remainder of section 316.1932. Although we are initially guided by the clear language of section 316.1932(1)(a)(1), we also look to the other provisions of the implied consent law to discern if there is any indication that the Legislature intended urine testing methods to be "approved." Indeed, in Mehl v. State, 632 So.2d 593, 594-95 (Fla.1993), this Court specifically recognized that provisions of the implied consent law should be read in pari materia as expressing a unified legislative purpose. See also M.W., 756 So.2d at 101 ("[A]ll parts of a statute must be read together in order to achieve a consistent whole.") (quoting Forsythe v. Longboat Key Beach Erosion Control Dist., 604 So.2d 452, 455 (Fla.1992)); T.R. v. State, 677 So.2d 270, 271 (Fla.1996) (all parts of a statute must be read together so that the statute is consistent in its entirety).

Reading section 316.1932(1)(a)(1) in pari materia with the remainder of the implied consent law leads to a logical and harmonious construction in which "approved" does not modify "urine test." The implied consent law as a whole consistently treats tests relating to breath and blood distinctly from urine tests.

For example, section 316.1932(1)(a)(2) confers on FDLE the responsibility for the regulation and approval of *blood and breath testing*. Specifically, sections 316.1932(1)(a)(2)(n) and 316.1932(1)(b)(2) grant FDLE the authority to *approve blood and breath testing techniques and methods*, respectively. Section 316.1932(1)(a)(2)(l) grants FDLE the authority to "[p]romulgate rules for the administration ... of [the] section, including definitions," and sections 316.1932(1)(a)(2)(f), (g), and (p) address F'LE's authority to "approve" operators, instruments, and repair facilities relating *to breath and blood testing*. Finally, sections 316.1933(2)(b) and 316.1934(3) both provide that chemical analysis of a person's *blood and breath* must be performed "substantially in accordance with methods approved by [FDLE]." Significantly, there is no mention of urine testing in *any* of these subsections of the implied consent law. As noted by the Fourth District in Montello, "[n]owhere in Chapter 316 has the Legislature given FDLE the authority to promulgate rules for urine testing for non-commercial drivers." 872 So.2d at 615.[10]

To construe section 316.1932(1)(a)(1) in the manner urged by Bodden would require the Court to "ignore the remainder of the statute, which, taken in its entirety, clearly conveys a contrary intent." Pierre, 854 So.2d at 233; see also Jones v. ETS of New Orleans, Inc., 793 So.2d 912, 914-15 (Fla.2001) ("A basic tenet of statutory interpretation is that a statute should be interpreted to give effect to every clause in it, and to accord meaning and harmony to all of its parts."). Accordingly, we hold that section 316.1932(1)(a), which requires that blood and breath tests be approved, does not similarly require that urine tests be approved through formal rule promulgation in accordance with the APA.

. . .

CONCLUSION

In conclusion, we hold that the implied consent law for operators of motor vehicles does not require that urine testing methods be approved in accordance with the APA. We emphasize that we do not decide whether it would be preferable for urine tests to be approved through rule promulgation. Rather, we resolve this case by applying well-established principles of statutory construction to effectuate the legislative intent of the statute. See Hawkins v. Ford Motor Co., 748 So.2d 993, 1000 (Fla.1999). Accordingly, we approve the Fourth and Fifth Distri'ts' reasoning in Montello and Pierre, answer the certified question in Bodden in the negative, and quash the Second Distr'ct's decision below. We remand this case for proceedings consistent with this opinion.

It is so ordered.

ANSTEAD, C.J., and WELLS, LEWIS, QUINCE, CANTERO, and BELL, JJ., concur.

NOTES AND QUESTIONS

1. Was this statute any clearer than the statute in Kasischke? Doesn't the fact that the Second and Fifth Districts interpret the statute differently imply that the language is ambiguous?

2. Does the Court split hairs when it separates the two clauses connected by "and"?

3. Does it makes sense that there should be uniform accepted rules for doing blood and breathalyzer tests but not for urine tests?

---

[10]...*An analysis of a person's breath,* in order to be considered valid under this section, *must have been performed substantially according to methods approved by the Department of Law Enforcement.* For this purpose, the department may approve satisfactory techniques or methods.
(Emphasis supplied.)

4. Why didn't the rule of lenity come in here to aid the defendant/ respondent?

F. CONSTRUCTION OF THE PART IN LIGHT OF WHOLE

FLORIDA DEP'T OF ENVTL. PROT. V. CONTRACTPOINT FLA. PARKS, LLC
986 So. 2d 1260 (Fla. 2008)

PARIENTE, J.

The issue in this case is whether the State is required to pay a lawful judgment arising from a breach of contract action. In order to decide this issue we must interpret section 11.066(3), Florida Statutes (2005), on which the Department of Environmental Protection relied in refusing to pay the judgment against it. In ContractPoint Florida Parks, LLC v. State, 958 So.2d 1035 (Fla. 1st DCA 2007), the First District Court of Appeal held that section 11.066 does not prevent the State or a state agency from paying a judgment in the absence of a specific appropriation but certified the following question to be one of great public importance:

> DOES SECTION 11.066, FLORIDA STATUTES, APPLY WHERE JUDGMENTS HAVE BEEN ENTERED AGAINST THE STATE OR ONE OF ITS AGENCIES IN A CONTRACT ACTION?

Id. at 1038. We have jurisdiction. See art. V, § 3(b)(4), Fla. Const.

For the reasons that follow, we conclude that section 11.066 was not intended to require a specific legislative appropriation before a governmental entity can be required to pay a valid judgment entered into for breach of contract with a private entity. We reach this decision not based on our own view of the "best" policy for the State, but by applying well-established principles of statutory construction. Accordingly, we answer the certified question in the negative and approve the decision of the First District.

FACTS AND PROCEDURAL HISTORY

This case involves a contract entered into between the State and a private entity at a time when the State sought to "privatize" many of its operations. In April 2001, the Florida Department of Environmental Protection (DEP) entered into a concessions agreement with ContractPoint Florida Parks, LLC (ContractPoint) whereby ContractPoint would finance, construct, and operate 143 vacation cabins and associated concessions in eight state parks. Under the concessions contract, ContractPoint was obligated to pay DEP fifteen percent of its gross sales for thirty years, with two ten-year renewal options based on satisfactory performance.

ContractPoint brought a suit against DEP for wrongful termination of the contract. In August 2005, a jury found that DEP breached the contract and judgment was entered in favor of ContractPoint for $628,543. ... The issue here concerns DEP's refusal to pay the judgment based on its assertion that section 11.066 prohibits a state agency from paying any judgment unless there is a specific appropriation by the Legislature for that judgment. In December 2005, ContractPoint filed a Petition for Writ of Mandamus in the trial court seeking to compel DEP and Florida's Chief Financial Officer to pay the judgment. Based on its interpretation of 11.066, the trial court denied ContractPoint's petition, finding no clear duty on the part of DEP to pay the judgment without a specific appropriation for that purpose.

On appeal, the First District reversed, relying on this Court's decision in Pan-Am Tobacco Corp. v. Department of Corrections, 471 So.2d 4 (Fla.1984), which held that when the State enters into a legislatively authorized contract with a private entity, "sovereign immunity will not protect the state from action arising from the state's breach of that contract." Id. at 5. The First District noted in ContractPoint that since Pan-Am, the Legislature has actually promoted public/private contracting projects through several statutes and that the interpretation urged by the State would defeat that very purpose by rendering "all public/private contracts illusory." ContractPoint, 958 So.2d at 1038. Accordingly, the First District concluded that the Legislature did not intend section 11.066 to apply to actions in contract and, therefore, held that the statute did not prohibit payment of the breach of contract judgment by DEP. Id.

The Contract

The contract between DEP and ContractPoint, entitled "Concession Agreement," is seventeen pages in length and comprises forty-five separate paragraphs. It imposes many obligations on ContractPoint and includes at least two paragraphs (paragraphs 31 and 32) wherein it waives certain types of claims for compensation by ContractPoint. The contract includes the following express remedies to the State for certain breaches by ContractPoint: (1) if ContractPoint does not pay the monthly concession fees on time, liquidated damages will be assessed (paragraph 25); (2) if the payments and damages are not received timely, DEP may take possession and cancel the agreement (paragraph 25); (3) DEP has a continuing lien on all ContractPoint personal property and in the event of default may take possession and sell the personal property (paragraph 28); (4) DEP may terminate the agreement at any time for failure to perform (paragraph 40); and (5) if the agreement is terminated and ContractPoint holds over, such shall constitute trespass for which DEP is entitled to receive liquidated damages of $300 per day (paragraph 40).

Thus, under the contract, not only does DEP have the right to compensation for breach, it also has a right to a lien against ContractPoint's personal property. And, of paramount importance to the issue in this case, there is no limitation contained in either the contract or the statutes on DEP's right to sue the contractor and enforce any judgment it might obtain. It is also noteworthy that the contract could have, but did not, contain provisions for liquidated damages against the agency or mandatory alternative dispute resolution procedures, such as arbitration. The Concession Agreement states that it "shall be interpreted in such manner as to be *effective and valid* under applicable law" and concludes that it "represents the entire agreement of the parties." (Paragraph 17; emphasis supplied.)

Statutes Related to the Contract with DEP

The Legislature expressly granted DEP contracting authority in section 258.007(3), Florida Statutes (2000), which authorizes DEP through its Division of Recreation and Parks to "grant privileges, leases, concessions, and permits for the use of land for the accommodation of visitors in the various parks, monuments, and memorials." This statute was in effect before enactment of section 11.066 and has remained in effect ever since. Section 258.007(3) is an explicit authorization by general law for DEP to enter into express, written concessions contracts with private parties and it was under this legislative authority that DEP contracted with ContractPoint in this case.

Moreover, the Legislature expressly encouraged and authorized DEP to contract with private entities for the specific type of project contemplated in the concessions contract between DEP and ContractPoint. Subsection (3)(a) of section 258.015, Florida Statutes (2000), enacted prior to the execution of the contract in this case, provides:

(3) PARTNERSHIPS IN PARKS.-

(a) The Legislature recognizes that many of the parks in the state park system need a variety of facilities to enhance their use and potential. Such facilities include, but are not limited to, improved access, camping areas, picnicking shelters, park management offices and facilities, and environmental education facilities. The need for such facilities has exceeded the ability of the state to provide such facilities in a timely manner with moneys available. The Legislature finds it to be in the public interest to provide incentives for partnerships with private organizations with the intent of producing additional revenue to help enhance the use and potential of the state park system.

The Legislature also appropriated $9.5 million to DEP in fiscal year 2000/2001, which DEP intended to use in its "cabins initiative," although under the Concession Agreement, the burden of financing and construction of cabins in eight state parks was placed on ContractPoint.

DEP's contract with ContractPoint appears to fall squarely within the purview of the Partnerships in Parks program. Under the terms of the contract, DEP would increase the use and potential of the state park system, while receiving fifteen percent of gross sales for the new facilities and without increasing the burden on the State to provide the facilities-a goal specifically encouraged by section 258.015. Under the contract, ContractPoint would receive profit incentives to build and operate the cabins and concessions. In fact, it was primarily ContractPoint's expenditures made toward performing under this contract that formed the basis of the final judgment in this case. We must now answer the question posed by the First District Court of Appeal and decide whether section 11.066 was intended to apply to breach of contract judgments and thus prohibits DEP from paying the judgment obtained by ContractPoint in this case.

ANALYSIS

Interpretation of Section 11.066

The question presented by the First District involves an issue of statutory interpretation, which is subject to de novo review. Heart of Adoptions, Inc. v. J.A., 963 So.2d 189, 194 (Fla.2007). Specifically, the Court must determine whether section 11.066(3), Florida Statutes (2005), applies to contract actions and bars enforcement of judgments entered on breach of contract claims against the State or its agencies if there is no specific legislative appropriation to pay the judgment. This is a case of first impression.

...The only question before us is whether section 11.066 plainly evinces an intent to shield the State from paying any valid judgment entered against it in a breach of contract action unless and until there is a specific legislative appropriation to pay that judgment.

The Florida Legislature originally enacted section 11.066 in 1991 as part of "An Act relating to fiscal affairs of the state." See ch. 91-109, § 40, Laws of Fla. Although located in a chapter dealing generally with "Legislative Organization, Procedures and Staffing," section 11.066 is entitled "Suits seeking monetary damages against the state or its agencies; payment of judgments; appropriations required" and provides:

> (1) As used in this section, the term "appropriation made by law" has the same meaning as in s. 1(c), Art. VII of the State Constitution and means money allocated for a specific purpose by the Legislature by law in a general appropriations act or a special appropriations act.
>
> (2) The state and each state agency, when exercising its inherent police power to protect the public health, safety, or welfare, is presumed to be acting to prevent a public harm. A person may rebut this presumption in a suit seeking monetary damages from the state or a state agency only by clear and convincing evidence to the contrary.
>
> (3) *Neither the state nor any of its agencies shall pay or be required to pay monetary damages under the judgment of any court except pursuant to an appropriation made by law.* To enforce a judgment for monetary damages against the state or a state agency, the sole remedy of the judgment creditor, if there has not otherwise been an appropriation made by law to pay the judgment, is to petition the Legislature in accordance with its rules to seek an appropriation to pay the judgment.
>
> (4) Notwithstanding s. 74.091, a judgment for monetary damages against the state or any of its agencies may not be enforced through execution or any common-law remedy against property of the state or its agencies, and a writ of execution therefor may not be issued against the state or its agencies. Moreover, it is a defense to an alternative writ of mandamus issued to enforce a judgment for

monetary damages against the state or a state agency that there is no appropriation made by law to pay the judgment.

(5) The property of the state, the property of any state agency, or any monetary recovery made on behalf of the state or any state agency is not subject to a lien of any kind.
(Emphasis supplied.)

This Court has long held that a "statute must be given its plain and obvious meaning." Holly v. Auld, 450 So.2d 217, 219 (Fla.1984) (quoting A.R. Douglass, Inc. v. McRainey, 102 Fla. 1141, 137 So. 157, 159 (1931)). If the language of the statute is "clear and unambiguous and conveys a clear and definite meaning" there is no need to resort to statutory construction. Id.; accord Forsythe v. Longboat Key Beach Erosion Control Dist., 604 So.2d 452, 454 (Fla.1992). In interpreting section 11.066, however, we cannot read subsection (3) in isolation, but must read it within the context of the entire section in order to ascertain legislative intent for the provision. Id. at 455 ("Every statute must be read as a whole with meaning ascribed to every portion and due regard given to the semantic and contextual interrelationship between its parts." (quoting Fleischman v. Dep't of Prof'l Reg., 441 So.2d 1121, 1123 (Fla. 3d DCA 1983))). A "statute should be interpreted to give effect to every clause in it, and to accord meaning and harmony to all of its parts" and is not to be read in isolation, but in the context of the entire section. Jones v. ETS of New Orleans, Inc., 793 So.2d 912, 914-15 (Fla.2001) (quoting Acosta v. Richter, 671 So.2d 149, 153-54 (Fla.1996)).

In Florida State Racing Commission v. McLaughlin, 102 So.2d 574, 575-76 (Fla.1958), this Court stated:

> [I]f a part of a statute appears to have a clear meaning if considered alone but when given that meaning is inconsistent with other parts of the same statute or others in pari materia, the Court will examine the entire act and those in pari materia in order to ascertain the overall legislative intent.

These principles apply to this statute. While subsection (3), standing alone, appears to be an absolute bar to the State's payment of all judgments, subsections (3) and (4) must be read with reference to subsection (2), which states:

> The state and each state agency, when exercising its inherent police power to protect the public health, safety, or welfare, is presumed to be acting to prevent a public harm. A person may rebut this presumption in a suit seeking monetary damages from the state or a state agency only by clear and convincing evidence to the contrary.

§ 11.066(2), Fla. Stat. (2005) (emphases supplied).

This express reference to suits "seeking monetary damages" made in the context of the State's exercise of its "police power to protect the public health, safety, or welfare" precedes the references in subsection (3) to "monetary damages under the judgment of any court" and "a judgment for monetary damages." The reference to police power also precedes the remaining subsections that discuss execution on State property and application of mandamus to enforce such judgments. Subsection (2) clearly focuses the thrust of the statute on judgments arising from claims based on the exercise of the State's police power and says nothing about claims arising from breach of contract. The references in subsection (3) to "monetary damages" echo the provisions of subsection (2) and accordingly relate to monetary damages contained in judgments arising from the exercise of the State's police powers. Therefore, the statute does not express a clear intent to bar payment of valid breach of contract judgments, but rather expresses an intent to limit payment of judgments arising out of the exercise of the State's police powers.

Moreover, "[t]o discern legislative intent, courts must consider the statute as a whole, including the evil to be corrected, the language, title, and history of its enactment, and the state of law already in existence on the statute." Bautista v. State, 863 So.2d 1180, 1185 (Fla.2003) (emphasis supplied) (quoting State v. Anderson, 764 So.2d 848, 849 (Fla. 3d DCA 2000)). When considered as a whole, with the express indication of the "evil to be corrected" in subsection (2), in the context of the broad statutory scheme conferring contracting authority upon its agencies, and in light of the legislative history of the enactment, the Legislature's apparent intent in section 11.066 is to preclude payment of judgments for monetary damages arising out of the State's exercise of its police powers unless an appropriation exists.

The legislative history of section 11.066 confirms that the provision addresses the State's exercise of its police powers. Chapter 91-109, section 40, Laws of Florida, was enacted in 1991 by the passage of House Bill 2313. The House of Representatives Committee on Appropriations Bill Analysis and Economic Impact Statement for HB 2313 (May 13, 1991) states that section 40 of the bill: "Provides that in suits seeking monetary damages against the state or its agencies, a court may not require the payment of monetary damages unless an appropriation has been made by law. Provides for a standard of clear and convincing evidence for a person to rebut the presumption that state agency, exercising its inherent police power, is acting to prevent public harm." It can be seen that the elements of the law given prominence in the staff analysis were suits for monetary damages stated in conjunction with the State's exercise of its police power. Other legislative materials relating to the original enactment of section 11.066 also suggest that one impetus for the statute was the many attempts to recover judgments for claims arising out of the State's exercise of its police powers during the Citrus Canker Eradication Program in the mid-1980s.

Subsequently, the Senate Staff Analysis and Economic Impact Statement for CS/SB 822 (Apr. 5, 2001), discussing the proposed amendment of section 11.066, explains generally that the statute "relates to suits seeking monetary damages against the state or state agencies." This staff analysis goes on to again explain: "When the state or a state agency is exercising its inherent police power to protect the public health, safety, or welfare, it is presumed to be acting to prevent a public harm." Immediately following this statement, the staff analysis states that "[t]he section permits payment of monetary damages under a court judgment by the state or its agencies only pursuant to an appropriation."

Nothing in either of the staff analyses or legislative history indicates in any way that the statute bars payment of breach of contract judgments entered upon legislatively authorized contracts. Instead, these legislative staff analyses, as do the other sections of the statute, focus on the police power aspect of monetary damage suits as the subject of the legislation.

Additionally, no contemporaneous amendments were enacted to limit or alter state agencies' contracting authority in the vast array of contracting statutes which then, and now, provide broad contracting authority to state agencies, including DEP. And despite DEP taking the position that section 11.066 broadly applies to all judgments entered against the State, there has been no contention made that the specific statutory scheme relating to tort suits and judgments against the State pursuant to section 768.28, Florida Statutes, is affected by section 11.066. In our view, this further supports the conclusion that section 11.066 was not intended to broadly limit the payment of all judgments, but only those entered against the State arising from actions it took in the exercise of its police powers.

. . .

Although the dissent asserts that it is ascribing a "plain language" meaning to the statute and that the majority thwarts the clear legislative intent, the dissent adds words to subsection (3) that are not contained in the statute by concluding that the only legislative prerogative is to control the timing of payment of the judgment and not the obligation to pay the judgment. We assume that this caveat was added in order to avoid the inescapable conclusion that, without an obligation to pay the judgment, the contract would be wholly illusory. Although this caveat would place constraints on the Legislature, it does so without any standards. How long is too long? Could the Legislature pay in installments? How should or would the Legislature prioritize? What rules would the judgment creditor follow? Would it have to obtain a claims bill? The fact that these questions must be asked further reinforces our conclusion that the Legislature would never have intended the result reached by the dissent, a result that authorizes the State to avoid its validly entered contracts and the monetary consequences resulting from any breach.

If we were to interpret section 11.066(3) in isolation as prohibiting payment of valid breach of contract judgments, thereby rendering express, written contracts entered into by the State under legislatively granted authority essentially illusory and unenforceable, that result would be untenable and contrary to the Legislature's overall intent. The sounder and more reasoned interpretation, viewing the statute in its entirety, in light of the overall legislative scheme of encouraging private/public partnerships, and keeping in mind the history of this provision, is that section 11.066 is not applicable to breach of contract judgments.

. . .

CONCLUSION

We note that the dissent has listed a "parade of horribles" for what might happen if the State is forced to choose between having to pay a large contract judgment and "funding critical State services that affect the whole population." Dissenting op. at 1278. We believe this type of "sky is falling" alarmist scenario, which is based on absolutely no evidence in substantiation, has no place in a statutory construction analysis. In fact, this is not a choice the State has been forced to make in any other case that has been called to our attention involving a lawful breach of contract judgment, either before or after section 11.066 was enacted in 1991. The State has been honoring its contract debts, and not forcing contractors to seek a special law to obtain payment on a court-entered judgment. Indeed, a statute that would require a contractor to seek a specific legislative appropriation to obtain payment on a lawful judgment would run the risk of creating a chilling effect on business between the State and the private sector. But that would be a legislative decision to reach after weighing all the policy considerations, both pro and con. In our view, that was not the basis for the enactment of section 11.066, which provides no clear indication that the Legislature intended it to apply to breach of contract judgments.

. . .

Having reviewed the actual language of the statute, the history of its enactment, and our prior case law, we conclude that section 11.066 was never intended to act as a shield to prevent a state agency from paying a lawful judgment arising from the breach of a contract that it was expressly authorized to enter. Accordingly, for all the reasons stated, we conclude that section 11.066 was not intended to and does not apply to valid judgments arising from the breach of a legislatively authorized express, written contract by the State or any of its agencies. Therefore, we answer the certified question in the negative, approve the decision of the First District, and remand for proceedings consistent with this opinion.

It is so ordered.

QUINCE, C.J., and ANSTEAD and LEWIS, JJ., concur. WELLS, J., dissents with an opinion, in which CANTERO and BELL, JJ., concur.

WELLS, J., dissenting.

. . .

I dissent. ...The plain language of section 11.066, Florida Statutes (2001), is applicable in the instant case and requires the conclusion that the trial court properly denied ContractPoint's petition for a writ of mandamus. I would answer the certified question in the affirmative and quash the decision of the First District Court of Appeal in ContractPoint Florida Parks, LLC v. State, 958 So.2d 1035 (Fla. 1st DCA 2007).

The question certified by the First District asks, "Does Section 11.066, Florida Statutes, apply where judgments have been entered against the State or one of its agencies in a contract action?" ContractPoint, 958 So.2d at 1038. The majority answers that "section 11.066 was not intended to require a specific legislative appropriation before a governmental entity can be required to pay a valid judgment entered into for breach of contract with a private entity." Majority op. at 1262. However, the issue before the First District was whether the trial court erred in denying ContractPoint's petition for a writ of mandamus that sought to compel the State's Chief Financial Officer (CFO) and the Florida Department of Environmental Protection (DEP) to pay a judgment resulting from a breach of contract action. Considering the certified question in the context of the issue on appeal in this case, the First District has asked this Court to decide whether section 11.066 is to be given its plain and obvious meaning where the statute states that a *valid defense* to a petition for a writ of mandamus seeking to compel the State or a State agency to pay a monetary judgment is that there is not a specific appropriation made by law to pay the judgment. I would answer that section 11.066 is to be given its plain and obvious meaning, and thus the trial court did not err in denying ContractPoint's petition for a writ of mandamus.

. . .

...The majority acknowledges that a "statute must be given its plain and obvious meaning" and that if "the language of a statute is 'clear and unambiguous and conveys a clear and definite meaning' there is no need to resort to statutory construction.' " Majority op. at 1265 (quoting Holly v. Auld, 450 So.2d 217, 219 (Fla.1984)). The majority and I part ways because I find that section 11.066 is clear and unambiguous.

Subsection (4) of section 11.066 expressly answers the question before this Court. That subsection provides that "it is a defense to an alternative writ of mandamus issued to enforce a judgment for monetary damages against the state or a state agency that there is no appropriation made by law to pay the judgment." § 11.066(4), Fla. Stat. (2001). Subsection (3) further provides that

> To enforce a judgment for monetary damages against the state or a state agency, the sole remedy of the judgment creditor, if there has not otherwise been an appropriation made by law to pay the judgment, is to petition the Legislature in accordance with its rules to seek an appropriation to pay the judgment.

§ 11.066(3), Fla. Stat. (2001). There is no ambiguity in these subsections or in the statute as a whole. The Legislature speaks in broad, general terms, apparently encompassing all monetary judgments against the State. The Legislature does not qualify or limit to judgments arising from any particular cause of action its proclamation that the lack of an appropriation to pay a judgment is a defense to a writ of mandamus and that, absent an appropriation, a judgment creditor's *sole* remedy is to petition the Legislature. There is a complete absence of language in the statute that excludes monetary damages liquidated in a breach of contract action.

The majority holds that the statute does not apply to monetary judgments from breach of contract actions because "the statute does not express a clear intent to bar payment of valid breach of contract judgments." Majority op. at 1266. This analysis does not defer properly to the Legislature's constitutional authority to draft legislation.

The statute repeatedly refers to "monetary damages under the judgment of any court" and "a judgment for monetary damages." § 11.066(3)-(4). Where the Legislature uses the term "a judgment for monetary damages" without further description or exception, this Court is obliged to read the statute as applying to all judgments for monetary damages, giving to "a judgment for monetary damages" its plain and obvious meaning. For example, in Aetna Casualty & Surety Co. v. Huntington National Bank, 609 So.2d 1315, 1316 n. 1 (Fla.1992), the Court applied the plain, literal meaning of section 324.021(9)(b), Florida Statutes (1987), which provided:

> Notwithstanding any other provision of the Florida Statutes or existing case law, the lessor, under an agreement to lease a motor vehicle for 1 year or longer which requires the lessee to obtain insurance acceptable to the lessor ... shall not be deemed the owner of said motor vehicle for the purpose of determining financial responsibility for the operation of said motor vehicle....

In that case, Aetna argued that the statute only applied to long-term leases that were "automobile financing substitutes" because during the legislative debate preceding passage of the bill later codified as section 324.021(9)(b), the sponsor of the proposed bill described long term leases as "an alternative way of financing an automobile." Aetna, 609 So.2d at 1317. This Court expressly rejected Aetna's argument, stating:

> In this case, the statute clearly states that "the lessor, under an agreement to lease a motor vehicle for 1 year or longer ... shall not be deemed the owner" of the vehicle for purposes of determining financial responsibility for the operation of the vehicle or for the acts of the operator of the vehicle. § 324.021(9)(b), Fla. Stat. (1987). The statute places two restrictions upon the type of motor vehicle lease that would exempt the owner/lessor from liability: 1) the lease must be "for 1 year or longer"; and 2) the lease must require the lessee "to obtain insurance acceptable to the lessor which contains limits not less than $100,00[0]/$300,000 bodily injury liability and $50,000 property damage liability." Id. The statute contains no language that would restrict its application to leases which are financing substitutes, as Aetna urges. Moreover, section 324.021(9)(b) specifically states that its terms are applicable "[n]otwithstanding any other provision of the Florida Statutes or existing case law."
>
> Aetna argues that the legislative debate evidences a legislative intent that section 324.021(9)(b) only applies to long-term leases which are financing substitutes. On the contrary, legislative intent must be determined primarily from the language of the statute. It must be assumed that the legislature knows the meaning of the words and has expressed its intent by the use of the words found in the statute. S.R.G. Corp. v. Department of Revenue, 365 So.2d 687 (Fla.1978). The legislative history of a statute is irrelevant where the wording of a statute is clear. Maryland Casualty Co. v. Sutherland, 125 Fla. 282, 169 So. 679 (1936).

Aetna, 609 So.2d at 1317; see also O'Leary v. Fla. Birth-Related Neurological Injury Comp. Ass'n, 757 So.2d 624, 627 (Fla. 5th DCA 2000) (finding that statutory language stating that "the administrative law judge has exclusive jurisdiction to determine whether a claim filed under this act is compensable" included jurisdiction to determine notice issues because "[n]otably, the determination of the adequacy of notice is not excluded from the duties of the administrative law judge"). In the instant case, the Court, in accord with abundant precedent on statutory construction, must trust that the Legislature knows the meaning of the words "a judgment for monetary damages" and has expressed its intent by the use of those words. The Legislature does not have an obligation to clarify that when it used the words "a judgment for monetary damages," it intended for that phrase to include monetary judgments from breach of contract actions. Rather, the Court has an obligation to apply the statute as written.

Similarly, even if the majority is correct in believing that citrus canker litigation inspired the drafting of section 11.066, there is no qualification in the statute limiting its effect to judgments arising from citrus canker-related causes of action. Subsection (2) discusses a plaintiff's burden of proof in an action challenging the State's use of its inherent police power, but the subsection does not discuss the process of executing a monetary judgment, the issue currently at hand. This Court is not at liberty to read extra provisions into a statute. The Legislature could have excluded monetary judgments from breach of contract actions and narrowed section 11.066 to judgments arising from the State's use of its police power mentioned in subsection (2), but it did not. In subsections (3) and (4), the Legislature defined the method by which a judgment creditor may enforce a judgment for monetary damages against the State or a state agency, and this Court must apply those dictates to all judgments for monetary damages unless and until told to do otherwise by the Legislature. Again, "[t]he legislative history of a statute is irrelevant where the wording of a statute is clear." Aetna, 609 So.2d at 1317.

The First District and the majority of this Court also determined that section 11.066 should be found inapplicable to judgments arising from breach of contract actions in part because the statute does not express a legislative intent to overturn twenty-two years of case law subjecting the State to breach of contract actions. ContractPoint, 958 So.2d at 1037; majority op. at 1268-70. Again, I disagree and would apply the plain language of section 11.066.

First, I disagree with the majority's theoretical approach. Where the plain language of a statute overturns the effect of prior case law, no express legislative finding of intent to replace the common law rule is necessarily required. Statutory language itself can overturn common law. See, e.g., Burchfield v. Realty Executives, 971 So.2d 138, 139 (Fla. 5th DCA 2007) (finding statute providing that transaction broker "does not represent [buyer or seller] in a fiduciary capacity" replaced fiduciary duty owed by real estate brokers at common law without requiring express statement of intent to abrogate common law). Detailed legislative findings such as those included in chapter 2004-93, section 1, Laws of Florida, see majority op. at 1269-70 n. 10, are helpful and informative where a statute would otherwise be subject to multiple meanings but gratuitous where the statutory language is clear.

. . .

Furthermore, contrary to the majority, I do not find that recognizing and applying the Legislature's decision to maintain sovereign immunity in the context of proceedings to execute judgments would render illusory all State contracts since 1991. See majority op. at 1270. In any contractual setting there is a risk that a breaching party may lack the resources needed to pay a judgment. The possibility that a party may ultimately turn out to be "judgment proof" does not render the contract a nullity. The likelihood that a judgment debtor will pay a legally binding judgment in the event of a breach is a practical factor to be considered when entering any contract but not a legally required element of a contract. Applying the plain language of section 11.066(4) would not relieve the State from obligations assumed by contract. Instead, it would permit the Legislature to choose the time and manner by which it will pay outstanding judgments by allowing the State to argue the lack of an appropriation as a defense in a mandamus proceeding, thereby preserving the Legislature's constitutionally granted authority over the State's budget. See Spangler v. Fla. State Turnpike Auth., 106 So.2d 421, 424 (Fla.1958) ("[T]he immunity of the sovereign is a part of the public policy of the state. It is enforced as a protection of the public against profligate encroachments on the public treasury.").

Arguably, the majority's decision that section 11.066 is not a defense to a mandamus proceeding to enforce a monetary judgment arising from a breach of contract action leads to an absurd result. While the majority seems to hold that a party may successfully seek a writ of mandamus to compel the State to pay a judgment where no appropriation has yet been made to pay that judgment, the majority does not address the First District's concern about how the CFO or DEP will be able to disburse legally public funds to pay the judgment if not authorized to do so by an appropriation or an express constitutional directive. See art. VII, § 1(c) ("No money shall be drawn from the treasury except in pursuance of appropriation made by law.").

. . .

Finally, I do not find that maintaining sovereign immunity as it relates to the collection of a judgment would render the right to sue for damages "meaningless." Majority op. at 1270. The contract action is the injured party's opportunity to prove the existence and terms of its contract, the fact of the State's breach, and the amount of damages. The contract suit allows the aggrieved party to establish that it has a "clear legal right" to damages. Cf. Coldiron v. Seminole County Sheriff's Dept., 936 So.2d 42, 43 (Fla. 5th DCA 2006) ("Mandamus may not be used to establish rights.... Instead, a party petitioning for a writ of mandamus must establish a clear legal right to the requested relief...."). Under the scheme set forth in section 11.066, the contract action is an important step toward recovery by means of a petition for a writ of mandamus where the Legislature *has* appropriated funds to compensate an injured party or by means of a petition in the Legislature where it *has not* yet appropriated funds to pay the judgment.

In conclusion, I think that the majority has erred by straying from our duty to apply the plain language of unambiguous statutes and by disregarding the distinction between a breach of contract action and post-judgment litigation to enforce a judgment. I would answer the certified question in the affirmative and quash the decision of the First District. The trial court did not err in denying ContractPoint's petition for a writ of mandamus on the basis that pursuant to section 11.066, the CFO did not have a clear legal duty to pay the judgment without an appropriation for that purpose.

CANTERO and BELL, JJ., concur.

NOTES AND QUESTIONS

1. Is section 11.066 clear on its own?

2. Does reading other provisions in the statute clarify or settle the meaning of section 11.066?

3. Do you think the majority looks to the whole statute because it does not like the consequences of a plain meaning approach to section 11.066?

4. Is the majority correct that the dissent's plain meaning reading requires that it write things into the statute?

5. Does the majority need to write things into section 11.066 in order to get the meaning it wishes from the statute?

6. The dissent argues that the majority not only violates the plain meaning rule, but that it does so in a way that would have absurd results. The majority argues that the dissent's approach would lead to untenable results that would be contrary to the Legislature's overall intent? Which has the better argument?

BROWN V. STATE

848 So.2d 361 (Fla. Dist. Ct. App. 4th Dist. 2003)

FARMER, J.

In a case involving theft of a purse, defendant was charged with strong arm robbery but convicted of robbery by sudden snatching. Because we find that the trial court erroneously instructed the jury and that, in any case, the evidence does not support the conviction, we reverse.

On the day in question, the victim sat on a park bench with a friend. The bench was partially bordered by bushes about three feet high. Victim placed her purse on the bench near her but apart from her person. Her friend noticed defendant riding a bicycle past them "a couple of times." Presently, they heard a rustling in the bushes. Her friend looked in that direction and saw defendant running away. Victim also turned and only then became aware that her purse had been taken. Her friend ran after defendant, who he noticed was carrying her purse. After an altercation, defendant was arrested at the scene.

With this evidence, the state rested. Defendant moved for judgment of acquittal on the strong arm robbery charge, arguing that victim had not been placed in fear, and was not herself the target of any violence, threat, or assault. The trial court granted the motion and reduced the charge to robbery by sudden snatching.[1] Defendant objected, arguing that the purse was not on victim's person when stolen, but was placed instead next to her on the park bench. The court overruled the objection, stating that because the purse was within her reach, it was tantamount to being on her person.

During the charge conference, the trial court proposed to instruct the jury with the definition of "possession" from the standard jury instruction on possession of controlled substances. Defendant objected. The trial court overruled the objection and gave the following instruction:

> "Actual possession means (A) that the thing is in the hands of or on the person, or (B) that the thing is in a container in the hands of or on the person, or (C) *the thing is so close as to be within ready reach and is under the control of the person."* [e.s.]

The jury convicted defendant of robbery by sudden snatching, and he now appeals.

The state argues that the text of the robbery by sudden snatching statute, section 812.131(1) ("from the victim's person"), does not require that the item be taken from the actual, physical possession of the victim. According to the state, the "from the victim's person" text requires only that the item be within the victim's reach and control. The state bases this argument on the doctrine "*in pari materia*." See Ferguson v. State, 377 So.2d 709, 710 (Fla.1979) ("[S]tatutes which relate to the same or to a closely related subject or object are regarded as in pari materia and should be construed together and compared with each other."). The contention is that the robbery by sudden snatching statute should be read *in pari materia* with the general robbery statute, which has been interpreted not to require actual, physical possession by the victim.[2]

---

[1] See § 812.131(1), Fla. Stat. (2000) (" 'Robbery by sudden snatching' means the taking of money or other property from the victim's person, with intent to permanently or temporarily deprive the victim or the owner of the money or other property, when, in the course of the taking, the victim was or became aware of the taking. In order to satisfy this definition, it is not necessary to show that: (a) The offender used any amount of force beyond that effort necessary to obtain possession of the money or other property; or (b) There was any resistance offered by the victim to the offender or that there was injury to the victim's person.").

[2] Section 812.13(1) defines "robbery" as "the taking of money or other property...from the person or custody of another." [e.s.] In Jones v. State, 652 So.2d 346, 350 (Fla.1995), the court held that the phrase "from the person or custody of another" does not require actual, physical possession. It is enough if the item is:

> "sufficiently under the victim's control so that the victim could have prevented the taking if she had not been subjected to violence or intimidation by the robber."

652 So.2d at 350 (quoting from 2 LAFAVE & SCOTT, SUBSTANTIVE CRIMINAL LAW § 8.11(c), at 443 (1986)). The court added that under the robbery statute:

The state emphasizes that legislative intent is the "polestar" for statutory interpretation. In this instance, the state argues, the Legislature has indicated an intent that the property suddenly snatched need not actually be on the victim's person. The state points out that the robbery by sudden snatching statute explicitly eliminates any requirement that the state prove that the offender used force in snatching the property or that the victim was injured or resisted the taking.[3]

The state's argument is invalid. In the first place, the *"in pari materia"* canon of statutory construction would be appropriate only if we found the statute ambiguous, and we do not. See McLaughlin v. State, 721 So.2d 1170 (Fla.1998) (when language of statute is clear and unambiguous and conveys clear and definite meaning, there is no occasion for resorting to the rules of statutory interpretation and construction; the statute must be given its plain and obvious meaning); see also Holly v. Auld, 450 So.2d 217, 219 (Fla.1984) (same); A.R. Douglass, Inc. v. McRainey, 102 Fla. 1141, 137 So. 157, 159 (1931) (same). Even if *"in pari materia"* were indicated-and we stress that it is not-it applies only when two different statutory provisions deal with the same specific subject or with subjects so connected that the meaning of the one informs the other. Here, one statute deals with robbery generally, but the other deals only with a specific form of robbery. Nothing about the *"in pari materia"* canon suggests that criminal statutes on a specific topic must necessarily be interpreted identically to statutes on a topic touching the same subject only generally.

Moving on from the canon of statutory construction, there is no basis for us to look to "polestars" when the ship of statutory interpretation is guided by clear text. That is to say, we look only to clear text for statutory meaning, not to the stars. The text of the specific crime of robbery by sudden snatching defines the offense differently than the general crime of robbery. The text pointedly omits any reference to the person's "custody," a term that would have indicated that a snatching might occur from nearby the person.

With the sudden snatching offense, the clear import of the statute's words is to require that the property be abruptly and unexpectedly plucked from the embrace of the person, not from that person's figurative biosphere. It also requires that the victim become aware of the sudden snatching while it is underway. The statute thus addresses the horror of a victim who is conscious of the startling seizure of something from her hand or person. It is not concerned with a surreptitious taking out from under the victim's senses. The erroneous instruction improperly allowed the jury to convict when the property snatched was not actually taken from the person of the victim.

> "If [the property] is away from the owner [or custodian], yet under his control, for instance in another room of the house, or in another building on his property, it is nevertheless in his personal possession; and if he is deprived thereof, it may well be said it is taken from his person."

Id. (quoting from Wood v. State, 98 Fla. 703, 124 So. 44, 46 (Fla.1929)).

[3] See § 812.131(1)(a) and (b) ("In order to satisfy this definition [of robbery by sudden snatching], it is not necessary to show that: the offender used any amount of force beyond that effort necessary to obtain possession of the money or other property; or there was any resistance offered by the victim to the offender or that there was injury to the victim's person.").

Because the evidence shows that the property was not on the victim's person, and that in any event the victim herself made it obvious that she was unaware of the snatching until after it had been accomplished, defendant should be acquitted of the charge of robbery by sudden snatching. Accordingly, the case is returned for such further proceedings as may be necessary.

REVERSED AND REMANDED FOR FURTHER PROCEEDINGS.

KLEIN, J., concurs.

LEVIN, STEVEN J., Associate Judge, dissents with opinion.

LEVIN, STEVEN, J., Associate Judge, dissenting.

I respectfully dissent from the majority as the taking of the victim's purse was a taking *from the victim's person*. The fact that the purse in the instant case was merely inches from the person does not prevent the taking from being from the victim's person. The jury properly found from the specific facts of this case that the purse was taken *from the person*. The purse was within arm's length of the victim. The trial court was correct in its interpretation of the statute and properly instructed the jury that an item is in possession of a person if "*the thing is so close as to be within ready reach and is under the control of the person*." (emphasis supplied). The exact distance needed to support the item being taken *from the person* is a factual determination made by the jury and that finding should not be disturbed on appeal absent a showing of an abuse of discretion.

In addition, the "Robbery by sudden snatching" statute requires the victim to be aware of the taking *in the course of the taking*. "In the course of the taking" can be subsequent to the taking. In the instant case, although the victim was unaware of the taking at the time of the taking, the victim did become aware of the taking as the defendant was fleeing after the taking. This fact satisfies the statutory requirement of section 812.131, Florida Statutes, as it was a "*continuous series of acts or events*." § 812.131(3)(b)(emphasis supplied). For these reasons, the conviction should be affirmed.

NOTES AND QUESTIONS

1. Why didn't the Court accept that the statutes in question were "*in pari materia*"? Was it only because there was no need to use the canon?

2. The 11th Circuit Court of Appeals in Belanger v. Salvation Army 556 F.3d 1153 C.A.11 (Fla. 2009) considered it appropriate to "...turn to any related statutory provisions that define[d] the word "person." Cason, 944 So.2d at 313; see also State v. Mitro, 700 So.2d 643, 645 (Fla.1997) ("In the absence of a statutory definition, resort may be had to case law or related statutory provisions which define the term, and where a statute does not specifically define words of common usage, such words are construed in their plain and ordinary sense")."

That case was a case involving the question of whether a corporation qualified as a "person" permitted to be a lawful beneficiary of a pay-on-death account. Is it more appropriate to turn to "any related statutory provision" in a case involving this issue than one involving a criminal matter? Does the rule of lenity impact the canon of "in pari material"?

3. Should the question of whether the purse was taken "from the victim's person" be a question of fact for the jury?

4. Is there something troubling about the fact that "from the person" is defined differently in different parts of the criminal code? Should we expect similar terms in a criminal code to be interpreted the same, or should we be pleased that the court interprets this phrase differently depending on what kind of code provision it is and where it is in the context of the code?

5. The general rule is that specific statutes trump general statutes and thus, one should not turn to a general statute to help define provisions in a more specific statute.

MADDOX V. STATE

923 So.2d 442 (Fla. 2006)

Charles J. Crist, Jr., Attorney General, Tallahassee, FL, Robert J. Krauss, Chief-Assistant Attorney General, Bureau Chief, Tampa Criminal Appeals and Donna S. Koch, Assistant Attorney General, Tampa, FL, for Respondent.

PER CURIAM.

We have for review the decision in Maddox v. State, 862 So.2d 783 (Fla. 2d DCA 2003), which certified conflict with the decision in Dixon v. State, 812 So.2d 595 (Fla. 1st DCA 2002). We have jurisdiction. See art. V, § 3(b)(4), Fla. Const. For the reasons more fully expressed below, we disapprove the decision of the First District Court of Appeal in Dixon, and approve the result reached by the Second District Court of Appeal in Maddox.

. . .

Facts

The instant action arises from the Second District Court of Appeal's decision in Maddox v. State, 862 So.2d 783 (Fla. 2d DCA 2003), affirming the circuit court's conviction of the petitioner (Maddox) and certifying conflict with the First District Court of Appeal's decision in Dixon v. State, 812 So.2d 595 (Fla. 1st DCA 2002). The facts of the instant case, summarized in Judge Davis's opinion below, are as follows:

> A Polk County Deputy Sheriff stopped Maddox for an improper lane change. Upon being asked for his driver's license and proof of insurance, Maddox advised

> the deputy that he did not have his license or proof of insurance with him. The deputy then asked for his name and date of birth, in response to which Maddox said his name was Nathaniel Lewis Maddox and his date of birth was November 1, 1980. Based on this information, the deputy issued two citations in the name of Nathaniel Lewis Maddox-one for improper lane change and the other for failure to produce proof of insurance. When Maddox was hesitant to sign the citations, the deputy advised that failure to sign was a criminal offense. Maddox then signed the citations.
>
> During the traffic stop, a second deputy arrived on the scene. The owner of the car, who had been riding in the front passenger seat, gave permission for the deputies to search the vehicle. During the search, the second deputy found an identification card that identified Maddox as Robert Edwin Maddox. A license check for Robert Edwin Maddox showed that his driver's license was suspended. The deputy retained possession of the two traffic citations issued to Nathaniel Maddox and issued a citation to Maddox charging him with driving while his licensed was suspended. Maddox initially refused to sign this citation but agreed to after the deputy issued him a subsequent citation for refusing to sign a citation. Later, while in custody, Maddox volunteered that Nathaniel Maddox was his brother. Accordingly, Maddox was charged with two counts of forgery for signing the citations issued in the name of Nathaniel and two counts of uttering a forged instrument.
>
> Maddox went to trial on the forgery and uttering counts, as well as on one count of giving false information to a police officer and one count of driving while license suspended. He was found guilty as charged.

Maddox, 862 So.2d at 783-84. Maddox appealed his convictions to the Second District Court of Appeal.

The Second District affirmed Maddox's convictions and sentences without comment but wrote to specifically address his contention that the forged traffic citations were inadmissible pursuant to section 316.650(9) of the Florida Statutes (2001). See id. at 783. The district court determined that the trial court did not err in allowing the forged traffic citations into evidence. See id. at 784. In support of its holding, the district court noted that "the purpose of the statute is to protect the person to whom the citation is issued." Id. The district court stated that the person to whom the citations were actually issued in the present case, Nathaniel Maddox (Maddox's brother), was not on trial for either of the infractions underlying those forged traffic citations, nor was Maddox himself on trial for those violations. See id. Further, the district court found that when the deputy issuing the citation learned that Maddox was not Nathaniel Maddox the deputy "withdrew the charges ... and retained the documents as evidence of the criminal offense of forgery." Id. Therefore, the district court determined that the charges were no longer pending against anyone and, as a result, the documents relating to those charges "were not 'citations' as contemplated by the statute, but rather were documentary evidence of Maddox's criminal conduct." Id. Accordingly, the district court held that section 316.650(9) of the Florida Statutes did not apply to the present case and certified conflict with the First District's decision in Dixon. See Maddox, 862 So.2d at 784.

Analysis

In analyzing the conflict that exists between the decision here and that of the First District in Dixon, it is helpful to consider a brief summary of the material facts presented to the First District in Dixon. The factual predicate in Dixon was essentially identical to that in the present case:

> Upon being stopped by a police officer following the commission of several traffic infractions, [Dixon] provided a false name to the officer. That name was placed on the traffic citation, which [Dixon] signed using the false name. When it was learned that [Dixon] gave a false name, he was charged with forgery under section 831.01 and driving without a valid driver's license.

812 So.2d at 595-96. However, contrary to the decision of the district court in the present case, the First District in Dixon determined that the language of section 316.650(9) of the Florida Statutes (2000),was unambiguous and for that reason was not subject to any judicial interpretation or construction whatsoever. See id. at 596. Therefore, the district court in Dixon simply determined without elaboration that the language contained in section 316.650(9)-that "traffic citation[s] 'shall not be admissible evidence in any trial' "-required the exclusion of forged citations in the State's prosecution for forgery. Id. (quoting § 316.350(9), Fla. Stat. (2000)).

Maddox urges this Court to approve and adopt the First District's approach and decision in Dixon and hold that the First District appropriately applied section 316.650(9) of the Florida Statutes (2000), when it concluded that the language of the section is unambiguous and, therefore, not subject to judicial interpretation. Maddox continues that the plain meaning of the particular section makes it absolutely clear that citations simply should not be admissible in *any* trial under any circumstance. The outcome of this case necessarily turns on the application of principles of statutory construction with regard to section 316.650(9) of the Florida Statutes. Turning to these principles, we note that we have previously held that "[i]t is a fundamental principle of statutory construction that where a statute is plain and unambiguous there is no occasion for judicial interpretation." Golf Channel v. Jenkins, 752 So.2d 561, 564 (Fla.2000) (alteration in the original) (quoting Forsythe v. Longboat Key Beach Erosion Control Dist., 604 So.2d 452, 454 (Fla.1992)). However, this Court has

> also stated that related statutory provisions should be read together to determine legislative intent, so that "if from a view of the whole law, or from other laws in pari materia the evident intent is different from the literal import of the terms employed to express it in a particular part of the law, that intent should prevail, for that, in fact is the will of the Legislature."

Id. (quoting Forsythe, 604 So.2d at 454); see also McGhee v. Volusia County, 679 So.2d 729, 730 n. 1 (Fla.1996) ("The doctrine of in pari materia requires the courts to construe related statutes together so that they illuminate each other and are harmonized."). Moreover, "a literal interpretation of the language of a statute need not be given when to do so would lead to an unreasonable or ridiculous conclusion." Holly v. Auld, 450 So.2d 217, 219 (Fla.1984).

The statute at issue here is found within chapter 316 of the Florida Statutes entitled "Florida Uniform *Traffic* Control Law." § 316.001, Fla. Stat. (2001). (emphasis supplied). The stated purpose of this chapter of the Florida Statutes was outlined by the Legislature in section 316.002:

> It is the legislative intent in the adoption of this chapter to make uniform *traffic* laws to apply throughout the state and its several counties and uniform *traffic* ordinances to apply in all municipalities.

§ 316.002, Fla. Stat. (2001) (emphasis supplied). Additionally, when section 316.650 was originally enacted by the Legislature in 1971, the description of the bill expressly stated that it was

> AN ACT relating to the regulation of *traffic* on highways; ... to provide for a uniform *traffic* citation; requiring its statewide use; prescribing duties of *traffic* officers and chief administrative officers in connection with the issuance, distribution and maintenance of records...

Ch. 71-321, preamble, at 1501, Laws of Fla. (emphasis supplied). When section 316.650 is read in the context within the chapter in which it is found, its related statutory provisions, and the legislative history surrounding its passage, it is clear that a strict literal reading of the phrase "any trial," as suggested by Maddox and endorsed by the First District in Dixon, would inappropriately extend the effects of this statutory provision far beyond the scope of that which was intended by the Legislature when it originally enacted this section. It would extend far beyond cases in which the operation, maintenance or use of a vehicle was an issue in controversy. In addition, we agree with Second District that the purpose of this statutory provision is to protect the person to whom the citation is issued which in this case was Nathaniel Maddox, the appellant's brother, who is not even a party in this matter. See Maddox, 862 So.2d at 784. We further conclude that the statute was intended to apply only in connection with matters directly associated with the substance of the charge upon which the citation is issued-a *traffic* infraction.

Another principle of statutory construction that compels our conclusion that the Second District appropriately determined that section 316.650 is inapplicable to the instant matter is the rule which recognizes that "[t]he legislative use of different terms in different portions of the same statute is strong evidence that different meanings were intended." State v. Mark Marks, P.A., 698 So.2d 533, 541 (Fla.1997) (quoting Dep't of Prof'l Regulation v. Durrani, 455 So.2d 515, 518 (Fla. 1st DCA 1984)); see also Beach v. Great W. Bank, 692 So.2d 146, 152 (Fla.1997) (quoting Leisure Resorts, Inc. v. Frank J. Rooney, Inc., 654 So.2d 911, 914 (Fla.1995) ("When the legislature has used a term ... in one section of the statute but omits it in another section of the same statute, we will not imply it where it has been excluded.")). Tellingly, in section 316.066(4) of the Florida Statutes (2001), located in the same chapter as the statutory provision at issue in this case, the Legislature enacted a provision that mandates that neither a crash report nor a statement made in connection with such a report "shall be used as evidence in any trial, *civil or criminal*." § 316.066(4), Fla. Stat. (2001) (emphasis supplied). . The Legislature's use of the language "civil or criminal" in section 316.066(4) to modify the phrase "any trial," and the exclusion of those same modifiers in the statutory provision under review here, compels us to conclude that the Legislature intended different meanings of the term "any trial" in each statute. If the Legislature had intended section 316.650(9) to include "any trial, *civil or criminal*," then the Legislature would have included that language within its enactment, as it did in section 316.066(4). However, the Legislature chose not to include these modifying terms in section 316.650(9), and we conclude that it would not be proper for us to imply this missing language where the Legislature has obviously intended that it be omitted. See State v. Bradford, 787 So.2d 811, 819 (Fla.2001); Beach, 692 So.2d at 152 (quoting Leisure Resorts, Inc., 654 So.2d at 914). Based on the foregoing analysis, we conclude that the Legislature intended that the phrase "any trial" in section 316.650(9) should not be interpreted to mean "any trial, civil or criminal," but instead that the phrase "any trial" in section 316.650(9), consistent with the statutory chapter in which that statutory provision is found, was intended to refer to the use of traffic citations in proceedings in which the manner or method of the operation, maintenance or use of a vehicle is the issue in controversy.

...

In summary, although the strict meaning of the words in the abstract employed by the Legislature when it drafted section 316.650(9) may admittedly support the outcome of the First District's opinion in Dixon v. State, 812 So.2d 595 (Fla. 1st DCA 2002), such a sterile literal interpretation should not be adhered to when it would lead to absurd results. See Parker v. State, 406 So.2d 1089, 1091 (Fla.1981). When section 316.650 is read in the context in which it is found and in conjunction with related statutory provisions, the reasonable construction of this statutory provision is that the Legislature intended only to exclude traffic citations in a more limited fashion in matters with issues related to the operation, maintenance or use of the motor vehicle. To hold otherwise would expand the scope of this statute unreasonably and lead to absurd results. Accordingly, we disapprove the decision of the First District Court of Appeal in Dixon v. State, 812 So.2d 595 (Fla. 1st DCA 2002), and approve the result reached by the Second District Court of Appeal in Maddox v. State, 862 So.2d 783 (Fla. 2d DCA 2003) for the reasons stated herein.

It is so ordered.

WELLS, ANSTEAD, LEWIS, and BELL, JJ., concur.

CANTERO, J., dissents with an opinion, in which PARIENTE, C.J., and QUINCE, J., concur.

CANTERO, J., dissenting.

I would apply the plain meaning of the statute, which prohibits the introduction of traffic citations "in any trial." Contrary to the majority, I agree with the First District Court of Appeal's conclusion in Dixon v. State, 812 So.2d 595 (Fla. 1st DCA 2002), that the statute at issue is unambiguous and therefore must be applied as written. I do not believe that we can, or should, circumvent the statute's plain language. Its directive that traffic "citations shall not be admissible evidence in any trial," § 316.650(9), Fla. Stat. (2001), is simple and clear. "Any trial" means literally *any* trial.

The majority instead interprets the statute as excluding citations from evidence only in trials "related to the operation, maintenance or use of the motor vehicle." Majority op. at 448. In other words, according to the majority, "any trial" must mean "any *traffic-related* trial." I do not agree that we must construe the statute in such a way to avoid an absurd result. I am not prepared to declare it absurd for the Legislature to make citations inadmissible in all cases. As I explain below, the Legislature could have a rational basis for excluding them, such as preventing undue prejudice to defendants. Because I believe the plain meaning of section 316.650(9) prohibits the introduction of traffic citations in any trial, and that such a reading does not lead to an absurd result, I must dissent.

In the following discussion, I will (A) analyze the plain meaning of the statute, (B) summarize the absurdity doctrine, and (C) explain why the plain meaning of the statute cannot be considered absurd. [parts B and C are deleted but will be addressed in the next section]

A. Plain Meaning

Florida is one of "[m]any states [that] have shown great reluctance to admit traffic citations into evidence." Hadley v. Maxwell, 144 Wash.2d 306, 27 P.3d 600, 604 (2001) (citing Martin v. Hackworth, 127 Idaho 68, 896 P.2d 976, 978 (1995), and Ruthardt v. Tennant, 252 La. 1041, 215 So.2d 805, 808 (1968)). Some states have made citations inadmissible where they carry the greatest risk of prejudice, such as in civil trials arising from the cited traffic offense. See, e.g., Ingrum v. Tucson Yellow Cab Co., 131 Ariz. 523, 642 P.2d 868, 872 (Ct.App.1981); Townsend v. Brantley, 163 Ga.App. 899, 296 S.E.2d 186, 187 (1982); Ferreira v. Gen. Motors Corp., 4 Haw.App. 12, 657 P.2d 1066, 1069 (1983); Hood v. Oakley, 519 So.2d 1236, 1239 (Miss.1988); Cotton v. Pyle, 400 S.W.2d 72, 75 (Mo.1966); Frias v. Valle, 101 Nev. 219, 698 P.2d 875, 876 (1985); Isaacs v. Plains Transp. Co., 367 S.W.2d 152, 153 (Tex.1963). Other states have rejected "a rule of blanket exclusion" in favor of a case-by-case approach. Getchell v. Lodge, 65 P.3d 50, 58 (Alaska 2003).

Florida has done the opposite. Until recently, our traffic citation statute broadly provided that "citations shall not be admissible evidence in any trial." § 316.650(9), Fla. Stat. (2001). The question in this case is whether "any trial" really means *any* trial.

. . .

Section 316.650(9) is as clear, definite, and unambiguous as statutory language gets. It states firmly and without exception that citations "*shall not* be admissible

evidence *in any trial.*" § 316.650(9), Fla. Stat. (2001). That, of course, includes forgery trials. The First District concluded as much, holding that "section 316.650(9) unambiguously provides that traffic citations are not admissible in any trial" and "contains no exceptions to this clear and unambiguous prohibition." Dixon, 812 So.2d at 595-96. Before this case, two separate panels of the Second District had reached the same conclusion. See State v. Veilleux, 859 So.2d 1224 (Fla. 2d DCA 2003), review denied, 880 So.2d 1212 (Fla.2004); State v. Martinez, 870 So.2d 18 (Fla. 2d DCA 2003).
. . .

First, the majority notes that section 316.650(9) appears in the Florida Uniform Traffic Control Law, whose opening provision expresses a "legislative intent ... to make uniform traffic laws to apply throughout the state," § 316.002, Fla. Stat. (2001), and whose original preamble focused on "the regulation of traffic on highways." Ch. 71-321, Laws of Fla. Highlighting the recurring word "traffic," the majority reasons that section 316.650(9) must have been intended to exclude citations only in traffic-related trials. This reasoning, however, is undermined by the crash report provision, contained in the same Uniform Traffic Control Law and furthering the same legislative intent. See § 316.066(4), Fla. Stat. (2001). As the majority acknowledges, that provision excludes crash reports even in trials unrelated to motor vehicle operation. It provides as follows:

> Except as specified in this subsection, each crash report made by a person involved in a crash and any statement made by such person to a law enforcement officer for the purpose of completing a crash report required by this section shall be without prejudice to the individual so reporting. *No such report or statement shall be used as evidence in any trial, civil or criminal.*

Id. (emphasis added).

Thus, notwithstanding the Legislature's stated goal of making "uniform traffic laws," it prohibited the introduction of crash reports in *any* trial, even those unrelated to traffic violations (specifically including civil or criminal trials). The Legislature obviously felt that the uniform exclusion of such reports was compatible with its creation of uniform traffic laws. Therefore, the exclusion of traffic citations from evidence in any trial must also be compatible with the general goal of creating uniform traffic laws, as well as with the more specific one of "provid[ing] for a uniform traffic citation; requiring its statewide use." Ch. 71-321, Laws of Fla.

The majority nevertheless concludes that the crash report provision supports its interpretation because the provision addresses admissibility in slightly different language than the provision at issue (using "any trial, civil or criminal" instead of simply "any trial"). The majority interprets the modifier "civil or criminal" as indicating that crash reports must be excluded from literally "any trial," whereas the omission of that modifier from the traffic citation provision indicates that citations need only be excluded from traffic-related trials. The majority claims that to conclude otherwise would be "to imply this missing language where the Legislature has obviously intended that it be omitted." Majority op. at 447.

I disagree that such a conclusion necessarily follows. One need not imply missing language to interpret the phrase "any trial" as encompassing all trials, including those unrelated to motor vehicle operation. The phrase is already as expansive as possible. Adding the modifier "civil or criminal," as the Legislature did in the crash report provision, would serve only to emphasize-or perhaps even *restrict*-the provision's scope. In fact, the Department of Highway Safety and Motor Vehicles has argued that the modifier "civil or criminal" renders the crash report provision inapplicable to administrative proceedings, such as license suspension hearings, that are neither civil *nor* criminal. This case does not require us to address that argument, which the district courts have consistently rejected. See Dep't of Highway Safety & Motor Vehicles v. Corbin, 527 So.2d 868, 872 (Fla. 1st DCA 1988) (holding that "to narrowly interpret the accident report privilege as being applicable only in criminal and civil 'trials,' in the literal sense of these terms, but not in administrative proceedings, would be to substantially diminish its effectiveness"); see also Dep't of Highway Safety & Motor Vehicles v. Perry, 702 So.2d 294, 295 (Fla. 5th DCA 1997) (holding that "the Corbin case is controlling" and therefore the crash report "statute must also be applied to administrative proceedings"); Nelson v. State Dep't of Highway Safety & Motor Vehicles, 757 So.2d 1264, 1265 (Fla. 3d DCA 2000) (citing Perry for the proposition that the crash report provision "is applicable to administrative proceedings"). Suffice it for these purposes to say that the modifier "civil or criminal" does not *expand* the scope of the phrase "any trial."

The majority itself adds language to section 316.650(9) to support its narrower construction, qualifying the phrase "in any trial" with the phrase, "in which the manner or method of the operation, maintenance or use of a vehicle is the issue in controversy." Majority op. at 447. According to the majority, the absence of the phrase "civil or criminal" in section 316.650(9) implicitly limits the provision to traffic-related trials. However, the civil/criminal distinction is not the same as the traffic/non-traffic distinction. A traffic offense can result in either civil or criminal proceedings. See, e.g., § 318.12, Fla. Stat. (2001) (expressing "the legislative intent ... to decriminalize certain violations" of the Uniform Traffic Control Law). Also, as I mentioned, some traffic offenses can result in administrative proceedings, which are neither civil *nor* criminal. Whether section 316.650(9) applies to civil or criminal trials is thus an entirely separate question from whether it applies to traffic-related trials.

Based on this analysis, I continue to believe that the plain meaning of section 316.650(9) is that traffic citations may not be admitted as evidence in any trial, even a forgery trial. Nothing in the statutory context casts doubt on this plain meaning.

. . .

D. Conclusion

I conclude from the plain meaning of section 316.650(9), Florida Statutes (2001), that traffic citations may not be admitted as evidence in any trial. This necessarily includes criminal trials for forgery of a traffic citation. I also conclude that such a result is not absurd and therefore the statute's plain language cannot be avoided.

For these reasons, I respectfully dissent.

PARIENTE, C.J., and QUINCE, J., concur.

NOTES AND QUESTIONS

1. Is the majority correct that "any trial" is narrower than "any trial, civil or criminal"?

2. What tools does the majority use to argue that "any trial" means "any traffic related trial"?

3. Why does the dissent think that "any trial" is more expansive than "any trial, civil or criminal"?

4. Under which exclusionary rule language would crash reports be excluded from administrative proceedings?

5. The general rule is that a statute that is passed later in time trumps an early statute. If the provisions of the two statutes are inconsistent the later statute supersedes the earlier. Nonetheless, as the Court in Woodgate Dev. Corp. v. Hamilton Inv. Trust351 So.2d 14 (Fla. 1977) held:

   > The courts presume that statutes are passed with knowledge of prior existing statutes and that the legislature does not intend to keep contradictory enactments on the books or to effect so important a measure as the repeal of a law without expressing an intention to do so. Where possible, it is the duty of the courts to adopt that construction of a statutory provision which harmonizes and reconciles it with other provisions of the same act. State ex rel. School Board v. Dept. of Education, 317 So.2d 68 (Fla.1975); State v. Putnam County Development Authority, 249 So.2d 6 (Fla.1971); Woodley Lane, Inc. v. Nolen, 147 So.2d 569 (Fla.2d DCA 1962).

G. AVOIDING ABSURD RESULTS

MADDOX V. STATE

923 So.2d 442 (Fla. 2006)

Defendant was convicted in the Circuit Court, Polk County, Judith J. Flanders, J., of committing forgery, uttering forged instruments, giving false information to a law enforcement officer, and driving with suspended license. Defendant appealed. The

District Court of Appeal, Davis, J., 862 So.2d 783, affirmed and certified conflict. [For a full statement of the facts see the treatment of the case in the section above.]

. . .

[C]ontrary to the dictates of this Court in Auld, if we were to agree with the view of the dissent and approve of the First District's interpretation of the phrase "any trial" and conclude that this phrase was intended to absolutely encompass all proceedings in a court of law, we would in essence be sanctioning a construction of this statutory provision that would lead to "unreasonable or ridiculous" results. Auld, 450 So.2d at 219. An example of the absurd results that could follow if we were to approve the First District's decision in Dixon was outlined by Chief Judge Altenbernd in his dissenting opinion in State v. Veilleux, 859 So.2d 1224 (Fla. 2d DCA 2003). He reasoned:

> Hypothetically, if Mr. Veilleux had been charged with first-degree murder and he wished to introduce a traffic citation as alibi evidence to establish that he was receiving a traffic ticket in another county at the time of the murder, it is inconceivable to me that a court could constitutionally prohibit him from introducing this document as evidence. Yet, if read literally, this statute would prevent anyone from introducing the traffic citation in *any* court proceeding.

Id. at 1231 (Altenbernd, C.J., dissenting). In a similar manner, under the dissenting opinion's view, a citation found at the scene of the murder of a police officer would be inadmissible to show the last person having contact with the officer when the substance of the particular citation was in no way in controversy.

We find further support for our conclusion in this matter when recognizing that the First District's interpretation of section 316.650(9) essentially eradicates all prosecutions for forgery of a traffic citation. Under Florida's statutory scheme, to obtain a conviction for forgery the State must demonstrate that the alleged document forged falls within the classes of documents specified in section 831.01 of the Florida Statutes (2005). See State v. Escobedo, 404 So.2d 760, 764 (Fla. 3d DCA 1981) ("Our forgery statute ... makes whoever 'forges' *documents of specified classes* 'with intent to injure or defraud any person' liable to a maximum of [five] years' imprisonment.") (quoting Green v. State, 76 So.2d 645, 646 (Fla.1954)). To accomplish this, the State must specifically prove that the allegedly forged document is in fact a "public document" and is therefore actionable under the statute. Such could never be accomplished in the context of the instant matter if the traffic citation could not be admitted into evidence. The dissent expresses concern that allowing traffic citations into evidence could be unduly prejudicial to defendants due to the potential that the citation may contain "unflattering, legally irrelevant information recorded on the citation," and that a citation will "invariably ... proclaim the officer's judgment that the defendant committed an offense other than forgery." Dissenting op. at 454. However, the dissent's concerns could be alleviated by merely redacting the portions of the citation that do not relate to the forgery charge and that could potentially prejudice a defendant, a practice that is used by trial courts throughout Florida when a critical piece of probative evidence also contains prejudicial information. When the First District's construction of section 316.650(9) is considered in light of the above, it is clear to us that the

Legislature surely did not intend for the phrase "any trial" to be construed so literally to exclude the use of traffic citations in all judicial proceedings-including proceedings other than those involving traffic control and related motor vehicle operation matters such as civil litigation flowing from motor vehicle operation.

In summary, although the strict meaning of the words in the abstract employed by the Legislature when it drafted section 316.650(9) may admittedly support the outcome of the First District's opinion in Dixon v. State, 812 So.2d 595 (Fla. 1st DCA 2002), such a sterile literal interpretation should not be adhered to when it would lead to absurd results. See Parker v. State, 406 So.2d 1089, 1091 (Fla.1981). When section 316.650 is read in the context in which it is found and in conjunction with related statutory provisions, the reasonable construction of this statutory provision is that the Legislature intended only to exclude traffic citations in a more limited fashion in matters with issues related to the operation, maintenance or use of the motor vehicle. To hold otherwise would expand the scope of this statute unreasonably and lead to absurd results. Accordingly, we disapprove the decision of the First District Court of Appeal in Dixon v. State, 812 So.2d 595 (Fla. 1st DCA 2002), and approve the result reached by the Second District Court of Appeal in Maddox v. State, 862 So.2d 783 (Fla. 2d DCA 2003) for the reasons stated herein.

It is so ordered.

. . .

WELLS, ANSTEAD, LEWIS, and BELL, JJ., concur.

CANTERO, J. dissents with an opinion in which PARIENTE, C.J., and QUINCE, J., concur.

. . .

B. The Absurdity Doctrine

As the majority notes, and I agree, we will deviate from a statute's plain language when necessary to avoid an absurd result. As we explained many years ago, "no literal interpretation should be given that lends to an unreasonable or ridiculous conclusion." State v. Sullivan, 95 Fla. 191, 116 So. 255, 261 (1928); see also State v. Burris, 875 So.2d 408, 414 (Fla.2004) (stating, more recently, that "[a] statute's plain and ordinary meaning controls only if it does not lead to an unreasonable result"). However, to prevent the appearance that we are merely substituting our own judgment for the Legislature's, we must invoke the exception only when absolutely necessary-that is, when otherwise the result truly would be absurd or patently unreasonable.

This canon of statutory construction has been one of the "fixed points" in American law, John F. Manning, The Absurdity Doctrine, 116 Harv. L.Rev. 2387, 2389 (2003), and has guided this Court's jurisprudence from the very beginning. See White v. Camp, 1 Fla. 94, 109 (1846) (Baltzell, J., dissenting) (stating, in the first volume of the Florida Reports, that "the reason and intention of the law giver will control the strict letter of the law, when the latter would lead to palpable injustice, contradiction and absurdity") (quoting Plowden's digest of English cases from the sixteenth century).

Yet the absurdity exception to the plain meaning rule is intended to be narrow. The Supreme Court, for example, "rarely invokes such a test to override unambiguous legislation." Barnhart v. Sigmon Coal Co., 534 U.S. 438, 459, 122 S.Ct. 941, 151 L.Ed.2d 908 (2002). In fact, the Court has come "to connect its absurdity analysis to the more forgiving standards of rationality review," Manning, supra, at 2452, meaning that it will enforce a statute's plain meaning as long as it can hypothesize a rational basis to support the textual policy. Id. at 2452 n. 244 (citing examples).

The absurdity doctrine should be reserved for cases where applying the plain meaning would border on irrationality. Only then can we be sure that a textual interpretation would yield "an absurd result totally incongruous with the will of the people." Plante v. Smathers, 372 So.2d 933, 937 (Fla.1979). If expanded beyond rational basis review, the absurdity exception would threaten to undermine the separation of powers by allowing judges to substitute their own views of wise public policy for the compromises struck by legislators. As one scholar recently explained:

> The legislative process is untidy, and the particular wording of a statute may have been, for unknowable reasons, essential to its passage. Thus, rather than identifying genuine legislative intent, application of the absurdity doctrine to disturb a clear statutory text risks displacing whatever bargain legislators actually reached through the complex and path-dependent legislative process.

Manning, supra, at 2486. In other words, there is a fine line between a judicious policy and a judicially imposed one. Unless we can say with absolute confidence that no reasonable legislature would have intended for the statute to carry its plain meaning, we should "presume that [our] legislature says in a statute what it means and means in a statute what it says there." BedRoc Ltd., LLC v. United States, 541 U.S. 176, 183, 124 S.Ct. 1587, 158 L.Ed.2d 338 (2004) (plurality opinion) (quoting Connecticut Nat'l Bank v. Germain, 503 U.S. 249, 253-54, 112 S.Ct. 1146, 117 L.Ed.2d 391 (1992)). The exception to the plain meaning rule should not be used to avoid an unintended result, only an absurd or patently unreasonable one.

C. Excluding Citations from Forgery Trials is not Truly Absurd

The majority claims it would be absurd to prohibit the admission of traffic citations as evidence of forgery. I am not so sure. While citations certainly have greater probative value in forgery trials than in ordinary traffic trials, they still pose a substantial risk of prejudice to the defendant. That the Legislature would decide that the costs of admitting citations outweigh the benefits, even in forgery trials, cannot be considered "unreasonable or ridiculous." Sullivan, 116 So. at 261. To explain this point, I first examine why the Legislature has excluded traffic citations in ordinary traffic trials. Then I demonstrate that the same rationales may justify their exclusion in forgery trials.

All traffic citations have potential value as evidence. They contain a contemporaneous record of what the officer observed, as well as a signature confirming the defendant's presence at the scene. Therefore, they could verify, refute, or supplement the testimony at trial. Also, they could be admitted as business records even without the officer's testimony, provided that a records custodian could verify their authenticity and that their admission would not violate the right to confrontation. See § 90.803(6), Fla. Stat. (2001); see also Veilleux, 859 So.2d at 1230 (Alternbernd, C.J., dissenting) (suggesting that, in the absence of other statutory restrictions, citations could be introduced as business records).

The Legislature, however, has prohibited citations from playing a substantive role by prohibiting their admission as evidence. Instead, they serve three procedural purposes. First, they document the traffic encounter. The statute requires citations to be issued in quintuplicate, § 316.650(1)(a), Fla. Stat. (2001), and meticulously explains where the copies must be sent and how long they must be kept. Id. § 316.650(3)-(8). Second, they give the accused notice to appear. Id. § 316.650(1)(a). The statute provides that the accused "must sign and accept a citation indicating a promise to appear." Id. § 318.14(2). Finally, they can serve as charging documents before the traffic court. See Fla. R. Traf. Ct. 6.165(a); Hurley v. State, 322 So.2d 506 (Fla.1975).

While the Legislature has not stated its reasons for relegating citations to a purely procedural role, I can think of three. First, excluding citations from evidence ensures that the officer who witnessed the alleged traffic offense will actually appear in court and offer firsthand testimony, rather than defer to what is written on the ticket. As a result, the defendant can confront the officer and expose any weaknesses in the testimony. The theory behind this policy is that factfinders can assess the credibility of firsthand, confrontational testimony more accurately than they can assess the credibility of an officer's written report. See Sheryl L. Musgrove & David W. Gross, Use of a Traffic Citation in a Subsequent Related Civil Proceeding, 33 Idaho L.Rev. 135, 144-45 (1996) (warning that "the jury may give undue credence to the decision of the investigating officer to issue the citation").

Another reason for excluding citations from evidence is to ensure that officers will testify only about the facts they witnessed, rather than their legal relevance. As the Idaho Supreme Court explained in holding that citations may not be admitted as evidence in traffic-related civil trials, "[a] citation constitutes a police officer's conclusion that a driver has violated a statute or an ordinance. While a police officer may testify about the observations which led the officer to issue the citation, it is improper for the officer to testify that the driver violated the law." Martin, 896 P.2d at 978; see also Getchell, 65 P.3d at 57-58 (noting that the exclusion of traffic citations in negligence cases is generally "based in part on the rationale that such testimony amounts to an opinion on an ultimate issue that is for the trier of fact to decide ... and in part on the undue weight concerns"). In Florida, too, citations express legal judgments. They contain various boxes that officers must check when they believe that a listed offense has been committed. See, e.g., § 316.650(1)(a), Fla. Stat. (2001) (requiring a special box for "aggressive careless driving as defined in s. 316.1923").

A third reason for excluding citations is to protect defendants in traffic trials, and subsequent civil suits, from the prejudice caused by unflattering, legally irrelevant information recorded on the citation. For example, the uniform citation used in this case included a space for "[o]ther violations or comments pertaining to the offense." What the officer deems factually pertinent, however, can differ from what a court will deem legally relevant. A blanket rule against the admission of citations frees officers to record any information they find helpful, without exposing defendants to undue prejudice.

The majority apparently accepts these rationales as applied to traffic-related cases, but concludes they do not justify the exclusion of citations as evidence of forgery. I agree that in forgery trials the balance changes. Because the citation is the document on which the alleged forgery occurred, it assumes greater probative value. If admitted into evidence, it would become the centerpiece of the State's case. Conversely, excluding citations from evidence "will make convictions for forgery of a traffic citation more difficult." Dixon, 812 So.2d at 596. Indeed, one district court has speculated they will be "all but impossible" to obtain, Martinez, 870 So.2d at 20, although perhaps "the State can bring in evidence from the officer who issued the citation and witnessed the false signature, as well as other evidence of the defendant's identity and intent." Veilleux, 859 So.2d at 1227.

Despite their probative value in forgery trials, citations still pose a substantial risk of prejudice. Invariably, the citation will proclaim the officer's judgment that the defendant committed an offense other than forgery. Sometimes the alleged offense will be relatively minor, but at other times it may be quite serious (for example, drunk driving or aggressive careless driving). If the citation is admitted as evidence of forgery, in deciding whether the forgery was proved the factfinder may be influenced by the unproven traffic charge. The factfinder also may be influenced by any other negative observations in the citation, even if they have no legal bearing on the forgery charge. Finally, to the extent the State relies on the written citation rather than firsthand testimony, the context of the alleged forgery may not be fully explored.

None of this discussion is to suggest that traffic citations should be excluded from forgery trials. The only issue is whether it would be *absurd* to exclude them. I conclude it would not be. Whether the probative value of admitting citations in forgery trials outweighs the risk of prejudice to defendants is, in my view, a policy decision for the Legislature. Earlier this year, the Legislature amended section 316.650(9) to allow the admission of traffic citations to prove forgery. This policy is sensible and should make it easier to prosecute citation forgery cases. Another sensible policy, which the majority suggests, would be to admit the citation into evidence but "merely redact[ ] the portions ... that do not relate to the forgery charge and that could potentially prejudice a defendant." Majority op. at 448. This policy would also be more convenient for prosecutors than the one in the statute at issue. But the Legislature is not required to make prosecutions as easy as possible. Sometimes what is easiest for prosecutors may be too hard on defendants. The Legislature must strike the balance it deems appropriate, within constitutional limits.

Here, the Legislature reasonably could have decided to accept fewer forgery convictions to prevent undue prejudice to defendants, knowing that most drivers who forge citations can also be charged with other crimes of misrepresentation that do not require the admission of unduly prejudicial documents. In this case, for example, the defendant faced additional charges of giving a false name or identification to a law enforcement officer and driving with a suspended or revoked license. Maddox, 862 So.2d at 783. Similarly, in the conflict case, the defendant faced a charge of driving without a valid license. Dixon, 812 So.2d at 595-96. Other charges might include misuse of a license, § 322.32, Fla. Stat. (2001), giving false oral reports under the traffic laws, id. § 316.067, or obstructing an officer, id. § 843.02.

Because the Legislature could have a rational basis for deciding that the costs of admitting traffic tickets in forgery trials outweigh the benefits, applying the plain meaning of section 316.650(9) cannot be considered absurd.[5] In the absence of absurdity, we have a responsibility to the Legislature, which carefully selected the words, and to defendants, whose liberty possibly hinges upon them, to enforce the statute as written.

D. Conclusion

I conclude from the plain meaning of section 316.650(9), Florida Statutes (2001), that traffic citations may not be admitted as evidence in any trial. This necessarily includes criminal trials for forgery of a traffic citation. I also conclude that such a result is not absurd and therefore the statute's plain language cannot be avoided.

For these reasons, I respectfully dissent.

NOTES AND QUESTIONS

1. Does the absurdity analysis make the majority's argument about the meaning of the statute more or less convincing?

2. Does the fact that three out of the seven judges think the plain meaning of the statute does not lead to an absurd result mean that the plain meaning of the statute is not absurd? Are the reasons for excluding this kind of evidence in normal trials also good reasons for excluding them in forgery trials?

---

[5] The majority claims it would be absurd to apply the statute's plain meaning in two other contexts: (1) where the citation is alibi evidence in a murder trial; and (2) where it is evidence of the last driver stopped by a murdered police officer. Majority op. at 447. As I explained earlier, however, the absurdity exception to the plain meaning rule is intended to be narrow. We should depart from the statutory text only to the extent necessary to avoid absurd results. Thus, even assuming it would be absurd to apply the statute's plain meaning in certain murder trials-an issue on which I would reserve judgment until those unusual circumstances actually arise-that would not be a justification for departing from the statute in forgery trials, where the plain meaning does not produce absurd results. The majority suggests that the statute's plain meaning might be unconstitutional as applied to the first situation above. However, constitutionality is a separate issue from absurdity.

3. Does the absurdity of the statute depend on the kind of case in which it is applied? Is a statute less likely to be found absurd in negligent accident cases, than in forgery cases, and less absurd in each of those cases, than in a murder case?

4. Is it fair or appropriate to point to absurd result that may occur in other types of cases?

5. What, if anything, is wrong with the Court fashioning a rule that would serve all the purposes of the exclusionary rule, while preserving good evidence?

BARBER V. STATE

988 So. 2d 1170 (Fla. Dist. Ct. App. 4th Dist. 2008)

TRAWICK, DARYL EVAN, Associate Judge.

The Appellant, Marvin Barber, has two convictions for sexual battery-one for an offense committed in February 1980, and the other for an offense committed in July 1990. Barber's 1990 conviction resulted in a fifteen-year prison sentence. Sometime between 1996 and 1998, Barber was released from prison and placed on conditional release by the Florida Parole Commission. Barber continued in this status until 2000, when he was returned to prison after the Parole Commission determined that he had violated the terms of his conditional release by testing positive for drugs and failing to abide by his curfew. In January 2006, the State filed a petition seeking to have Barber civilly committed under the Jimmy Ryce Act. Ultimately, Barber was found to be a sexually violent predator and committed to the custody of the Department of Children and Family Services. In this appeal, Barber argues that the trial court lacked the authority to order such commitment because he was neither in custody on the effective date of the act, January 1, 1999, or sentenced to "total confinement" after that date. We reject Barber's argument and affirm the order appealed.

The Jimmy Ryce Involuntary Civil Commitment for Sexually Violent Predator's Treatment and Care Act (the "Act") became effective on January 1, 1999. See Ch. 98-64, § 24, at 455, Laws of Fla.; §§ 916.31-.49, Fla. Stat. (Supp.1998). The Act has since been renumbered and now appears in Florida Statutes Chapter 394, Part V, "Involuntary Civil Commitment of Sexually Violent Predators" (2006). At all times relevant to the instant appeal, section 394.925, the so-called "jurisdictional" section of the Act, provided as follows:

> This part [part V or chapter 394 governing the involuntary civil commitment of sexually violent predators] applies to all persons currently in custody who have been convicted of a sexually violent offense, as that term is defined in § 394.912(9), as well as to all persons convicted of a sexually violent offense and sentenced to total confinement in the future.

§ 394.925, Fla. Stat. (2008).

There are thus two classes of persons subject to involuntary commitment as provided for in the Act: (1) those who have been convicted of a sexually violent offense and who were "*in custody*" [emphasis added] on January 1, 1999 (Clause One) and (2) those who have been convicted of a sexually violent offense and who are "*sentenced to total confinement* [1] [emphasis added] *in the future* [post January 1, 1999]" (Clause Two). See § 394.925, Fla. Stat.; Ward v. State, 986 So.2d 479, 481 (Fla.2008) (answering certified question in the affirmative).

Barber contends that he does not fall within either class of persons defined by section 394.925. Barber believes that he does not fall within Clause One because on January 1, 1999, he was on conditional release and not in a "physically secure facility." He also maintains that he does not fall within Clause Two because the revocation of his conditional release did not constitute a "sentence to total confinement in the future" within the meaning of the Act.

In determining whether the facts before us fall within the ambit of Clause One, we must answer this question: Are the terms "in custody" and "total confinement," as used in separate clauses of section 394.925, synonymous in the context of a person on conditional release? Barber, and the dissent, concludes that they are, citing State v. Siddal, 772 So.2d 555 (Fla. 3d DCA 2000), and Gordon v. Regier, 839 So.2d 715 (Fla. 2d DCA 2003), disagreed with on other grounds in Larimore v. State, 917 So.2d 354 (Fla. 1st DCA 2005), review granted in 935 So.2d 1220 (Fla.2006). In reaching this conclusion, these cases rely on a "plain and ordinary meaning" analysis of the term "in custody." While such an analysis is normally warranted, the use of different terms in different clauses of the same statutory provision-"in custody" in Clause One, and "total confinement" in Clause Two-creates an inherent ambiguity requiring the court to look beyond the plain and ordinary meaning of the term "in custody." Further, even if this language could be construed to be unambiguous, the plain meaning analysis should not be used when to do so would clearly defeat the intent of the legislature. "'It is a fundamental rule of statutory construction that legislative intent is the polestar by which the court must be guided, and *this intent must be given effect even though it may contradict the strict letter of the statute.*' " Knowles v. Beverly Enters.-Fla., Inc., 898 So.2d 1, 6 (Fla.2004) (quoting State v. Webb, 398 So.2d 820, 824 (Fla.1981)) (emphasis added). None of the above-cited authorities dispel the concern that legislative intent would be preempted by the interpretation Barber and the dissent urge we afford the term "in custody."

In considering the legislature's use of the term "in custody" in Clause One and "total confinement" in Clause Two, we should be mindful of the maxim of statutory

---

[1] "Total confinement" is defined as follows:

> "Total confinement" means that the person is currently being held in any physically secure facility being operated or contractually operated for the Department of Corrections, the Department of Juvenile Justice, or the Department of Children and Family Services. A person shall also be deemed to be in total confinement for applicability of provisions under this part if the person is serving an incarcerative sentence under the custody of the Department of Corrections or the Department of Juvenile Justice and is being held in any other secure facility for any reason.

§ 394.925(11), Fla. Stat

interpretation that where certain language is used in one part of a statute and different language is used in another, it will be assumed that different meanings were intended. Norman J. Singer, Statutes & Statutory Construction § 46:06, at 194 (6th ed. 2000). Additionally, absent evidence of a contrary conclusion, legal terms in a statute will be presumed to have been used in their legal sense. Id. § 47:30 at 361-62.

A careful reading of the cases relied on by Barber and the dissent reveal no discussion or analysis of the significance of the legislature's use of the terms "in custody" in Clause One and "total confinement" in Clause Two. These cases instead rely on the "plain and ordinary meaning" of the term "in custody," and, by the use of a dictionary, they conclude that "in custody" and "total confinement" are synonymous. See Siddal, 772 So.2d at 556; Gordon, 839 So.2d at 718. Such a conclusion dismisses without discussion the ambiguity created by the use of these terms in difference clauses of the same provision. It also ignores the presumption that the legislature intended different meanings by its use of different terminology in the two clauses of section 394.925. The use of the undefined term "in custody" by the legislature in this context cloaks it with legal significance that cannot be ignored. As the Gordon court stated, "[i]n the legal arena, the term 'custody' is a term of art...." Id. at 718. Thus, we cannot casually dismiss the possibility that the legislature intended that this term encompass more than its colloquial meaning.

In Echols v. State, 201 So.2d 89 (Fla. 2d DCA 1967), the Second District Court of Appeal discussed the legal status of a paroled, or conditionally released, prisoner. Our sister court found that while such a prisoner was not in actual custody, the prisoner remained in "legal" or "constructive custody." Id. at 93-94 (citing 67 C.J.S. Pardons § 22(b), p. 610). This concept, in the context of persons on parole, is well established in our jurisprudence. See United States v. Presley, 487 F.3d 1346, 1349 (11th Cir.), cert. denied, --- U.S. ----, 128 S.Ct. 414, 169 L.Ed.2d 290 (2007); see also Sherman v. United States Parole Comm'n, 502 F.3d 869, 884 (9th Cir.2007); United States v. Brown, 117 F.3d 471, 475 (11th Cir.1997); Howse v. Tenn. Dep't of Correction, No. M2004-01497-COA-R3CV, 2007 WL 2198188 (Tenn.Ct.App. July 23, 2007); Jenner v. Ortiz, 155 P.3d 563, 565 (Colo.Ct.App.2006), cert. denied, --- U.S. ----, 127 S.Ct. 2976, 168 L.Ed.2d 708 (2007). Thus, the term "in custody" can be interpreted to mean both *actual* and *constructive* custody. Such an interpretation would comport with the assumption that the legislature intended different meanings in using different terminology in Clause One and Clause Two, as well as the presumption that the legislature understood the full meaning and implication of the language it used. See Ward v. State, 936 So.2d 1143, 1146 (Fla. 3d DCA 2006), aff'd, 986 So.2d 479 (Fla.2008).

How then can it be presumed that the legislature intended the term "in custody" to include "constructive" custody? A contrary conclusion would create a serious anomaly within the Jimmy Ryce Act. If a person was on probation on the effective date of the Act, and that person was later found to have violated his probation, resulting in a sentence of "total confinement" by a court, that individual may be subject to civil commitment under Clause Two. However, a person who was on conditional release on the effective date of the Act, as Barber was here, and was later found to have violated his release conditions, would not likewise be subject to commitment under the Act. Since the offender would already have been sentenced to a prison term *prior* to the effective date of the Act, a decision by the Parole Commission to return the offender to custody to complete a sentence may not constitute a sentence of "total confinement in the future." Thus, persons conditionally released from prison terms and who later violate their release conditions would be treated in a more lenient manner under the Act than persons who violate conditions of their probationary sentences. Yet, a person originally sentenced to probation can, in most circumstances, be presumed to be a less serious offender than a person originally sentenced to prison and on conditional release. Absent a departure sentence, only less serious offenders would be eligible for probation under Florida's Sentencing Guidelines, Florida Statutes section 921.001, et. seq. See also Duncan v. Moore, 754 So.2d 708, 712 (Fla.2000) (due to prior criminal history, conditional release upon release from prison justified).

It is a basic tenet of statutory construction that a court must interpret a statute in a manner that would avoid an absurd result. See Smith v. Krosschell, 937 So.2d 658, 663 (Fla.2006); V.K.E. v. State, 934 So.2d 1276, 1289 (Fla.2006) (Cantero, J., dissenting); Warner v. City of Boca Raton, 887 So.2d 1023, 1033 n. 9 (Fla.2004); State v. Atkinson, 831 So.2d 172, 174 (Fla.2002); Ross v. State, 947 So.2d 699, 701 (Fla. 4th DCA 2007); Velde v. Velde, 867 So.2d 501, 507 (Fla. 4th DCA 2004); DR Lakes Inc. v. Brandsmart U.S.A. of W. Palm Beach, 819 So.2d 971, 974 (Fla. 4th DCA 2002); Dillard v. State, 820 So.2d 994, 996-97 (Fla. 4th DCA 2002); City of Margate v. Singh, 778 So.2d 1080, 1081 (Fla. 4th DCA 2001). A broad interpretation of the term "in custody," as used in the Act, would avoid such a result and support the clear legislative intent to protect the public. See State v. Robinson, 873 So.2d 1205, 1210 (Fla.2004); Ward, 936 So.2d at 1149 (the purpose of the Act is to provide mental health treatment and protect the public from sexually violent predators) (citing Westerheide v. State, 831 So.2d 93, 112 (Fla.2002)). Indeed, the supreme court's discussion of the purpose of the Act in Ward supports such a broad interpretation:

> [T]here is no rational basis to classify potential sexually violent predators differently based on whether they were incarcerated on the effective date of the Act. The purpose of the Act is to remove the threat posed to society by sexually violent predators by means of involuntarily committing them to long-term care and treatment facilities. This purpose is served equally when the Act is applied to those individuals who were in custody on its effective date and who had been convicted of a sexually violent offense in the past, see Hale, and when the Act is applied to those individuals who were not in custody on the effective date but have also been convicted of a sexually violent offense in the past. *Classification as a sexually violent predator does not rest on the vagaries of whether an individual was in custody on the date the Act became effective.*

986 So.2d at 483 (emphasis added).

If the legislative intent is to protect the public, it becomes quite logical and reasonable to conclude that the legislature, while intending that less serious offenders who are on probation be included under the Act, did not intend that the more serious offenders on conditional release be excluded. As a result, the term "in custody," as used in Clause One of the Jimmy Ryce Act, must be interpreted to include persons in both actual and constructive custody in the context of conditional release. Thus, Barber falls within the ambit of this clause.

A thorough analysis of the cases primarily relied on by the dissent, namely Siddal and Gordon, supports the conclusion that they are not dispositive of the issue before us. In Siddal, the appellee was on probation on the effective date of the Jimmy Ryce Act. The State argued that the term "in custody" should include persons on probation. The Third District Court of Appeal rejected that argument, utilizing a plain meaning analysis and relying on a dictionary definition of the term. The court thus affirmed the trial court's finding that Clause One did not apply to persons on probation on the Act's effective date. Unlike Siddal, the case before us involves conditional release and constructive custody. To extend the Siddal holding under the circumstances presented here would, as discussed earlier, ignore the significant differences between probation and conditional release.

Despite such differences, Gordon extended Siddal to a conditional release circumstance. The petitioner, who had been convicted of a lewd and lascivious act in the presence of a child under the age of sixteen, was sentenced to fifteen years in prison in 1992. He was released from prison on conditional release in 1998. He was found to have violated his release conditions and was returned to custody. On April 6, 2000, the petitioner was reinstated to conditional release by the Florida Parole Commission and released from custody. After this second release, the Department of Corrections determined that the petitioner might be subject to the Jimmy Ryce Act and issued a warrant for his arrest. He was arrested two days after the second release date. The issue presented to the Second District Court of Appeal was whether the Act applied to a person who was not in custody *at the time a petition for involuntary commitment was filed*. The court answered this question in the negative. The court placed great reliance on the accomplishment of certain procedural prerequisites under the Act "while the person [is] still in prison." Gordon, 839 So.2d at 718. In other words, the procedural review process must be accomplished prior to the completion of a person's sentence and while the individual is still incarcerated. Gordon found that since these prerequisites could only be accomplished in a total confinement setting, i.e., prison, "in custody," as used in Clause One, must necessarily equate to "total confinement." The court noted approvingly Siddal's reliance on a dictionary definition of "custody" in reaching this conclusion, id. at 718, and extended the custody analysis of Siddal, made in the context of a probationary sentence, to a custodial release circumstance.

While it is true that civil commitment prerequisites cannot take place unless a defendant is in total confinement, the Gordon court's blanket extension of Siddal to custodial release circumstances is unwarranted. The key point in the Gordon analysis was the fact that the petitioner was not incarcerated at the time the Act's procedural prerequisites were commenced. "[T]he Legislature intended that ordinarily the review process of potential sexual predators would be concluded while the person was still in prison." Id. at 718. Thus, Gordon found that a person on conditional release cannot be civilly committed under the Jimmy Ryce Act since that person is not in total confinement. The question of whether the petitioner was incarcerated or in "actual custody" on the Act's enactment date was not addressed by the Gordon court. Yet the dissent here relies on Gordon in concluding that the Act does not apply unless an individual is in actual custody, i.e., total confinement, on the Act's enactment date, regardless of whether the individual is in actual custody when civil proceedings are commenced. This would be an unwarranted extension of the overbroad language in Gordon and would clearly be contrary to the intent of the Legislature. Instead, we interpret Gordon as being limited to those circumstances in which an individual is not in actual confinement, i.e., total confinement, when civil commitment proceedings are commenced, regardless of whether the individual was in actual or constructive custody on the Act's enactment date. Not only would this interpretation comport with the intent of the legislature, it would be in line with the conclusion of the supreme court in Ward, quoted above, that the determination of whether a person is a sexual predator under the Act should not "rest on the vagaries of whether an individual was in custody on the date the Act became effective." Ward, 986 So.2d at 483.

Our analysis of the term "in custody" would not be complete without considering the full impact of Ward, even though it was a Clause Two decision. Ward was convicted of two sexually violent offenses in 1976, and he was released from prison in 1993. He was later convicted for non-sexually related offenses and sentenced to thirty-six months in prison in 2004. In 2005, the State commenced commitment proceedings under the Act. Ward moved to dismiss the petition because he had not been in custody on the effective date of the Act and he had not been convicted of a sexually violent offense after that date. The trial court denied his motion, and Ward filed for a writ of prohibition with the Third District Court of Appeal. The Third District, in analyzing Clause Two, found that the Act applied to persons in "total confinement" even if the reason for such confinement was not a sexually related offense. Ward, 936 So.2d at 1145. The supreme court agreed with this conclusion, rejecting the petitioner's argument that both the qualifying offense and total confinement requirements of Clause Two must occur "in the future"-after the effective date of the Act. In reaching its decision, the court relied in part on its holding in Hale v. State, 891 So.2d 517 (Fla.2004). Hale, important to our analysis here, involved an interpretation of Clause One of section 394.925 of the Act prior to the May 1999 amendment. The petitioner argued that when the State filed its civil commitment petition, he was not in custody for a sexually violent offense. The Hale court found that "the Act applies to all persons who are currently incarcerated and who at some point in the past have been convicted of a sexually violent offense." Id. at 522. The Hale court reasoned that this interpretation " 'give[s] effect to *all* statutory provisions ... in harmony with one another.' " Id. (quoting Forsythe v. Longboat Key Beach Erosion Control Dist., 604 So.2d 452, 455 (Fla.1992)). The Ward court, in its discussion of Hale, noted that Hale involved Clause One and the pre-May 1999 version of the Act. However, Ward applied Hale's reasoning to Clause Two, finding that the Act's scope includes persons who committed a sexually violent offense in the past, regardless of what the offense was they were being incarcerated for when a commitment petition was filed. Ward, 986 So.2d at 481-83.

Ward, despite the Third District's conclusion that "total confinement" and "in custody" are interchangeable, is not dispositive of the issue presented here, since, as we noted earlier, the issue before the Ward court involved Clause Two and not Clause One. Additionally, Hale, the reasoning of which was relied upon by Ward, was decided *prior* to the amendment of the jurisdictional provision of the Act, which added the term "total confinement" to Clause Two. This amendment substantively changed the interpretation of the term "in custody" by creating two separate groups of persons-an undefined group which must be "in custody" and a specifically defined group which must be in "total confinement." The ambiguity created by the use of these terms and the intent of the legislature in creating these separate groups, until now, has never been fully addressed.

As each of the cases discussed above is distinguishable on its facts from the subject case, they do not bar the interpretation of the term "in custody" reached here. We therefore conclude that Barber does fall within the scope of Clause One of the Act, and that the trial court was correct in finding that Barber was subject to involuntary commitment. Given this conclusion, we need not reach Barber's arguments regarding the inapplicability of Clause Two.

Affirmed.

STONE, J., concurs.

STEVENSON, J., dissents with opinion.

STEVENSON, J., dissenting.

I must respectfully dissent. Because appellant was out of prison on conditional release he was not "in custody" *on* the effective date of the Jimmy Ryce Act (the Ryce Act) and because appellant was later returned to prison by the Parole Commission for a conditional release violation he was not "sentenced" to confinement *after* the effective date of the Ryce Act. Thus, I would reverse and hold that the trial court had no authority to civilly commit appellant under the Ryce Act.

A person is subject to civil commitment proceedings under the Ryce Act if he has been convicted of a sexually violent offense and was "in custody" on the effective date of the Ryce Act, January 1, 1999. See § 394.925, Fla. Stat. (2008) (so-called clause one). During the course of this appeal, and below, both appellant and the State have correctly agreed that clause one of the jurisdictional provisions of the Ryce Act is not applicable because appellant was on conditional release on the effective date of the Ryce Act. This position is supported both directly and indirectly by at least two other districts. See State v. Siddal, 772 So.2d 555 (Fla. 3d DCA 2000) (finding that petitioner on probation on January 1, 1999, was not "in custody" for purposes of the Ryce Act); Gordon v. Regier, 839 So.2d 715, 718 (Fla. 2d DCA 2003), disagreed with on other grounds in Larimore v. State, 917 So.2d 354 (Fla. 1st DCA 2005) (concluding that petitioner on conditional release on January 1, 1999, was not "in custody"), review granted in 935 So.2d 1220 (Fla.2006).

I have no quarrel with the concept of "constructive custody" addressed in the majority opinion and discussed in Echols v. State, 201 So.2d 89, 93 (Fla. 2d DCA 1967) (" '[A] a paroled prisoner, although conditionally released from actual custody, remains in legal custody and is constructively a prisoner of the state or nation, as the case may be.' ") (quoting 67 C.J.S. Pardons § 22(b), p. 610). I also acknowledge that a person freed from prison on conditional release remains under a degree of supervision by the state. I simply do not agree that the legislature intended to include the legal fiction of "constructive custody" when it used the term "in custody" in section 394.925 of the Ryce Act. As a well-accepted principle of statutory interpretation, where the legislature has not defined words or phrases used in a statute, they should be "construed in the plain and ordinary sense." Dadeland Depot, Inc. v. St. Paul Fire & Marine Ins. Co., 945 So.2d 1216, 1225 (Fla.2006). I believe that if the legislature had intended such an expansive and hyper-technical meaning for the term "in custody," it would have explicitly said so. As the court in State v. Siddal remarked, "especially considering the serious consequences of the statutory section at issue, the liberal reading of the term advocated by the state is not supported by the terminology employed or the section's legislative history." 772 So.2d at 556. Neither the common meaning nor the general legal understanding of the term "in custody" conjures up the esoteric notion of "constructive custody."

Further, I do not believe that appellant was "*sentenced*" to total confinement after the effective date of the Ryce Act.[1] The second clause of the jurisdictional provisions of the Ryce Act applies to those who have been convicted of a sexually violent offense and "sentenced to total confinement in the future [i.e., post January 1, 1999]." § 394.925, Fla. Stat. Appellant was returned to prison post-January 1, 1999, as a consequence of the Florida Parole Commission's revocation of his conditional release. The Conditional Release Program Act is governed by Florida Statutes section 947.1405. "[C]onditional release is not a form of sentence, and it is not imposed by a court" and an inmate's "placement on conditional release is required, not by the sentencing court, but by the Parole Commission." Mayes v. Moore, 827 So.2d 967, 971 (Fla.2002). As explained in Evans v. Singletary, 737 So.2d 505, 507 (Fla.1999):

> Conditional Release is an extra post-prison probation-type program. In other words, when an inmate is released due to gain time from a sentence that is eligible for Conditional Release, instead of going free as other offenders would do (unless they have probation or some other supervision to follow), these offenders are placed on supervision for the amount of time equal to the gain time they have accrued. If they violate their supervision, gain time is forfeited and the inmate is returned to prison to continue serving the sentence(s). See § 947.1405(2), Fla. Stat. (1997).

A Parole Commission panel may revoke conditional release if it finds that the violations of conditional release have been sustained and may "return the releasee to prison to serve the sentence imposed." § 947.141(4), Fla. Stat.; see also Sutton v. Fla. Parole Comm'n, 975 So.2d 1256 (Fla. 4th DCA 2008).

According to appellant, the word "sentenced," as used in section 394.925, requires a judicial action and, thus, he is not subject to the Ryce Act since he had been

---

[1] By statutory definition, "total confinement" is a more restrictive term than "custody." In Ward v. State, 986 So.2d 479, (Fla.2008), our supreme court noted that under the Ryce Act, "total confinement means that the person is in state custody." Id. at 481 (emphasis add- ed). Thus, the legislature's use of the term "custody" in clause one and "total confine- ment" in clause two has differing implications for amenability to commitment under the Ryce Act. Appellant doesn't argue that he was not in total confinement post-January 1, 1999; his claim is that he was not "sentenced" to total confinement post-January 1, 1999.

"sentenced" to confinement many years prior to the Ryce Act's effective date. I am constrained to agree. The word "sentenced" is not defined in chapter 394. It is, however, defined by the Florida Rules of Criminal Procedure and its meaning is limited to a punishment handed down by a court. Rule 3.700(a) provides that "[t]he term sentence means the pronouncement by the court of the penalty imposed on a defendant for the offense of which the defendant has been adjudged guilty." The word "sentence" used as a legal term of art refers to the punishment imposed by a court. See Waite v. City of Fort Lauderdale, 681 So.2d 901, 903 n. 3 (Fla. 4th DCA 1996). " '[T]he legislature is presumed to know the existing law when a statute is enacted.' " Crescent Miami Ctr., LLC v. Fla. Dep't of Revenue, 903 So.2d 913, 918 (Fla.2005) (quoting Wood v. Fraser, 677 So.2d 15, 18 (Fla. 2d DCA 1996)). Further, the plain and ordinary meaning of the word "sentenced" also denotes the judicial act of imposing a penalty or punishment.

In revoking conditional release, the Parole Commission returns a defendant to serve the remainder of a sentence previously imposed by a judge; it does not impose a new sentence. To conclude that the Parole Commission "sentenced" appellant might well amount to a separation of powers violation.[2]

Appellant was sentenced to total confinement by the court in 1990 and not by the Parole Commission when he was returned to prison post-January 1, 1999. The State claims that this interpretation creates a statutory "loophole," and treats persons returned to prison by the Parole Commission after conditional release differently than persons sentenced to prison by a judge after a probation violation; however incongruous that consequence may seem to the State, this court is not free to re-write the statute. See State v. Globe Commc'ns Corp., 622 So.2d 1066, 1080 (Fla. 4th DCA 1993) ("[I]t is a time-honored principle of Florida law that it is not the role of a court to rewrite a statute."), aff'd, 648 So.2d 110 (Fla.1994).

Accordingly, I would reverse the order committing appellant to the custody of DCF under the Ryce Act.

NOTES AND QUESTIONS

1. Marvin Barber is not a very sympathetic party. Is it the fact that he is a "sexual predator" that makes it absurd that he could benefit from this apparent gap in the statute?

2. Would the Court find it equally absurd if this was a statute that allowed for involuntary civil commitment for people with a gambling addiction?

3. Does the dissent come up with any rational basis for this loophole in the law? Could there be?

---

[2] See Art. II, § 3, Fla. Const. ("No person belonging to one branch shall exercise any powers appertaining to either of the other branches unless expressly provided herein.").

4. Even if there is no rational basis for the loophole, should someone who may be involuntarily incarcerated get every benefit of gaps in the law?

CHILDERS V. CAPE CANAVERAL HOSP., INC.

898 So.2d 973 (Fla. Dist. Ct. App. 5th Dist. 2005)

PLEUS, J.

This is an appeal of the trial court's dismissal with prejudice of a wrongful death action filed by William Childers on behalf of himself and his four year old son, Jason Childers. The claim arose from the death of Sandra Childers, William's wife and Jason's mother, who died allegedly from a misdiagnosed ovarian cancer. At the outset, we find that William's individual claim is barred by Ash v. Stella, 457 So.2d 1377 (Fla.1984). As to Jason's claim, the issue on appeal is whether the statute of repose in section 95.11(4)(b), Florida Statutes, for cases "brought on behalf of a minor," applies only to cases brought on behalf of a child injured by medical malpractice or also extends to cases brought on behalf of a child for the wrongful death of a parent. We believe it applies only to the former and therefore affirm.

In September of 1997, Sandra Childers had some ovarian cysts removed. The biopsy report found no abnormal pathology. In March of 2000, her ovarian cancer was properly diagnosed, but by then it had metastasized. She died in April of 2001, within the four year statute of repose for medical malpractice claims. Suit was filed in April of 2003. Appellants' complaint alleged that the appellees erroneously and negligently interpreted the 1997 pathology slides. It further alleged that appellants did not learn of the 1997 misdiagnoses until June of 2002.

Appellees filed motions to dismiss the suit based on the ground that it was barred by the statutes of limitations/repose. The trial court found that the suit was barred by the statute of repose found in section 95.11(4)(b), Florida Statutes.

Section 95.11(4)(b) now provides:

> An action for medical malpractice shall be commenced within 2 years from the time the incident giving rise to the action occurred or within 2 years from the time the incident is discovered, or should have been discovered with the exercise of due diligence; however, in no event shall the action be commenced later than 4 years from the date of the incident or occurrence out of which the cause of action accrued, except that this 4 year period shall not bar an action *brought on behalf of a minor* on or before the child's eighth birthday. An "action for medical malpractice" is defined as a claim in tort or in contract for damages because of the death, injury, or monetary loss to any person arising out of any medical, dental, or surgical diagnosis, treatment, or care by any provider of health care. The limitation of actions within this subsection shall be limited to the health care provider and persons in privity with the provider of health care. In those actions covered by this paragraph in which it can be shown that fraud, concealment, or intentional

> misrepresentation of fact prevented the discovery of the injury the period of limitations is extended forward 2 years from the time that the injury is discovered or should have been discovered with the exercise of due diligence, but in no event to exceed 7 years from the date the incident giving rise to the injury occurred, except that this 7 year period shall not bar an action *brought on behalf of a minor* on or before the child's eighth birthday. (Emphasis added).

The legislature did not define the phrase "brought on behalf of a minor." No Florida cases have previously defined this phrase, or explained when, or under what circumstances, the statute of repose is extended to seven years for actions "brought on behalf of a minor."

When interpreting a statute and attempting to discern legislative intent, courts must first look at the actual language used in a statute. See, e.g., Joshua v. City of Gainesville, 768 So.2d 432 (Fla.2000). If the language contained in a statute is clear and unambiguous, courts must derive legislative intent from the words used without involving rules of construction or speculating as to what legislature intended. See, e.g., State v. Dugan, 685 So.2d 1210 (Fla.1996). Courts must give statutory language its plain and ordinary meaning, and is not at liberty to add words that were not placed there by the legislature. See, e.g., Exposito v. State, 891 So.2d 525 (Fla.2004).

However, as in this case, where reasonable differences arise as to the meaning or application of a statute, rules of statutory construction control. See, e.g., Lowry v. Parole and Probation Com'n, 473 So.2d 1248 (Fla.1985). Courts should not construe a statute so as to achieve an absurd result. See, e.g., McKibben v. Mallory, 293 So.2d 48 (Fla.1974). A literal interpretation of the statutory language used is not required when to do so would lead to an unreasonable conclusion, defeat legislative intent or result in a manifest incongruity. See Las Olas Tower Co. v. City of Fort Lauderdale, 742 So.2d 308, 312 (Fla. 4th DCA 1999), rev. dismissed, 783 So.2d 1056 (Fla. 2001). "[I]f from a view of the whole law, or from other laws in pari materia the evident intent is different from the literal import of the terms employed to express it in a particular part of the law, that intent should prevail, for that, in fact is the will of the Legislature." Forsythe v. Longboat Key Beach Erosion Control District, 604 So.2d 452 (Fla.1992).

Here, the plain meaning of the phrase "brought on behalf of a minor" is unclear and subject to multiple interpretations. Appellants assert that because this action was "brought on behalf of a minor [Jason]" prior to his eighth birthday, Jason has up until his eighth birthday on August 11, 2006, to file a suit for damages relating to the alleged malpractice in September of 1997. As support for this argument, appellant speculates that the Florida Legislature created this eight year old extension in response to Ash v. Stella, 457 So.2d 1377 (Fla.1984), which held that the medical malpractice statute of limitations applies to wrongful death actions arising from medical malpractice. Appellees counter that the legislature intended to extend the statute of repose only in those instances where the minor suffers injury as the result of medical negligence. A careful review of the legislative history leading to the 1996 amendment to section 95.11(4)(b) indicates that the appellees are correct.

Section 95.11(4)(b) was amended as a result of Senate Bill 454 (SB 454). The prologue to SB 454 provides that the amendment was intended to toll the statute of limitations and statute of repose "with respect to claims of medical malpractice by certain minors...." According to the staff analysis related to SB 454, the amendment "will increase the number of suits primarily against OB/GYNs and pediatricians." Appellees assert that because OB/GYNs and pediatricians are the most likely candidates to be sued for injuries to children, the legislature must have intended the "brought on behalf of a minor" language to apply only to claims brought on behalf of injured children.

Appellees' argument is supported by language contained in section VII of the staff analysis. That section provides commentary on issues related to the amendment and cites to information provided to the legislature by the Academy of Florida Trial Lawyers and the American Tort Reform Association regarding the then national trend toward tolling the statute of limitation and statute of repose for actions brought on behalf of a minor under certain circumstances. Section VII provides in relevant part, "[i]n California, the statute of limitations for a plaintiff *injured* under the age of six years to bring a medical malpractice action is within 3 years or before the 8th birthday, whichever is later...." (Emphasis added). That section also cites to a Massachusetts statute that tolls the time statute of limitations for medical malpractice claims brought "by a minor" and an Ohio statute that tolls the statute of limitations "for minors to bring a medical malpractice action." Collectively, these citations indicate that the legislature intended to amend section 95.11(4)(b) to provide children under the age of eight that are injured as a result of medical malpractice with additional time to file a claim.

This proposition finds strong support in the staff analysis for House Bill 43 ("HB 43"), a companion bill to SB 454. HB 43 contained a proposal to amend section 95.051, Florida Statutes to toll the statute of limitations and statute of repose for medical malpractice actions "brought on behalf of a minor child" until the child reached 5 years of age. The language contained in the staff analysis for HB 43 closely tracks that contained in the staff analysis for SB 454, and provides additional insight into the intent behind the phrase "brought on behalf of a minor."

Section II of the staff analysis to HB 43 provides

> Florida does not have a tolling provision for the statute of limitations for medical malpractice claims involving children. Approximately 40 other states have enacted legislation which extends the statute of limitations for minors entitled to sue under a medical malpractice claim due to the difficulty in detecting or determining the extent of injuries caused by medical malpractice in children. The limitation periods range from three years from the date of injury, to tolling the statute of limitations until the minor reaches 18 years of age.

Subsection C of the staff analysis provides that HB 43 "tolls the running of the statute of limitations with respect to medical malpractice claims that *occur to children* under the age of five until the child's fifth birthday." (Emphasis added)[6] Subsection B compares the differences between the then-current law and the amendment proposed in HB 43 and explains that the time extension applies to those situations where "*medical malpractice is committed on a child.*" (Emphasis added). These facts provide further evidence that the 1996 amendment to section 95.11(4)(b) was directed to claims brought on behalf of a minor who suffered personal injury as the result of medical negligence.

In addition, appellants' interpretation undermines the purpose of the statutes of limitations and repose. Under appellants' scenario, a child would have up until his or her eighth birthday to individually bring suit, regardless of the date of the alleged malpractice. Theoretically, appellants could bring suit "on behalf of" Jason even if the date of the alleged malpractice against Jason's mother was 20 years ago and Jason was not even born yet. This possibility produces an absurd result and runs contrary to the basic premise behind the time limitations on lawsuits. Under this proposed reading, health care providers, regardless of the age of their patients and the time of the relevant treatment, would be constantly concerned about the possibility that a child could come into a position to bring a derivative claim.

In summary, appellants are asking this Court to create new law based on their unfortunate and sympathetic circumstances. The creation of new law is better left to the Florida legislature. We have considered the other arguments raised by the appellants and find them to be without merit.

AFFIRMED.

PALMER and MONACO, JJ., concur.

NOTES AND QUESTIONS

1. Is the phrase: "except that this 4 year period shall not bar an action brought on behalf of a minor on or before the child's eighth birthday" unclear?

2. Does the fact that the statute reads: "An *action for medical malpractice* is defined as a claim in tort or in contract for damages because of the death, injury, or monetary loss to any person arising out of any medical, dental, or surgical diagnosis, treatment, or care by any provider of health care" clarify the scope of the exception?

3. Did the legislative history make the language unclear, or was it unclear before the court turned to the legislative history?

4. Was this a case where the plain meaning really resulted in an "absurd result?" Would it lead to "an unreasonable conclusion, defeat legislative intent or result

---

[6] Although this statement does not include the statute of repose, the immediately paragraph provides, "this tolls the statute of limitations and the statute of repose for medical malpractice claims for minors."

in a manifest incongruity." Are these all the same thing? Do they equally justify moving away from the plain meaning of the statute?

5. Do you agree that the appellants were asking the Court to create new law, or was it the Court that created new law in this case?

SECTION II: SUBSTANTIVE TOOLS

Introduction

The substantive tools of statutory interpretation are often cast in terms of reading different kinds of statutory provisions either strictly (narrowly) or liberally (broadly). Generally, Florida judges follow the traditional substantive canons. The judges often interpret public interest and remedial statutes liberally. On the other hand, statutes that alter the common law, criminal statutes, statutes that may raise constitutional issues, and statutes that abrogate state sovereign immunity, are often interpreted strictly or narrowly.

As they stand, these tools guide the interpreter to abandon the plain meaning of the statute. This is done by either expanding the meaning of the text to affect its remedial purpose, or by constricting the text to avoid infringing a defendant's rights, avoid conflicts with the Constitution, or to avoid undermining state sovereignty. The canons are substantive in that they embody values that add weight to one interpretive choice over another. Putting it this way implies that there must be two or more ways of interpreting the text. Florida's general rule is that if the statute is clear, the judge will not turn to these canons. Thus, Florida does not use canons to operate as presumptions that one brings to an otherwise clear text, but uses them as a tie breaker between two or more competing interpretations of an ambiguous text.

As noted in the introduction, some Florida justices do not think reference to the substantive tools of construction is legitimate.[1] This issue is not often addressed in the cases. Rather, judges will sometimes invoke the canons, and sometimes they simply ignore them without a great deal of deep justification either way. However, the cases, notes, and questions below do engage this issue. Nonetheless, it is worthwhile canvassing the general criticisms of this set of tools of construction at the outset so that one might test the criticisms against the cases and the cases against the criticisms.

The criticisms include:

1. There are almost always competing canons that pull in the opposite direction on very point.[2]

---

[1] Peter D. Webster, Sylvia H. Walbolt, and Christine R. Davis, Statutory Construction in Florida: In Search of a Principled Approach, 9 Fla. Coastal L. Rev. 435, 519-521 (2008). Note the authors approved method is "First, always start with the words. Second, assume a reasonable Legislature. Third, search for the legislative purpose. Fourth, shun substantive canons of statutory construction. Fifth, respect the legislature's coequal status." Id at 523. Note that one of the substantive canons, "interpret remedial statutes liberally," has been argued to be a product of the author's third step, namely to give full effect to the "legislative purpose." See, Justice Farmer, in his concurrence in Blankfeld v. Richmond Health Care, Inc., 902 So. 2d 296 (Fla. 4th DCA 2005) where he argued that the remedial canon carried out the holding in Heydon's Case, namely, that "the function of judges was 'to make such construction as shall suppress the mischief and advance the remedy ...'" Heydon's Case, 76 Eng. Rep. 637 (Ex. 1584). Legislative purpose is addressed below when dealing with "external tools."

[2] See Webster et. al. supra note 23 at 519-20 (quoting from Karl N. Llewellyn, Remarks on the Theory of Appellate Decision and the Rules or Canons About How Statutes are to be Construed, 3 Vand. L. Rev. 395, 401 (1950) and RICHARD A. POSNER, THE PROBLEMS OF JURISPRUDENCE 280 & 282 (1990)).

2. They amount to folk wisdom and really are not very helpful in interpreting statutes.[3]
3. They are ill-reasoned or ill-suited to modern times.[4]
4. They are political and the choice of one canon over the other will often determine the outcome.[5]

I will leave it up to the reader to decide if these criticisms are valid, and if they are equally valid as applied to all of the substantive canons of construction. The cases, notes, and questions should help you determine if the tools are outdated, merely political, or if they are useful and embody meaningful modern legal values. The materials below might also help you decide if having competing tools means that the use of one over the other is necessarily a political choice favoring one outcome over the other.[6] The alternative view is that the substantive canons have weight or pull and that they must be balanced in every case.

A. Liberal Construction of Public Interest and Remedial Statutes

KING V. KING MOTOR CO. OF FORT LAUDERDALE
780 So.2d 937 (Fla. Dist. Ct. App. 4th Dist. 2001)

GROSS, J.

The narrow issue we consider in this case is whether a consumer must be able to furnish clear title to and possession of a motor vehicle in order to bring a circuit court action for damages under section 681.112, Florida Statutes (2000), Florida's Lemon Law, and 15 U.S.C. § 2310(d) (2000) of the Magnuson-Moss Warranty Act.

---

[3] Webster et. al. supra note 23 at 520. (quoting among others, Posner, supra note 2, at 279-80).

[4] See id at 520-21 (quoting Richard A. Posner, Statutory Interpretation--in the Classroom and in the Courtroom, 50 U. Chi. L. Rev. 800, 806 (1983)).

[5] See id at 521.

[6] It should be noted that Llewellyn, in the article cited above not only argued that there were two opposing substantive canons on every point, but his list included most every canon, including the linguistic canons that Webster et. al. approve. See Karl Llewellyn, Remarks on the Theory of Appellate Decision and the Rules or Canons About How Statutes are to be Construed, 3 Vand. L. Rev. 395, 401-406 (1950) (listing 28 pairs of opposing canons, or 56 canons). However, Llewellyn did not stop with the canons of construction. The first half of his article addressed the numerous legitimate opposing ways that the courts deal with precedent as well. Id at 395-399. Llewellyn's point was not that this practice was illegitimately political, but that it was inescapable. For Llewellyn, there simply is no single correct meaning to either precedent or to statutory provisions – no single correct way to interpret precedent or statutes. Id. at 396, 399. As Llewellyn stated just before listing the canons, "every lawyer must be familiar with them all: they are still needed tools of argument.... Plainly, to make any canon take hold in a particular instance, the construction contended for must be sold. This is essentially done by means other than the use of the canon: The good sense of the situation and simple construction of the available language to achieve that sense, by tenable means, out of the statutory language. Id. at 401 (emphasis in original).

Appellant Martin Luther King appeals a final order granting with prejudice Kia Motors of America, Inc.'s ("Kia") motion to dismiss three counts against Kia in King's second amended complaint.

Considering an appeal from an order granting a motion to dismiss, we must "treat the factual allegations of the [second amended complaint] as true and consider them in the light most favorable to the appellant." B0urtman v. Tech. Chems. & Prods., Inc., 724 So.2d 672, 673 (Fla. 4th DCA 1999).

According to the second amended complaint, King purchased a new 1997 Kia Sephia from King Motor Company of Fort Lauderdale ("King Motor") for a price in excess of $15,000. Kia manufactured the car and warranted that it "was mechanically new, factory furnished and was free of substantial defects."

After King took possession of the car, "numerous problems" arose. King took the vehicle to King Motor to have the problems corrected. After "numerous and/or reasonable opportunities" to fix the defects, King Motor failed to do so. Acting on the manufacturer's behalf, King Motor "continuously represented ... that the automobile would be properly repaired."

On or about December 12, 1998, "after a series of unsuccessful repair attempts," the car "became inoperable and was towed to [King Motor] for repair." King Motor wrongfully refused to repair the vehicle without appellant's agreement to pay for the repairs. While the inoperable car sat on King Motor's lot, the lender repossessed and resold the vehicle.

King brought suit against Kia under Chapter 681, Florida Statutes (2000), the Motor Vehicle Warranty Enforcement Act, also known as the Lemon Law. Although King did not timely file for arbitration under sections 681.109 and 681.1095, he contended that this failure was caused by Kia's noncompliance with section 681.103(3), regarding a manufacturer's obligation to "inform the consumer clearly and conspicuously in writing how and where to file a claim with a certified procedure." He also alleged that Kia violated section 681.104(2), by not giving him the option of replacement or refund, and section 681.103(4), by not providing a "fully itemized, legible statement or repair order." The Chapter 681 count sought money damages, costs, and attorney's fees.

King's second amended complaint also sought recovery against Kia under the Magnuson-Moss Warranty Act, 15 U.S.C. §§ 2301-2312 (1998). He alleged that Kia breached an express warranty that the car "would be free from defects in material and workmanship" and an implied warranty that the car "would be merchantable and at least fit for the ordinary purposes for which such vehicles are used." The Magnuson-Moss counts sought compensatory damages, costs, and attorney's fees.

Citing eleven decisions from Florida New Motor Vehicle Arbitration Boards created under section 681.1095, Florida Statutes, the circuit judge dismissed the Lemon Law claim. The court ruled that because King no longer owned or possessed the Kia, he was not able to furnish clear title to and possession of the motor vehicle to the manufacturer, so that he was not entitled to the statutory remedy of refund or replacement under section 681.104(2)(a). For a similar reason, the court also dismissed the Magnuson-Moss counts, since King was not able to make the car "available" to Kia within the meaning of 15 U.S.C. § 2304(b)(2).

I

The Lemon Law applies to the purchase of new motor vehicles. See § 681.102(15), Fla.Stat. (2000). A stated intent of the statute is

> to provide the statutory procedures whereby a consumer may receive a replacement motor vehicle, or a full refund, for a motor vehicle which cannot be brought into conformity with the warranty provided for in this chapter.

§ 681.101, Fla.Stat. (2000).

For a nonconforming vehicle that the manufacturer cannot conform to the warranty, the primary statutory remedy is either a replacement vehicle or a refund, at the consumer's option. See § 681.104(2)(a), Fla.Stat. (2000). The Lemon Law also sets out a procedure for enforcing the consumer's rights to a replacement or refund. In certain circumstances, the Lemon Law provides relief other than the replacement/refund option. See §§ 681.111 & 681.112, Fla.Stat. (2000).

An earlier version of the statute defined a nonconforming vehicle to include a broader, more subjectively determined class of motor vehicles. Section 681.104(2)(a), Florida Statutes (1987), applied where a manufacturer was unable to repair or correct "any default or condition which impairs the use, market value, or safety of the motor vehicle to the consumer." (Italics supplied). An earlier version of the Lemon Law entitled consumers to a full refund or replacement, but rights under the statute "could only be enforced by filing suit in the appropriate court." Duane A. Daiker, Note, Florida's Motor Vehicle Warranty Enforcement Act: Lemon-Aid for the Consumer, 45 Fla.L.Rev. 253, 255 (1993); see § 681.104(5)(a), Fla.Stat. (1987).

In 1988, the legislature extensively revised the Lemon Law to create a more consumer friendly statute. See Ch. 88-95, Laws of Fla.; Daiker, 45 Fla.L.Rev. at 255-56. One significant change was the creation of the Florida New Motor Vehicle Arbitration Board as part of a statutory procedure to secure the replacement/refund remedy described in sections 681.101 and 681.104(2)(a). See § 681.109, Fla.Stat. (2000); Ch. 88-95, § 6, at 438, Laws of Fla.

The Arbitration Board is a neutral forum where consumers may obtain relief without having to go through the expense and delay of filing a lawsuit. Abbreviated time frames control arbitrations before a Board. See § 681.1095(6), Fla.Stat. (2000). The statute authorizes a board to "grant relief, if a reasonable number of attempts have been undertaken to correct a nonconformity or nonconformities." § 681.1095(8), Fla.Stat. (2000). Consistent with the language of section 681.104(2)(a), the "relief" contemplated by section 681.1095 is the "delivery of an acceptable replacement motor vehicle or the refund specified in the arbitration award." § 681.1095(9), Fla.Stat.

(2000). The "relief" also includes "all reasonably incurred collateral and incidental charges." § 681.104(2)(a), Fla.Stat. (2000).

A party may appeal a decision by the Board to the circuit court, which reviews the matter by "trial de novo." § 681.1095(12), Fla.Stat. (2000). The party appealing the Arbitration Board's decision carries the burden of proof in the circuit court. See Chrysler Corp. v. Pitsirelos, 721 So.2d 710, 713 (Fla.1998). Where the circuit court upholds a decision of the Board "in favor of the consumer," recovery by the consumer "shall include the pecuniary value of the award, attorney's fees incurred in obtaining confirmation of the award, and all costs and continuing damages in the amount of $25 per day for each day beyond the 40-day period following the manufacturer's receipt of the board's decision." § 681.1095(13), Fla.Stat. (2000). The statute allows the circuit court to double or triple the amount of the total award if it "determines that the manufacturer acted in bad faith." Id.

The Lemon Law favors resolution of cases outside of the court system in either dispute settlement procedures established by a manufacturer under section 681.108 or arbitration before the Board pursuant to section 681.109-681.1095. This preference is implemented by section 681.1095(4), which provides:

> Before filing a civil action on a matter subject to s. 681.104, the consumer must first submit the dispute to the [Division of Consumer Services of the Department of Agriculture and Consumer Services], and to the [B]oard if such dispute is deemed eligible for arbitration.

Section 681.1095(4) furthers the intent of the Lemon Law "to resolve motor vehicle warranty disputes in expedited proceedings at less cost to consumers than traditional court proceedings." Chrysler Corp., 721 So.2d at 712.

Obviously, the term "civil action" in section 681.1095(4) cannot refer to the petition appealing an arbitration decision under section 681.1095(10)-(14), since such an appeal presumes a previous submission to arbitration.

Section 681.1095(4) covers an action brought pursuant to section 681.109(7), where the division has rejected a dispute and the consumer "may file a lawsuit to enforce the remedies provided under" Chapter 681. Additionally, another "civil action" contemplated by section 681.1095(4) is that provided in section 681.112, Florida Statutes (2000), which states:

> (1) A consumer may file an action to recover damages caused by a violation of this chapter. The court shall award a consumer who prevails in such action the amount of any pecuniary loss, litigation costs, reasonable attorney's fees, and appropriate equitable relief.
>
> (2) An action brought under this chapter must be commenced within 1 year after the expiration of the Lemon Law rights period, or, if a consumer resorts to an informal dispute-settlement procedure or submits a dispute to the division or board, within 1 year after the final action of the procedure, division, or board.

(3) This chapter does not prohibit a consumer from pursuing other rights or remedies under any other law.

Section 681.112 provides for an action for damages caused by a statutory violation, apart from the replacement/refund remedy that is available by following the procedural pathway through arbitration contained in sections 681.109 and 681.1095. By requiring submission to the division and to arbitration, if appropriate, section 681.1095(4) guides consumers in the direction of the broadest remedy and the most streamlined procedure.

Section 681.112(1) uses the term "damages" and indicates that a prevailing consumer may recover "the amount of any pecuniary loss." When discussing the replacement/refund option, the statute uses the terms "refund," "replacement," "relief," and "compliance" with an arbitration decision. See §§ 681.104(2)(a), 681.1095(8) & (9), Fla.Stat. (2000). This difference in terminology indicates that the statute uses the term "damages" to mean something other than the replacement/refund option. As used in section 681.112(1), "damages" should be given its plain and ordinary meaning of pecuniary compensation recovered by a person who has suffered a loss caused by a violation of Chapter 681.

Section 681.112 thus allows for a Chapter 681 damages case in circumstances where a refund or replacement is not an option. Such circumstances might include: (1) a warranty violation under section 681.103 which does not rise to the level of a "nonconformity" under section 681.104 because it does not *substantially* impair the use, value, or safety of a motor vehicle within the meaning of section 681.102(16); (2) a violation of a provision of Chapter 681 other than sections 681.104 or 681.103, such as section 681.114, pertaining to the resale of returned vehicles; (3) where the refund/replacement remedy does not fully compensate the consumer, see Maserati Autos., Inc. v. Caplan, 522 So.2d 993, 996 (Fla. 3d DCA 1988); or (4) the situation presented in this case, where the consumer cannot take advantage of the refund/replacement option because he cannot furnish clear title to and possession of the motor vehicle.

This interpretation of section 681.112 is consistent with the policy that a statute "enacted in the public interest" should be given a "liberal construction in favor of the public." Dep't of Envtl. Regulation v. Goldring, 477 So.2d 532, 534 (Fla.1985); see Singer v. Land Rover N. Am. Inc., 955 F.Supp. 359, 363 (D.N.J.1997) (construing New Jersey Lemon Law "liberally to achieve its remedial purpose"); Harmon v. Concord Volkswagen, Inc., 598 A.2d 696, 703 (Del.Super.Ct.1991) (finding "no justification for imposing a technical restraint upon [the Delaware lemon law] whose purpose is to provide relief for the buying public from defective products").

Chapter 88-95 made the Lemon Law more consumer friendly by expanding the reach of Chapter 681 in three ways. First, it provided for an expedited, out-of-court arbitration process to afford consumers the most complete relief. Second, section 9 of Chapter 88-95, rewrote section 681.111 to enlarge the number of Chapter 681 violations that might give rise to a cause of action for an unfair or deceptive trade practice under part II of Chapter 501, Florida Statutes (2000). Third, Chapter 88-95, section 10 added section 681.112, which created a pecuniary remedy for consumers damaged by Lemon Law violations.

We therefore hold that King's inability to "furnish to the manufacturer clear title to and possession of" the Kia under section 681.104(2)(a), did not, for that reason alone, bar a cause of action for damages under section 681.112.

This result is consistent with the Arbitration Board cases cited by Kia. Those decisions indicate that when a vehicle is not available for return to the manufacturer, the consumer is not eligible for relief under Lemon Law arbitration. The *only* relief provided for in a Chapter 681 arbitration is the replacement/refund option plus collateral and incidental charges. See §§ 681.104(2)(a), 681.1095(8) & (9), Fla.Stat. (2000). Replacement or refund requires the purchaser to return the motor vehicle. The damage remedy is available in circuit court when the arbitration cannot provide relief or is otherwise inappropriate.

. . .

STEVENSON, J., and LABARGA, JORGE, Associate Judge, concur.

NOTES AND QUESTIONS

1. Did the Court need to appeal to the public interest to decide this case?

2. If not, then why did the Court below get it wrong? Was the Court below relying on extra-legal values when it decided that because the Plaintiff did not have title and possession he had no remedy under the Lemon Law?

3. In Vocelle v. Knight Bros. Paper Co.118 So.2d 664, 668 Fla.App. 1960 the Court stated:

> We are not unmindful of the rule that a liberal construction should be given to legislation of the character involved to the end that the benefits intended thereby shall not be withheld. And we are cognizant of the power and duty of the authority administering such laws to initially interpret them to that purpose when the provisions are vague, indefinite, or contradictory, neither of which conditions exists here. The rule is equally well established that neither the courts nor the administrative agencies have power to modify the plain purpose and intent of the Legislature as expressed by the language employed in the statutes and thus to bring about what may be conceived in the minds of the judges or the administrators to be a more practical or proper result.

Are there clear boundaries between giving a liberal construction to laws intended to benefit society and the plain purpose and intent of the Legislature?

4. The Supreme Court of Florida in Knowles v. Beverly Enters.-Fla., Inc., 898 So.2d 1 (Fla. 2004), addressed the issue of remedial statutes. As the Court stated:

> Petitioner contends that section 400.023(1) is remedial in nature and therefore should be liberally construed. Indeed, we have held that where a statute is remedial in nature, it should be liberally construed to "preserve and promote access to the remedy intended by the Legislature." Joshua v. City of Gainesville, 768 So.2d 432, 435 (Fla.2000) (holding that chapter 760, Florida Statutes, relating to employment discrimination, is remedial and requires a liberal construction to preserve and promote access to the remedy intended by Legislature); see also Golf Channel v. Jenkins, 752 So.2d 561, 566 (Fla.2000) (liberally construing Whistle-Blower Act in favor of granting access to remedy provided by Legislature). As mentioned above, section 400.023(1) provides a remedy to those residents whose rights have been deprived or infringed upon by the nursing home. Under this analysis, petitioner asserts that a liberal interpretation of the statute would permit suit by the personal representative of the estate of a deceased resident whose death did not result from a violation of the act but who was injured by said violation.
>
> However, it is apparent that such an interpretation would alter the clear and unambiguous language of section 400.023(1) by either injecting a different circumstance upon which suit may be brought or by ignoring the language expressly used in the statute. In other words, to give the statute the liberal interpretation urged by petitioner, this Court would have to add words to the statute stating that the cause of death is irrelevant or it would have to ignore the term "when death resulted from." The law is well settled that courts in this state are "without power to construe an unambiguous statute in a way which would extend, modify, or limit, its express terms or its reasonable and obvious implications." Holly, 450 So.2d at 219 (quoting Am. Bankers Life Assurance Co. of Fla. v. Williams, 212 So.2d 777, 778 (Fla. 1st DCA 1968)). Thus, while petitioner is correct that section 400.023(1) should be liberally construed, such construction does not mean that this Court may rewrite the statute or ignore the words chosen by the Legislature so as to expand its terms. See id.

5. Justice Farmer, in his concurrence in Blankfeld v. Richmond Health Care, Inc., 902 So. 2d 296 (Fla. Dist. Ct. App. 4th Dist. 2005) was highly critical of the rule that remedial statutes should be interpreted liberally. As he stated:

> In my view, reading a statute as remedial has little real meaning.
>
> . . .
>
> There are many instances in which the Supreme Court has qualified the remedial canon. Sometimes the canon may mean an expansive interpretation, but it may not. Along with those decisions, there is another body of Supreme Court decisions referring to remedial statutes as procedural. In some, the fact that the statute is both remedial and

procedural may lead to special treatment, but it may not. There is yet a third body of opinions referring to remedial statutes, but this time only to distinguish them from penal statutes...

All these variations on remedial rob the canon of any real interpretive weight. The fact that one statute is remedial never leads to annulling another. Because all civil statutes are remedial in one sense or another, the cases really suggest that reliance on the remedial canon is little more than a subjective rationalization for a particular outcome, a post hoc justification.

The canon's actual meaning is found in its origins. It was born when the common law was the primary source of social ordering. Most rule-making was by the common law. Statutes filled gaps or addressed conflicts untouched by the common law. Judges used statutes warily because they were few and judges were not accustomed to them.

Early interpretation was limited to these questions: "What was the mischief and defect for which the Common Law did not provide; [and] What remedy the Parliament hath resolved and appointed to cure the disease of the commonwealth ..." Heydon's Case, 76 Eng. Rep. 637 (Ex. 1584). The function of judges was "to make such construction as shall suppress the mischief and advance the remedy ..." Id. These two guides emerged: the remedial canon, and the derogation canon against implied repeals of the common law. The derogation canon would be used for a statute changing the common law, while the remedial canon carried out the holding in Heydon's Case.

Statutes then were not created from common law methodology. Indeed, 18th century judges felt them rather subject to tyrannical majorities and shifting whims. England had suffered through the civil wars of the 17th Century and the abuses of unchecked majorities in Parliament. The beheading of Charles I was followed by the post-restoration instability leading to the Glorious Revolution in 1685. They viewed the common law as a source of social stability, cast from the wisdom of the ages and forged in cases evolving over the long sweep of history. Statutes often emerged from ephemeral, narrow and parochial interests, but the common law was eternal and universal.

In this country, the Progressive Movement at the turn of the 19th into the 20th Century, the legal upheavals resulting from the 20th Century's two World Wars, the Great Depression and the Civil Rights Movement, all had a profound effect on the sources of law. Statutes have assumed a much greater role in making legal and social policy. Indeed statutes have displaced the common law in most areas of American life. Nevertheless, our rules for reading them are filled with relies of the English monarchy, and the remedial canon is one of them.

Some in the Academy think the remedial canon was effectively killed by the legal realists. Karl Llewellyn prominently demonstrated that each canon was offset by a contrary canon, that the derogation canon nullified the remedial canon. If the substantive canons feed on one another, how is the judge to use them sensibly? Some judges have thus been critical of the use of the substantive canons (303-305) (footnotes and references omitted).

B. Lenity in the Interpretation of Criminal Statutes

WALLACE V. STATE

860 So.2d 494 (Fla. Dist. Ct. App. 4th Dist. 2003)

WARNER, J.

Appellant was convicted of arson and possession and discharge of a destructive device. Based upon the jury's finding that appellant discharged a destructive device, the court felt obligated to sentence appellant to twenty years in prison under the 10/20/Life statute. Appellant contends that because the destructive device did not explode, it did not discharge within the meaning of the sentencing statute, so his sentence should only be ten years for possessing a destructive device. We construe the sentencing statute under the rule of lenity and hold that where the destructive device did not explode, it did not "discharge." Therefore, at most, the defendant could be sentenced to ten years for possession of a destructive device. We therefore reverse.

The charge against appellant was based upon the discovery of a blue bottle containing a rag used as a wick laying next to an SUV owned by Anthony Collins. The detective who investigated the scene testified that the bottle contained "some type of ignitable liquid." The bottle was intact except for a crack caused by heat from it being on fire. Collins noted a mark on his SUV that was not there the night before, and there was a scorch mark on the grass. There was no other indication of damage.

A neighbor of Collins led the detectives to appellant. The neighbor, Stephanie Williams, had dated appellant but wanted him to stop calling. She had a friend call appellant to tell him to stop calling and listened in on the conversation. According to testimony, appellant believed that Collins had a romantic relationship with Williams. In the phone conversation, appellant told Williams's friend that he had messed up Collins's car. Williams's brother-in-law testified that appellant told him that he had thrown "some kind of a little bomb" at the SUV. Williams's sister testified that she overheard the confession appellant made to her husband.

No physical evidence was found linking appellant to the crime. A crime lab analyst from the State Fire Marshall's Fire and Arson Laboratory testified that both the bottle and cloth found at the scene tested positive for the presence of gasoline.

Appellant presented an alibi defense at trial. He was living with his mother and Tawana Smith at the time of the offense. Both women testified that he was home that night. Appellant also testified that he was at home, taking care of Smith's sick child. He denied confessing anything about the incident. His attorney argued that Williams and her family members were not credible and were only trying to "get rid" of appellant.

The jury found appellant guilty on both counts as charged in the information. As to the destructive device count, the jury found appellant actually possessed and discharged a destructive device. Based on the jury's finding, the trial court felt obligated to sentence appellant to a mandatory minimum term of twenty years on the discharge of a destructive device count, pursuant to section 775.087(2)(a)2., Florida Statutes (1999). The court also sentenced appellant to five years on the arson count, concurrent with the twenty-year sentence. Because the trial court believed that a twenty-year sentence was unduly harsh in light of the very limited damage caused by appellant's actions, it recommended the governor grant appellant relief.

Appellant moved to correct a sentencing error pursuant to Florida Rule of Criminal Procedure 3.800(b)(2). He alleged that the trial court erred in sentencing him to the mandatory minimum term of twenty years for discharging a destructive device when it was not proven at trial that the device was actually discharged. The trial court did not rule on the motion. Therefore, it is deemed denied for purposes of this appeal.

As to the propriety of his conviction, appellant argues that the trial court erred in permitting a detective to testify that the items found at the scene constituted a destructive device under Florida law when the detective was not qualified as a legal expert. While it was error to allow the detective to so testify, the error was harmless as another investigator gave essentially the same testimony under questioning of defense counsel. Moreover, appellant never argued that the object was not a destructive device.

Contesting his sentence, appellant argues that the court erred by sentencing him under section 775.087(2)(a)2 to a mandatory minimum term of twenty years for discharging a destructive device when it was not proven that the device "discharged," as it did not explode. The state contends that "discharge" is not synonymous with "explosion," and there is substantial evidence to support a "discharge." The resolution of this issue requires us to construe the statutory provision.

Appellant was charged with and convicted of a violation of section 790.161, Florida Statutes (1999), which provides that "[a] person who willfully and unlawfully makes, possesses, throws, projects, places, discharges, or attempts to make, possess, throw, project, place, or discharge any destructive device" is guilty of a second degree felony when there is an intent to damage property. § 790.161(2). Section 775.087(2) provides for the penalty:

> (a)1. Any person who is convicted of a felony or an attempt to commit a felony, regardless of whether the use of a weapon is an element of the felony, and the conviction was for:
>
> . . .
>
> 6. Arson; or
>
> m. Unlawful throwing, placing, or discharging of a destructive device or bomb;
>
> . . .

> and during the commission of the offense, such person actually possessed a "firearm" or "destructive device" as those terms are defined in s. 790.001, shall be sentenced to a minimum term of imprisonment of 10 years. . . .
>
> 2. Any person who is convicted of a felony or an attempt to commit a felony listed in sub-subparagraphs (a)1.a.-q., regardless of whether the use of a weapon is an element of the felony, and during the course of the commission of the felony such person discharged a "firearm" or "destructive device" as defined in s. 790.001 shall be sentenced to a minimum term of imprisonment of 20 years.

A "destructive device" is defined as:

> any bomb, grenade, ... or similar device containing an explosive, incendiary, or poison gas and includes any frangible container filled with an explosive, incendiary, explosive gas, or expanding gas, which is designed or so constructed as to explode by such filler and is capable of causing bodily harm or property damage. . . .

§ 790.001(4), Fla. Stat. (1999).

Although the Legislature provided a definition of a "destructive device," no definition is provided for the term "discharge." We conclude that "discharge" must mean something different than "makes, possesses, throws, projects, places," as the statute provides those as alternative means of committing the substantive crime. See § 790.161. Moreover, from the definition of "destructive device", it is clear that such a device is intended to explode. See § 790.001(4). As noted in Judge Sharp's dissenting opinion in Stacey v. State, 660 So.2d 1083, 1085 (Fla. 5th DCA 1995), the key characteristic of a destructive device, as with a firearm, is that the device is explosive.

Looking to the dictionary, multiple definitions of "discharge" appear: 1) to relieve of a charge, load or burden; 2) to shoot or give an outlet or vent; 3) to throw off or deliver a load, charge or burden; 4) to put forth fluid or other contents. See Merriam Webster's Collegiate Dictionary (10th ed.1995). There is no one common definition of the word.

The Legislature committed itself to the "Rule of Lenity" in the construction of criminal statutes, providing in section 775.021(1), Florida Statutes (1999), that "[t]he provisions of this code and offenses defined by other statutes shall be strictly construed; when the language is susceptible of differing constructions, it shall be construed most favorably to the accused." See also McLaughlin v. State, 721 So.2d 1170, 1172 (Fla.1998) (realizing that it "is a well-established canon of construction that words in a penal statute must be strictly construed"); State v. Williams, 776 So.2d 1066 (Fla. 4th DCA 2001). Application of that rule means that if there is a reasonable construction of a penal statute favorable to the accused, the court must employ that construction. See Williams, 776 So.2d at 1070.

Because there are many and varied definitions of what constitutes the "discharge" of a destructive device, we interpret that statute most favorably to the accused and conclude that to discharge a destructive device for purposes of 775.087(2) providing for a mandatory minimum twenty-year sentence, the device must explode, i.e., function as it was intended. If the Legislature intended a different or more expansive definition, then it can certainly amend the statute. See State v. Houck, 652 So.2d 359, 359-60 (Fla.1995) (applying ordinary meaning of "weapon" where Legislature failed to define the term in 10/20/Life statute, and noting that if Legislature wanted the word to mean something other than the common definition, it could amend the statute).

The evidence here most favorable to the state demonstrated that appellant threw a bottle containing gasoline and a wick at Collins's vehicle. The bottle did not break but fell to the ground. The bottle neck was cracked from heat and not an explosion. It caused no damage other than a small mark on the vehicle and a small burn mark on the grass, which could indicate that the device may have been lit but did not explode. Neither the detective nor the arson investigator testified that the device exploded. While the jury found that the object "discharged," it was not given any definition of that term by the judge. As the supreme court recognized under similar circumstances in Houck, "The failure of the statute to broadly define the term 'weapon' cannot be cured by jury speculation." 652 So.2d at 360. Construing the statute most favorably to the defendant, we conclude that the state did not prove that the destructive device discharged so as to mandate sentencing appellant under the 10/20/Life statute to twenty years for this crime.

For the foregoing reasons, we affirm appellant's convictions but reverse his sentence under section 790.161 and remand for resentencing.

GUNTHER and MAY, JJ., concur.

NOTES AND QUESTIONS

1. Should a defendant's sentence depend on whether the explosive devise fully detonates as the defendant indented or if it merely fizzles out after being lit and thrown at the intended target?

2. If the Court uses the dictionary to look up any term, will it find a common meaning? See how many words you can find in the dictionary that have only one common meaning.

3. What is the relevance of the fact that there was no physical evidence linking the defendant to the crime, or of the fact that he had an alibi, or that there was very little physical damage?

4. The rule of lenity has a mixed record in the Federal Courts. Some judges and Courts use it as a strong presumption, while others view it as a weak tie breaker when the statute is grievously ambiguous. For instance, in the 5-4 decision of Muscarello v. U.S., 524 U.S. 125 (1998), Justice Breyer, for the majority, held the later view. Id at 138-39. On the other hand, Justice Ginsburg, for the four person dissent, held the former view. Id at 148. A recent study argues that the rule of lenity is only used by the Court in cases where a broad reading would lead to the punishment of 'innocent conduct' See Note, 119 Harv.

L. Rev. 2420, 2421 (2006). This is consistent with the idea that court are more likely to apply the rule in cases involving malum prohibitum crimes than malum in se crimes. Are the facts in question 3 above linked to this idea?

5. Some states have abrogated the common law rule of lenity through legislation requiring that courts construe statutes according to the "fair import of their terms." See WAYNE LAFAVE, CRIMINAL LAW 5th ed (2010) at 94. What are the policy reasons for choosing either the "fair import" rule or the "lenity rule"?

6. What should the Court do in cases that involve statutes that are enacted for the public benefit, (i.e. statutes that generally get a liberal or generous interpretation) but which have penal provisions (i.e. statutes that are narrowly construed in favor of the defendant)? Are not all penal statutes enacted for the public benefit? If so, should the rule of lenity not trump? The Supreme Court of Florida in State v. Hamilton 388 So.2d 561 (Fla. 1980), held that "A statute enacted for the public benefit should be construed liberally in favor of the public even though it contains a penal provision." (citing City of Miami Beach v. Berns, 245 So.2d 38, 40 (Fla. 1971). This case pitted the vague application of a penal provision making it illegal to "contaminat[e] state waters with any substance injurious to human health" and environmental protection legislation passed for the public benefit. As the Court stated, "We agree with other jurisdictions which have found that the nature of pollution control inhibits detailed descriptions of proscribed standards of conduct." Id. at 563 Thus, even though the statute may have not been clear enough to put a person of common intelligence on notice, the Court did not find it unconstitutionally vague.

C. CONSTRUCTION IN FAVOR OF CONSTITUTIONALITY

SANDLIN V. CRIMINAL JUSTICE STANDARDS & TRAINING COMM'N
531 So.2d 1344 (Fla. 1988)

McDONALD, Justice.

A district court of appeal has certified the following question as being of great public importance:

> Does a full pardon under chapter 940, Florida Statutes (1985), which restores the civil rights of a person convicted of a felony, relieve the pardoned person from the disqualification from certification as a law enforcement officer imposed by section 943.13(4), Florida Statutes_(1985), on a person who has been convicted of any felony?

Sandlin v. Criminal Justice Standards & Training Commission, 518 So.2d 1292, 1297 (Fla. 1st DCA 1987). We have jurisdiction. Art. V, § 3(b)(4), Fla. Const. With the caveats that a pardoned felon must demonstrate rehabilitation and good moral character and fitness to the commission's satisfaction and that the commission may decline to certify an applicant because of a character flaw as evidenced by the prior felony conviction, we answer the certified question in the affirmative and quash Sandlin.

In the early 1960s, and while still a very young man, Sandlin was convicted of robbery, escape, and assault. After being paroled in 1965, he received a full pardon from the governor in 1968. Sandlin is employed by the Jacksonville sheriff's office and, since 1971, has been a circuit court bailiff. In 1985 the sheriff's office asked the commission to certify Sandlin as a police officer. To support this request Sandlin submitted numerous letters from judges and attorneys averring his fitness to be a law enforcement officer. In discussing Sandlin's case various members of the commission noted Sandlin's rehabilitation and his moral and general fitness and qualifications. Based on its interpretation of section 943.13, Florida Statutes (1985), and subsection 112.011(1)(b), Florida Statutes (1985), however, the commission refused the certification. The district court affirmed and certified the question set out above, stating that

> the legislature does not intend to allow [a pardoned felon] to hold the sensitive position of law enforcement officer, or to give the Commission discretion to consider such a person for certification, notwithstanding his subsequent history. We hold that such a determination by the legislature is within its police power, and does not unconstitutionally impinge upon the executive's clemency power.

518 So.2d at 1297.

Section 943.13 provides that any law enforcement officer shall:

> (4) Not have been convicted of any felony or of a misdemeanor involving perjury or a false statement or have received a dishonorable or undesirable discharge from any of the Armed Forces of the United States. Any person who, after July 1, 1981, pleads guilty or nolo contendere to or is found guilty of a felony or of a misdemeanor involving perjury or a false statement is not eligible for employment or appointment as an officer, notwithstanding suspension of sentence or withholding of adjudication.

Moreover, subsection 112.011(1)(b) provides:

> A person whose civil rights have been restored shall not be disqualified to practice, pursue, or engage in any occupation, trade, vocation, profession, or business for which a license, permit, or certificate is required to be issued by the state, any of its agencies or political subdivisions, or any municipality solely because of a prior conviction for a crime. However, a person who has had his civil rights restored may be denied a license, permit, or certification to pursue practice, or engage in an occupation, trade, vocation, profession, or business by reason of the prior conviction for a crime if the crime was a felony or first degree misdemeanor and directly related to the specific occupation, trade, vocation, profession, or business for which the license, permit, or certificate is sought.

Sandlin argues that these statutes are an unconstitutional legislative incursion into the executive's power over pardons and that they should either be struck down or else be interpreted so that an unconstitutional result does not occur.

A pardon is an act of grace, and the pardoning power is a function exclusive to the executive, derived from the state constitution. Art. IV, § 8(a), Fla. Const.; Sullivan v. Askew, 348 So.2d 312 (Fla.), cert. denied, 434 U.S. 878, 98 S.Ct. 232, 54 L.Ed.2d 159 (1977); In re Advisory Opinion of the Governor, 334 So.2d 561 (Fla.1976); Singleton v. State, 38 Fla. 297, 21 So. 21 (1896). A full pardon removes all disabilities resulting from a crime. In re Florida Board of Bar Examiners, 183 So.2d 688 (Fla.1966); Page v. Watson, 140 Fla. 536, 192 So. 205 (1938); Singleton v. State. Neither the legislature nor the judiciary may infringe upon the executive's authority to grant pardons. E.g., In re Advisory Opinion (the administrative procedures act is not applicable to clemency proceedings); Fields v. State, 85 So.2d 609 (Fla.1956) (fully and unconditionally pardoned felony conviction cannot be used as a prior conviction under the habitual offender statute); Singleton (legislature does not have power to grant a pardon). Persons seeking to practice certain professions or employments, however, can be required to demonstrate their good moral character, even though they may have been fully pardoned for previous crimes. E.g., Page v. Watson; In re Bar Examiners; Lee v. Department of Health & Rehabilitative Services, 518 So.2d 364 (Fla.3d DCA 1987). See also Calhoun v. Department of Health & Rehabilitative Services, 500 So.2d 674 (Fla. 3d DCA 1987).

Subsection 943.13(7) provides, as one of the minimum requirements for becoming a law enforcement officer, that an applicant must have a "good moral character as determined by a background investigation." The prohibition against certifying pardoned felons (subsection 943.13(4)) has been applied absolutely, creating a nonrebuttable presumption that pardoned felons are not of good character. Sandlin. See also 1970 Op.Att'y Gen.Fla. 070-157 (Oct. 30, 1970). This legislative disqualification, as interpreted by the commission and the district court, diminishes the effect of a pardon and imposes a legal disability. Such literal reading of subsection 943.13(4) creates a head-on confrontation between the legislature's power to enact laws to protect the public and the executive's power to pardon convicted felons. Contrary to the district court, we do not find that this statute should be held to override the executive's pardon power.

The legislature will be presumed to have intended a constitutional result. Marsh v. Garwood, 65 So.2d 15 (Fla.1953). Moreover, courts will avoid declaring a statute unconstitutional if such statute can be fairly construed in a constitutional manner. Industrial Fire & Casualty Insurance Co. v. Kwechin, 447 So.2d 1337 (Fla.1983). Such a construction is possible in this case.

We thus approach the question of whether or not section 943.13 and the concept of pardons can coexist. We believe they can, but in doing so we must select one of contrary views on the effect of a pardon on an eligibility statute for employment.

> Crucial to the determination whether a pardon will restore eligibility to hold a particular office is the view that the court takes as to the general effect of a pardon.

> Thus, some courts have taken the view that the pardon eliminates both the punishment resulting from the conviction and any moral guilt or blame which may have accompanied the commission of the crime. Under this view, it would appear that a pardon would restore eligibility for public office. On the other hand, it has been said that while the pardon removes the punishment resulting from the conviction, it does not remove the moral guilt resulting from the commission of the crime; under this view, if a disqualification to hold public office is based merely upon a conviction of a crime, the pardon restores the one pardoned to eligibility for the office, although he is not restored to eligibility where character is a qualification for the office. In considering the eligibility of a pardoned person for public office, other courts have concluded that the pardon eliminates neither the fact of conviction nor the moral guilt accompanying the conviction. Such a view would appear to lead to the conclusion that the pardon does not restore eligibility.

Annotation, Eligibility for Public Office After Pardon, 58 A.L.R.3d 1191, 1195 (1974) (footnotes omitted).

In Page v. Watson this Court adopted the middle ground, i.e., that a pardon removes punishment, but not moral guilt. 140 Fla. at 543-49, 192 So. at 208-10. Massachusetts also adopted this view in Commissioner of Metropolitan District Commission v. Director of Civil Service, 348 Mass. 184, 203 N.E.2d 95 (1964), which is factually similar to this case. The Massachusetts court stated:

> [W]e think that the absolute disqualification or ineligibility, imposed by such a statute, is to be regarded as removed by a full pardon, so that the pardoned person (1) may apply for appointment to the office for which he was formerly disqualified, and (2) may hold that office if he is able to sustain the heavy burden of satisfying the electorate or an appointing authority of his good character and suitability at the time of seeking office. We think also that, in considering such a pardoned applicant's qualifications and suitability, the events underlying the pardoned conviction may be and should be evaluated, and relied upon reasonably, by the proper public body or authority.

Id. at 196, 203 N.E.2d at 103. See also Slater v. Olson, 230 Iowa 1005, 299 N.W. 879 (1941). The court continued and held that, although the applicant had ceased to be ineligible under the statute, it was open, and remained open, for the commission to refuse to appoint him as a police officer because of the serious character of the criminal conduct underlying his conviction. We approve this reasoning and find that it should be applied in Florida. It is imperative that law enforcement officers be of good character. Thus, it is entirely appropriate and necessary to review closely a pardoned felon's character.

Therefore, we answer the certified question in the affirmative and conclude, as did the Supreme Court of Massachusetts, that the commission has the broad discretion to certify Sandlin for appointment as a law enforcement officer, but may refuse to do so if it deems him to be of bad character, a poor moral risk, or an otherwise unfit appointee. In determining whether to certify Sandlin the commission may take into account and rely upon the facts of Sandlin's pardoned convictions and may give weight to the general policy expressed in section 943.13. We direct the district court to instruct the commission to reconsider Sandlin's request for certification consistent with this opinion.

It is so ordered.

EHRLICH, C.J., and OVERTON, SHAW, BARKETT and GRIMES, JJ., concur.

KOGAN, J., concurs in result only.

NOTES AND QUESTIONS

1. The Court claims to have avoided the constitutional conflict by adopting the middle ground between two extreme views, namely that while the pardon removes the punishment resulting from the conviction, it does not remove the moral guilt resulting from the commission of the crime. Could the Court have avoided the conflict by taking either of the other two approaches, i.e., (a) that the pardon eliminates both the punishment resulting from the conviction and any moral guilt or blame which may have accompanied the commission of the crime, or (b) that the pardon eliminates neither the fact of conviction nor the moral guilt accompanying the conviction?

2. Does the middle ground interpretation of the meaning of a pardon really avoid the conflict between the power to pardon and the statutory language in subsection 112.011(1)(b), which provides:

   > ...However, a person who has had his civil rights restored may be denied a license, permit, or certification to pursue practice, or engage in an occupation, trade, vocation, profession, or business by reason of the prior conviction for a crime if the crime was a felony or first degree misdemeanor and directly related to the specific occupation, trade, vocation, profession, or business for which the license, permit, or certificate is sought.

3. Is the real issue not the question of what "may" means in the context of denying the license, permit, or certification?

4. Is the Court writing a provision into the statute that requires that a pardoned person applying to be a police officer may not be denied on the basis of the felony conviction itself, but still may denied on the basis of their moral character (including the moral blight that may have been caused by their conduct which lead to the conviction)?

5. Did the literal reading of subsection 943.13(4) necessarily create a head-on confrontation between the Legislature's power to enact laws to protect the public and the Executive's power to pardon convicted felons? Could this conflict not have been avoided if it interpreted pardons as merely removing punishment and not the fact of conviction or moral guilt?

6. Why did the Court not simply strike down the law as unconstitutional?

D. CONSTRUCTION IN FAVOR OF STATE SOVEREIGN IMMUNITY

STATE EX REL. DAVIS V. LOVE
99 Fla. 333 (Fla. 1930)

BROWN, J.

Both of these cases turn upon the same questions. They arise out of separate petitions for writs of prohibition directed to Hon. E. C. Love, as circuit judge, and C. J. Lytle, as respondents in one case, and to the same judge and the Massachusetts Bonding & Insurance Company, as respondents in the other case, seeking peremptory writs of prohibition to restrain Judge Love from proceeding to hear and determine two certain suits pending before him in the circuit court of Leon county, Fla., in which Lytle and the bonding company, respectively, are plaintiffs and the state road department is defendant. Alternative writs of prohibition were issued by this court in each of the cases, and in due course Judge Love filed his separate answers in each case, and Lytle and the bonding company respectively filed motions to quash the alternative writs, and likewise filed, subject to the motion to quash, answers to the alternative writs.

Each of the two suits pending in the circuit court of Leon county was a suit on 'claim arising under contract for work done,' within the meaning of section 4, of chapter 9312, Laws of Florida, Acts of 1923, which purports to authorize the maintenance of suits against the state road department on claims of that character.

Each of the petitions for writs of prohibition were filed by the state, on the relation of the Attorney General, and each of them alleged that the state road department by its attorneys had appeared specially in such circuit court and moved to quash the writ of summons ad respondendum issued in each of said causes and to contest the jurisdiction of the court on the ground that no lawful provision had been made for the maintenance of suits against the state road department, which department was an agency and component part of the state government; which motions to quash the said judge had overruled, and had required the respective defendants to plead or demur on or before a named date. The petition further alleged that, unless prevented from so doing, the respondent circuit judge would proceed to entertain said causes and thereby put members of the state road department to great expense and inconvenience in preparing for and attending the trial, including the gathering of witnesses, the taking of the employees from the various departments of the defendant's activities, and thereby putting the state to a great deal of inconvenience, trouble, and expense without authority of law, inasmuch as said circuit court was without power or jurisdiction to entertain or adjudicate said causes. It is further alleged that said sec. 4 of chapter 9312, Laws of Florida, is unconstitutional and void, in that the subject-matter of said section is not embraced in the title of the act, but deals with a separate and distinct subject, to wit, the surrender of the state's sovereign immunity from suit, which is controlled by section 22 of article 3 of the Constitution, and also because said section is a special law relating to a certain class of contractors, hence in violation of both sections 20 and 22 of article 3 of the Constitution.

The answer of Circuit Judge Love sets up, among other things, that said section 4 is valid and duly evidences the legislative consent for the maintenance of suits of this character; that the circuit court is a court of general jurisdiction and had jurisdiction of these causes under the Constitution and laws of Florida. It is also alleged that no member of the state road department would be injured in person, property, or rights by the maintenance of said suit, and that it thus appears that neither said department nor any member thereof had any right to question the constitutionality of section 4 of chapter 9312.

The respondents Lytle and the bonding company, respectively, filed answers and motion to quash, in which motions, in addition to the questions above mentioned, it is denied that the relator, the Attorney General, has any right to question the validity of said statutory provisions.

. . .

We come now to the main question in the case, the constitutionality vel non of section 4 of chapter 9312, which is section 1651, C. G. L. That section reads as follows:

'Sec. 4. Suits at law and in equity may be maintained by and against the State Road Department on any claim arising under contract for work done. Provided, no suit in tort shall be maintained against the Department.'

This court has already held that the state road department is an agency of the state and a component part of the state government. It follows that suits against such department of the kind named in said section would be in effect suits against the state.

It was contended on the argument that such a provision as the one in question would put into effect a wise public policy; that it would afford contractors doing construction work for the road department an assurance of protection of their contractual rights which would tend to command the services of the highest class of contractors, and would also have an economical value in that it might tend to lower bids for construction work on account of the assurance of such protection, and that the state had nothing to fear, as it would certainly be accorded justice in its own courts. We do not question the public policy of this section; such is not within our province. But it might also be proper to observe that the rule is that statutes in derogation of state sovereignty are to be strictly construed. 25 R. C. L. 416, 617. The legal doctrine that a sovereign state is immune from suit is an ancient one. While it probably had its origin in the old theory that sovereignty was inherent in the crown, and that the king could do no wrong, and hence could not be sued, though as a matter of grace a petition could be addressed to him in the high court of chancery, still this doctrine was quite jealously preserved in this country by the various states after they had by united action secured their independence from the monarchical government of England. It will be recalled that very soon after our federal Constitution was adopted, the Supreme Court of the United States held, in the case of Chisholm v. Georgia, 2 Dall. 419, 1 L. Ed. 440, that under the federal Constitution a state could be sued in assumpsit by a citizen of another state. This decision brought about the prompt adoption of the Eleventh Amendment to the federal Constitution, to the effect that the judicial power of the United States should not extend to any suit at law or in equity against any state by citizens of another state or of any foreign country. It was, whether wisely or not, deemed that certain practical considerations warranted continued adherence to this ancient rule that a sovereign state was immune from suit, even when brought by one of its own citizens. Thus it had been said by many of our courts that inconvenience and perhaps danger might result from its abrogation; that the public service would be hindered and the public safety endangered if the supreme authority could be subjected to suit at the instance of every citizen, and consequently controlled in the use and disposition of the means required for the proper administration of the government. 25 R. C. L. 413. We are not here concerned with those modifications or distinctions related to, but not vitally affecting this time honored principle, such, for instance, as those cases holding that persons holding public office, who, under color of supposed authority, unlawfully invade the rights of the citizen, may in proper cases be proceeded against by suits appropriate to the purpose. This was an echo of an ancient doctrine. It was long ago recognized that, 'While the King can do no wrong, his ministers may.' Suffice it to say, that this principle of the state's immunity from suit is not only well settled, but has long been regarded as a matter of considerable importance. This is further exemplified by the fact that, although we have had a constitutional provision since the Constitution of 1868 authorizing the Legislature to permit suits against the state by general law, the Legislature has not in all that time, so far as the writer has been able to find, seen fit to pass any general law on the subject, unless the statutory provision now under consideration can be held to be such.

Section 22 of article 3 of the Constitution of 1885, which was section 19 of article 4 of the Constitution of 1868, is as follows:

'Provision may be made by general law for bringing suit against the state as to all liabilities now existing or hereafter originating.'

A few years ago the Legislature, by a provision in a special statute relating to a particular drainage district, attempted to permit the state to be sued in the foreclosure of drainage tax liens, but, the statute being special and local, this provision of the statute was held to be invalid. Southern Drainage Dist. v. State, 93 Fla. 672, 112 So. 561.

It is contended by the respondents in this case that the statute here involved is a general law, and that section 4 thereof, being a part of such general law, and germane to the subject expressed in the title thereof, complies with both sections 16 and 22 of article 3 of the Constitution. The title of the statute, chapter 9312, Laws of 1923, is:

"An Act Relating to the State Road Department Imposing Certain Duties Upon Said Department and Conferring Certain Powers Upon the Same."

It is also contended that the general character of this act is emphasized by the fact that this act is one of a series of several acts passed at the same session establishing the system of laws under which the road department, though itself created by a prior statute, was to operate, and has operated since that time, with very little material change.

We think it must be conceded that chapter 9312, dealing as it does with the powers and duties of a department with state-wide powers and duties, and constituting a component part of the state government, may be regarded as a general law, as distinguished from a special or local law.

It is also contended that the title refers to the conferring of 'powers' upon the road department, and that the power to sue and be sued is generally recognized as a power in acts relating to both public and private corporations, and that therefore section 4 is within the scope of the title and fairly indicated thereby, and thus in compliance with section 16 of article 3 of the Constitution. The 'power' to be sued, as well as to sue, may doubtless be correctly termed a 'power' when used in acts incorporating or providing for the incorporation of ordinary corporate entities, even of quasi public or public corporations, which form no part of the state government (see Arundel Corp. v. Griffin, 89 Fla. 128, 103 So. 422); but an act dealing with the powers and duties of a component part, or a department, of the state government comes within a somewhat different category. The use of the words 'Conferring Certain Powers' upon such a department, when used in the title of such an act, could hardly be held to constitute fair notice that in the body of the act the state's immunity from suit would be taken away, as to suits of a certain nature, against such state agency or department. The state road department was not a corporation at the time this act was passed. It was not until the Act of 1925, c. 10118, was adopted, that it was declared to be a body corporate, and then only for the purpose of that particular act, which purported to vest such department with the power of eminent domain and the right to maintain condemnation proceedings for certain specific purposes. The waiver, or taking away, in whole or in part, of the state's immunity from suit, which would otherwise protect such state agency from suits of every nature, can hardly be termed the 'conferring' of a 'power' upon such state agency. It is in fact, more in the nature of the imposition of a burden or liability than the granting of a power. The power, so far as there is a power, is conferred upon the courts and upon contractors of a certain class dealing with the road department, and not upon the department. In this connection, see Hampton v. State Board of Education, 90 Fla. 88, 105 So. 323, 42 A. L. R. 1456.

But it is contended by respondents that the first part of the title to chapter 9312, reading, 'An Act Relating to the State Road Department,' is broad and comprehensive enough to cover the disputed section 4; that these words state the broad subject of the act, and that their comprehensive meaning is not to be restricted by the remaining language of the title, as to 'Imposing Certain Duties' and 'Conferring Certain Powers.'

In State ex rel. Attorney General v. Burns, 38 Fla. 367, 21 So. 290, quoting the first and second headnotes, it was said:

'1. A leading purpose of section 16, art. 3, of the constitution is to prevent the incorporation into one act of legislation of more than one subject and matter properly connected therewith. A further object of the requirement is to avoid surprise or fraudin legislation by means of provisions in bills of which the titles give no sufficient notice, and to this end a title of an act should fairly apprise not only the members of the legislature, but the people to be affected, of the subject of legislation being enacted.

'2. When the title of an act clearly expresses the whole object of the legislature, and the provisions in the body of the act are germane to the subject expressed in the title, an essential requirement of the constitution has been met, but a general subject may become restricted in details in the body of the act by the title; and where one is so framed as to indicate that matters connected with the subject, generally considered, are not to be treated of in the bill, it is misleading as to any legislation on such matters.'

Even though we had no such constitutional provision as section 22 of article 3, it is extremely doubtful whether section 4 of chapter 9312 could be held valid under section 16 of art. 3, as construed in the case just quoted from. But when section 22 of article 3 is taken into consideration, we think the invalidity of said section 4 of the act, if section 16 of art. 3 of the constitution be applied thereto becomes plain, as hereinafter shown.

We take it that, if full force and effect be given to section 22 of article 3 of the Constitution, providing that 'provision may be made by general law for bringing suit against the State,' it means, among other things, that, if the Legislature sees fit to legislate upon that subject at all, it must do so by 'general law' dealing with that subject. It is by the Constitution undoubtedly considered of sufficient importance to be made a subject for legislation of a general, rather than a special or local, nature; and it would be inconsistent with the intent of the Constitution to deal with this subject merely incidentally in acts relating to other subjects. This is consistent, too, with the historical background above alluded to. In other words, the effect of the constitutional provision is to make this matter of legislative waiver of the state's immunity from suit sufficient, in and of itself, to constitute an independent subject of legislation, general in its character. And in view of section 16 of the same article 3, providing that each act shall embrace *but one subject*, we are inclined to agree with the Attorney General's contention that the legislation authorized by section 22 of that article can only be dealt with in an act or acts having that matter as its subject, and that to embrace it in some other act pertaining to some other subject, though there might be some reasonable connection between the two, would result in making such other act embrace two subjects. In any view that might be reasonably taken, it would hardly be consistent with the language and intent of section 22 of article 3 to hold that the immunity of the state from suit, which the Legislature may provide for by general law pursuant to that section, can be taken away by a mere provision incidentally embraced in an act dealing with another subject, the title of which act, however broad and comprehensive, makes no mention whatever of removing the state's immunity from suit and fails to fairly apprise the members of the Legislature and the people that such an important matter is one of the matters to be dealt with in such act.

As was well said in the relator's brief:

"To take any other view of this provision must necessarily mean that the Legislature can disregard the provision entirely and by consistent whittling of a small part at a time, each chip hidden out in a section of an act dealing with some other subject, eventually destroy the entire provision so incorporated by the framers of our organic law and brought down from the common law to protect all the people of the State and to preserve its immunity."

...

The motions to quash the alternative writs will be denied and a peremptory writ of prohibition will be granted, as prayed, in each of the two cases.

It is so ordered.

WHITFIELD, ELLIS, STRUM, and BUFORD, JJ., concur.

TERRELL, C. J., not participating.

WHITFIELD, J. (concurring).

...

In effect the subject expressed in the title of chapter 9312, Acts of 1923, is: 'Imposing certain duties, and conferring certain powers upon the State Road Department.' The words of the title do not fairly indicate that the act might contain a provision that 'suits at law and in equity may be maintained by and against the State Road Department.' The state road department is an agency of the state, as a suit against it would be in effect a suit against the State. Hampton v. State Board of Education, 90 Fla. 88, 105 So. 323, 42 A. L. R. 1456. The state, by virtue of its sovereignty, is immune from suit against it, unless it consents thereto. Under the Constitution, 'provision may be made by general law for bringing suits against the State.' If it be assumed that under section 22, art. 3, Constitution, provision for suits against state agencies may be made in a law dealing with any other subject, such provision is an unusual subject-matter of legislation and is in derogation of state sovereignty; and when provision for bringing suit against the state is included in a bill to be enacted into law, the title of the act should contain language sufficiently definite and comprehensive to indicate that such provision to bring suit against the state is the subject of the act, or that such subject is included in the subject expressed in the title of the act, or that such subject is matter properly connected with the subject expressed in the title of the act, or that such subject is a necessary or proper incident to the subject expressed in the title. Titles to acts are intended to apprise legislators and the public of the subject being legislated upon. Matters properly connected with the subject stated in the title may be included in the act without being stated in the title, but under section 16, art. 3, Constitution, an act cannot legally contain incongruous and unrelated matters or matters not fairly covered by a single subject expressed in the title of matters not properly connected with such subject.

. . .

NOTES AND QUESTIONS

1. Is state sovereign immunity a relic of pre-democratic law, a leftover from feudal times when the king or sovereign was thought to be above the law? Is the notion compatible with modern democracy, the rule of law, and the idea that no one is above the law?

2. If Florida's Constitution allows the legislature to waive immunity and provide for suits against the State, then why does the Court appear to guard state sovereign immunity so fiercely?

3. What are the policy arguments for safeguarding sovereign immunity?

SECTION III: EXTRINSIC TOOLS

A. Common Law

VANNER V. GOLDSHEIN

216 So.2d 759 (Fla. Dist. Ct. App. 3rd Dist. 1968)

HENDRY, Judge.

Plaintiffs below have appealed from a summary judgment entered in favor of two of the three defendants, Joseph and Anna Goldshein, by the Circuit Court of Dade County. Plaintiffs brought several actions, consolidated both at trial and on this appeal, based on the tragic deaths of two five-year old boys which occurred on August 30, 1966, when those children suffocated in a built-in ice-box section of a small trailer. We must note at the outset that this case involves the first judicial construction of a state statute, and therefore feel justified in giving a detailed rendering of the facts.

The defendants, Joseph and Anna Goldshein, are the fee simple owners of a certain piece of business property. On August 30, 1955, they and the American Oil Company entered into a ten-year lease, such term to begin on April 1, 1956. This leasehold was later extended by a recorded renewal to run for an additional term, scheduled to expire on March 31, 1976. American Oil Company, the lessee, subleased the premises to Mr. Omelia Diaz for a term which began in April, 1962, and was subject to successive annual renewals. Diaz did in fact renew the sub-lease for the term of April 1, 1966, through March 31, 1967, during which time the accident occurred.

The trailer was owned by the third defendant, Miss Elena Guasp. Some time between January 1 and March 1, 1966, she left it with the manager of the gas station in order to display it for sale to the general public, and this was done directly on the premises. The trial court found as a fact that at no time were the Goldsheins directly apprised of the situation, and that they never received knowledge of it until after the accident had occurred. This trailer measured 13 feet in length, had side walls which were about 4 or 5 feet in height, and rested on two wheels. It had no roof, but within its structure, it contained an ice-cooled type of icebox which was one and a half feet high, one foot deep and one foot wide. Somehow, the boys became entrapped in this icebox and died.

We are immediately confronted with a statutory mandate which at first appears to provide a ready answer to the question of liability. F.S. s 823.07, F.S.A. begins by setting forth the statutory intent in these words: '* * * (1) The purpose of sections 823.07-823.09 is to prevent deaths due to suffocation of children locked in abandoned or discarded ice boxes, refrigerators or deep freeze lockers from which the doors have not been removed.' This creates an initial issue of whether '* * * ice boxes, refrigerators, or deep freeze lockers * * *' referred to also include the built-in icebox in this case. We specifically decline to answer this problem in this opinion. Instead, we predicate our decision on the more basic problem, which may be stated thusly: whether the lessor of a long term leasehold is liable for acts committed by its lessee, or the lessee's sub-lessee? We are compelled to answer that question in the negative, and therefore must affirm the trial court.

In 1965, the provision of the statute directed to the question of liability had been worded thusly: '* * * (2) It shall be unlawful for any person to allow any used icebox * * * to remain on *his property or property under his control* * * *' (Emphasis added.) Then, at the next legislative session in 1967, that section was amended to read: '* * * (2) It is unlawful for any person to knowingly abandon or discard or to permit to be abandoned or discarded on premises *under his control* any icebox * * *' (Emphasis added.)

Viewing these two versions, we may begin to see the Legislature's intent as it sought to establish liability for violation of the statutory provisions. By omitting the words, '* * * on his property * * *', and yet continuing to retain the phrase, '* * * under his control * * *', the Legislature seems to have intended to make liable those vested with the right of control, rather than those holding title but removed from any position of control.

However, we cannot rely on semantics alone, and are required to look to the common law when the statutory intent is in doubt. The general rule is that statutes are to be construed with reference to appropriate principles of the common law, and when possible, they should be so construed as to make them harmonize with existing law and not conflict with long settled principles. 30 Fla.Jur., Statutes s 106, and cases cited therein. Here we have a lessor, tenant, and sub-tenant. One of the earliest rulings in this area came in Simms v. Kennedy, 74 Fla. 411, 76 So. 739, L.R.A.1918C, 297, where the court stated:

> 'A lessor landlord may be liable to third persons for injuries caused by defects in leased premises during the term of the lease, when the defect in or condition of the premises at the time of the lease was a violation of law, or was in the nature of a nuisance existing or incipient because of negligent construction or otherwise, or when the lessor has entire or partial control of the premises, or is required by law or undertakes to keep or to assist in keeping the premises in repair, or where his negligence or participation is a proximate cause of the injury. Liability of the lessor may also flow from the special circumstances or from applicable provisions of law.
>
> 'But prima facie where the lessee is in entire possession, occupancy, and control of the premises under a lease, and the premises were in good condition when leased, the lessor is not liable in damages for injuries to third persons caused by defects in the premises. And where an action for damages is brought against the lessor, he may plead specially the lease to and the possession, occupancy, and control of the premises by another, in bar of the action, in each case setting up the facts affording the bar.' Id. at 740.

The Sims case has been continually reaffirmed in a multitude of factual settings, most recently in Dabney v. Yapa, Fla.App.1966, 187 So.2d 381. There, the landlordlessor was held not liable for injuries caused by a condition over which he had no control. See also City of Daytona Beach v. Baker, Fla.App.1957, 98 So.2d 804, cert. denied, 105 So.2d 365, wherein the municipal corporation, in its status as a lessor of certain premises, was held not liable for damages caused by defects in those premises when the lessee was shown to be in possession, occupancy and control of same.

In conclusion then, we must agree with the appellee's position that the words of the 1967 statute, '* * * premises under his control * * *', can only reasonably mean, in the light of the long history of law on this point, that the person who is in possession and/or control of the premises must be regarded by the public as that person who uses the premises with the rights and powers incident to possession. It is that person who should occupy the position of liability, in the instance of F.S. s 823.07(2), F.S.A.

. . . .

Affirmed.

NOTES AND QUESTIONS

1. How did two five year olds get trapped in an icebox that was only 18 inches high, 12 inches deep and 12 inches wide? Does the fact that these facts must be wrong give you any insight into the Court's thinking? Does it indicate that the facts relating to the death of these children are irrelevant to the case? Are they?

2. Recall the comments of Justice Farmer, in his concurrence in Blankfeld v. Richmond Health Care, Inc., 902 So. 2d 296 (Fla. Dist. Ct. App. 4th Dist. 2005) quoted above under the substantive canons. Not only was he critical of the rule that remedial statutes should be interpreted liberally, he also seemed to question the relevance of the rule that statutes abrogating the common law should be interpreted narrowly. As he noted, the derogation cannon, like the remedial cannon were:

   > ...born when the common law was the primary source of social ordering. Most rule-making was by the common law. Statutes filled gaps or addressed conflicts untouched by the common law. Judges used statutes warily because they were few and judges were not accustomed to them.
   >
   > Early interpretation was limited to these questions: "What was the mischief and defect for which the Common Law did not provide; [and] What remedy the Parliament hath resolved and appointed to cure the disease of the commonwealth ..." Heydon's Case, 76 Eng. Rep. 637 (Ex. 1584). The function of judges was "to make such construction as shall suppress the mischief and advance the remedy ..." Id. These two guides emerged: the remedial canon, and the derogation canon against implied repeals of the common law. The derogation canon would be used for a statute changing the common law, while the remedial canon carried out the holding in Heydon's Case.

Statutes then were not created from common law methodology. Indeed, 18th century judges felt them rather subject to tyrannical majorities and shifting whims. England had suffered through the civil wars of the 17th and the abuses of unchecked majorities in Parliament. The beheading of Charles I was followed by the post-restoration instability leading to the Glorious Revolution in 1685. They viewed the common law as a source of social stability, cast from the wisdom of the ages and forged in cases evolving over the long sweep of history. Statutes often emerged from ephemeral, narrow and parochial interests, but the common law was eternal and universal.

In this country, the Progressive Movement at the turn of the 19th into the 20th Century, the legal upheavals resulting from the 20th Century's two World Wars, the Great Depression and the Civil Rights Movement, all had a profound effect on the sources of law. Statutes have assumed a much greater role in making legal and social policy. Indeed statutes have displaced the common law in most areas of American life. Nevertheless our rules for reading them are filled with relies of the English monarchy, and the remedial canon is one of them.

Some in the Academy think the remedial canon was effectively killed by the legal realists. Karl Llewellyn prominently demonstrated that each canon was offset by a contrary canon, that the derogation canon nullified the remedial canon. If the substantive canons feed on one another, how is the judge to use them sensibly? Some judges have thus been critical of the use of the substantive canons (303-305) (footnotes and references omitted).

3. Somewhat implicit in the above remarks is the notion that while these canons may have been appropriate when created, their legitimacy in our modern democratic society is questionable. There is a trend to view judge-made law as "activist," "undemocratic" or contrary to the separation of powers, while legislation is seen as "legitimate" and "democratic." Some, like Richard Abel, argue that the opposite is in fact the case. See, Richard L. Abel, Questioning the Counter-Majoritarian Thesis: The Case of Torts, 49 Depaul L. Rev. 533, 556 (1999) where he argues that in the confrontation between Courts and legislators in the arena tort reform "that courts tend to be populist and deliberative, whereas Legislatures tend to be captured by special interests, secretive, hasty, and unwilling or unable to offer reasons for their actions." I have also argued at length that the bulk of legislative "tort reform" since the 1980s has been undemocratic. See, Christopher J. Roederer, Democracy and Tort Law in America: The Counter-Revolution, 110 W. Va. L. Rev. 647 (2008).

More explicitly, Justice Farmer argues that these two canons pull in opposite directions and one can often be used to offset the other. Which one is to trump? There did not appear to be such a conflict in Vanner above, because the legislation was not treated as being remedial and in the public interest. Could one argue that the statute in question was one that was created in the public interest, namely to: "to prevent deaths due to suffocation of children locked in abandoned or discarded ice boxes, refrigerators or deep freeze lockers from which the doors have not been removed." Is there not the further argument that the statute was designed to be remedial in that it provided that it would be "unlawful for any person to knowingly abandon or discard or to permit to be abandoned or discarded on premises under his control any icebox." If so, should the Court not have given the statute a broad or generous reading so as to allow the Plaintiffs to obtain the remedy they were seeking? Note that the Plaintiffs likely wanted to sue the owners of the property rather than merely the gas station owner, because commercial property owners, in general, are more likely to have the resources to make Plaintiffs whole than those who lease their property (e.g. gas station operators). A generous reading may have allowed for this.

B. Purpose or Policy Behind the Law

Introduction

It is very common for the courts in Florida to explore the purpose(s) behind a given statute or provision as a useful or helpful tool for understanding and interpreting the meaning of the statute or statutory provision under consideration.[1] IFlorida courts regularly go further and hold that courts are required to find, and give effect to, the purpose of the law.[2] Arguably, no text has a plain or clear meaning without ascribing, explicitly or implicitly, one or more purposes for the text. Sometimes the purpose of any given provision or statute is straight forward, but often there is more than one viable purpose for any given provision or statute.[3]

Although many cases refer to the need to determine and give effect to the purpose(s) of the law, there is very little analysis concerning the most appropriate way to determine the purpose or purposes served by a statute, except in cases where the Legislature has stated the purpose in the legislation itself. The purpose of a statute may be determined by the same method the Courts use to identify "the legislative intent," namely, by simply reading the text. However, there are many instances when the plain meaning of the text appears to conflict with one or more purposes behind the law. As noted in the introduction, a statute can have many purposes, some of which may have been envisioned and intended at the time of drafting, and some not. Statutes serve

---

[1] See, e.g. Maddox v. State, 923 So. 2d 442 (Fla. 2006), Cason v. Florida Dept. of Mgmt. Servs., 944 So. 2d 306 (Fla. 2006), Knowles v. Beverly Enter.-Fla, Inc., 898 So. 2d 1 (Fla. 2004), Young v. Progressive Se. Ins. Co., 753 So. 2d 80 (Fla. 2000), Barber v. State, 988 So. 2d 1170 (Fla. Dist. Ct. App. 4th Dist. 2008), Smalbein v. Volusia County Sch. Bd., 801 So. 2d 169 (Fla. Dist. Ct. App. 5th Dist. 2001), and the cases in this section.

[2] See, e.g. Cason v. Florida Dept. of Mgmt. Servs., 944 So. 2d 306 (Fla. 2006), Knowles v. Beverly Enter.-Fla, Inc., 898 So. 2d 1 (Fla. 2004), and Smalbein v. Volusia County Sch. Bd., 801 So. 2d 169 (Fla. Dist. Ct. App. 5th Dist. 2001).

[3] There are often a range of purposes with differing degrees of generality and specificity. There are the general principles and purposes that underlie most any legal system, e.g rule of law principles of consistency, transparency, notice. Then there are more specific principles that tend to underlie any given area of the law, be it the criminal law, torts, contracts, corporate law, etc. Of course, even at these levels of generality there are conflicts and tensions between the various purposes that the law serves in any given area. Any particular legislative choice will often have these more general purposes as a backdrop against which the given law or particular provision is cast. Particular provisions often serve more particular purposes along with these more general purposes.

many competing needs, interests, or goals. This makes it difficult to tell which purpose(s) the legislature had in mind when it passed a given law. As time goes by, the original purposes may no longer be compelling or make sense. Sometimes, this results in statutes falling into disuse, but other times, the statute is adapted to new purposes. Should a court only interpret the text in light of the context in which it was written, and only as serving the purpose or purposes that the drafters intended? Or, rather, should judges view themselves as partners with the legislature. Should they fill in the gaps in the law, and interpret legislation's flexibly to keep up with changing context and societal needs? [4] Should judges attempt to apply the law in each case so as to make it the best that it can be? Note that as long as the legislature acts constitutionally, it can always return to the law and make its purposes clearer by amending the law.

The authors of *Statutory Construction in Florida: In Search of a Principled Approach*, offer the following advice:

> One should look to anything that, in the words of Justice Frankfurter, "is logically relevant" to the endeavor. Chief Justice Marshall was of a similar view. He said, "[w]here the mind labors to discover the design of the legislature, it seizes everything from which aid can be derived . . . ." One must keep in mind, however, that this search is an objective one, not subjective--it has nothing to do with attempting to psychoanalyze the draftsmen in an effort to divine what was in their minds. Moreover, in conducting this analysis, it is important that judges refrain from substituting their ideas regarding what the legislature's purpose ought to have been for the purpose that is manifested by the available evidence. [5]

Thus, the purpose here to be identified is neither the specific intent of the various legislators, nor is it the purpose or purposes that the judge thinks the statute ought to serve. As you go through the cases below and review the cases that have been addressed above, see if you can tell if the judge is either engaged in psychoanalysis, or is imposing her or his view of what purposes the law serves. Are the justices in these cases acting responsibly and legitimately or are they usurping the role of the legislature?

---

[4] Sometimes statutes are drafted so as to be ambiguous because of compromise, or because of the political costs of making a clear choice. Sometimes legislation is written with an open texture so that courts can fill in the gaps as cases arise, and sometimes statutes become unclear because it is difficult to determine how they should be applied to a new set of facts and conditions. Just as the text is sometimes left unclear, so are the statute's purposes.

[5] Judge Peter D. Webster of the Florida First District Court of Appeal in Peter D. Webster, Sylvia H. Walbolt, and Christine R. Davis, Statutory Construction in Florida: In Search of a Principled Approach, 9 Fla. Coastal L. Rev. 435, 519 (2008) (references omitted).

DEP'T OF ENVTL. PROT. V. MILLENDER

666 So.2d 882 (Fla. 1996)

SHAW, Justice.

We have for review a final declaratory judgment of the Circuit Court in Franklin County, construing article X, section 16, Florida Constitution, limiting marine net fishing. The First District Court of Appeal certified the trial court order to be of great public importance, requiring immediate resolution by this Court. We have jurisdiction. Art. V, § 3(b)(5), Fla. Const. We affirm the judgment of the trial court and hold that the trial court's construction of article X, section 16 of the Florida Constitution is correct, and that the Golden-Crum net meets the specifications of the amendment.

The controversy at issue involves the method of measuring trawl nets used for fishing in nearshore and inshore waters. Article X, section 16 states in pertinent part:

SECTION 16. Limiting Marine Net Fishing.-

(a) The marine resources of the State of Florida belong to all of the people of the state and should be conserved and managed for the benefit of the state, its people, and future generations. To this end the people hereby enact limitations on marine net fishing in Florida waters to protect saltwater finfish, shellfish, and other marine animals from unnecessary killing, overfishing and waste.

(b) For the purpose of catching or taking any saltwater finfish, shellfish or other marine animals in Florida waters:

(1) No gill nets or other entangling nets shall be used in any Florida waters; and

(2) In addition to the prohibition set forth in (1), no other type of net containing more than 500 square feet of mesh area shall be used in nearshore and inshore Florida waters. Additionally, no more than two such nets, which shall not be connected, shall be used from any vessel, and no person not on a vessel shall use more than one such net in nearshore and inshore Florida waters.

(c) For purposes of this section:

(1) "gill net" means one or more walls of netting which captures saltwater finfish by ensnaring or entangling them in the meshes of the net by the gills, and "entangling net" means a drift net, trammell net, stab net, or any other net which captures saltwater finfish, shellfish, or other marine animals by causing all or part of heads, fins, legs, or other body parts to become entangled or ensnared in the meshes of the net, but a hand thrown cast net is not a gill net or an entangling net;

(2) "mesh area" of a net means the total area of netting with the meshes open to comprise the maximum square footage. The square footage shall be calculated using standard mathematical formulas for geometric shapes. Seines and other

rectangular nets shall be calculated using maximum length and maximum width of the netting. Trawls and other bag type nets shall be calculated as a cone using the maximum circumference of the net mouth to derive the radius, and the maximum length from the net mouth to the tail end of the net to derive the slant height. Calculations for any other nets or combination type nets shall be based on the shapes of the individual components;

. . .

Art. X, § 16, Fla. Const. (effective July 1, 1995).

The following factual background is pertinent. Ronald Crum hired Buford Golden, an experienced net maker, to construct a shrimp trawl[1] which would meet the amendment's specifications ("Golden-Crum net"). In light of the state's[2] assertion that the Golden-Crum net does not comply with article X, section 16, of the Florida Constitution, appellees Bruce Millender, Ronald Crum, and other commercial shrimpers along with intervenors Wakulla and Franklin Counties asked the circuit court to determine: (1) the appropriate method of measuring trawl nets under the amendment; (2) the meaning of "with the meshes open;" and (3) whether the Golden-Crum net was prohibited.

The trial court concluded that the Golden-Crum net contained less than 500 square feet of mesh area as determined by application of subsections (b)(2) and (c)(2) of the amendment. In reaching its determination, the court found that: (1) the amendment intends to limit not prohibit trawl nets in the nearshore and inshore waters of Florida; (2) the amendment contains an internal inconsistency within its terms, but the various provisions must and can be construed together in harmony granting import to each; (3) trawl nets must not contain more than 500 square feet of mesh area using the formula for the area of a cone (circumference of the mouth of the net times the slant height length divided by two); and (4) the slant height equals the mid-point of the headrope (net mouth) to the tail of the net, with the meshes of the net in an open rather than closed or stretched position.

The basis of this appeal is a disagreement relative to the measurement of slant height. The state, FCA, and Millender present three different methods of calculating slant height[4] FCA argues that the stretched mesh measurement should be used because the specific language of the fourth sentence in subsection (c)(2) governs over the general language of the first sentence of subsection (c)(2):

---

[1] A shrimp trawl is a conical shaped, bag type net that is dragged along the ocean bottom with the shrimp being funneled through the open mouth of the net and captured in the closed end or bag of the net.

[2] The Florida Department of Environmental Protection, the Florida Marine Patrol, and the Florida Marine Fisheries Commission are the state regulatory agencies named as defendant parties. The Florida Conservation Association ("FCA") intervened on the defendants' behalf.

[4] FCA's method: The stretched mesh measurement is always twice the bar measurement. The bar length is one side of one square mesh, and on the Golden-Crum net it is .75 inches; thus the stretched mesh measurement equals 1.5 inches. All parties agree that the length of the net measured by the tape in the stretched mesh position is 29 feet. FCA's calculation uses 29 feet as the slant height. According to FCA, the area of the Golden-Crum net is (65.75 x 29) / 2 = 953.3 square feet.

> Sentence 1: '[M]esh area' of a net means the total area of netting with the meshes open to comprise the maximum square footage.
>
> Sentence 4: Trawls and other bag type nets shall be calculated as a cone using ... the maximum length from the net mouth to the tail end of the net to derive the slant height.

Art. X, § 16(c)(2), Fla. Const. FCA contends that because the slant height of a net cannot be measured with all the meshes open, the language in the first sentence requiring measurement "with the meshes open" is overridden by the language in the fourth sentence requiring the net to be stretched to its "maximum length."[5]

The state argues that the "meshes open" language can be harmonized with the "maximum length" language by using its calculations to obtain slant height and is the correct method because the net mesh is oriented and hung on the diagonal.[6] Millender agrees that the "open mesh" language must be harmonized with the "maximum length" language. He uses the measurement across the bar (one side of one square) of the mesh because he claims it is the industry-accepted method of measuring open mesh and most nearly approximates the amount of raw net stock actually contained in the trawl.[7]

It is undisputed that Golden used less than 500 square feet of netting to construct the net. Notwithstanding the actual raw stock used, the FCA (stretched mesh method) measures the net at 953 square feet; the state (open mesh diagonal) measures the net at 673 square feet; and Millender (open mesh across the bar) measures the net at 476 square feet. The trial court found that Millender's method of measurement more closely complies with the amendment's specifications. The state raises two issues on appeal.

The state first argues that there is no evidence in the record to support the court's finding that the open mesh length is one half the stretched length. After examining the language of the amendment, we find that the first and fourth sentences within subsection (c)(2) are subject to varying interpretations. In construing article X, section 16, the trial judge was obviously attempting to ascertain and give effect to the intent of the drafters and those who voted on the amendment. Intent is traditionally discerned

---

5 State's method: The state's conversion factor equals the ratio of the length of the diagonal of one mesh square (1.06) to the length of a stretched mesh (1.5). The state calculates the length of the diagonal using the Pythagorean Theorem: a2 + b2 = c2. The length of one side of one square of mesh equals .75, thus .752 + .752 = .5625 + .5625 = 1.125, and $\sqrt{1.125}$ = 1.06. The conversion factor, (1.06 / 1.5 = .706), is multiplied by the stretched mesh length (29 feet) to derive the state's slant height: .706 x 29 = 20.49. By the state's measure, the area of the Golden Crum net is (65.75 x 20.49) / 2 = 673.6 square feet.

6 Millender's method: Millender's conversion factor is exactly one half of the stretched mesh length. Because it is undisputed that the stretched mesh length of the net is 29 feet, using Millender's conversion factor (1/2), the slant height is one half of 29 feet, to wit: 14.5 feet. According to Millender, the area of the Golden Crum net is (65.75 x 14.5) / 2 = 476.6 square feet.

7 " 'Bar measurement' means the mesh size of a net as measured by the distance from the center of a knot to the center of an adjacent knot." Fla.Admin.Code R. 46-31.006(2).

> from historical precedent, from the present facts, from common sense, and from an examination of the purpose the provision was intended to accomplish and the evils sought to be prevented. Furthermore, we may look to the explanatory materials available to the people as a predicate for their decision as persuasive of their intent.

Plante v. Smathers, 372 So.2d 933, 936 (Fla.1979) (citation omitted). The amendment should also be construed as a whole in order to ascertain the general purpose and meaning of each part; each subsection, sentence, and clause must be read in light of the others to form a congruous whole so as not to render any language superfluous. Less latitude is permitted when construing constitutional provisions because it is presumed that they have been more carefully and deliberately framed than statutes. City of Jacksonville v. Continental Can Co., 113 Fla. 168, 172, 151 So. 488, 489 (1933).

In light of these principles of construction, we examine the first sentence in subsection (c)(2) which states: " 'mesh area' of a net means the total area of netting with the meshes open to comprise the maximum square footage" and the fourth sentence in subsection (c)(2) which states: "Trawls and other bag type nets shall be calculated as a cone using ... the maximum length from the net mouth to the tail end of the net to derive the slant height."

We conclude that had the drafters intended the maximum length from the net mouth to the tail end of the net to be measured using the stretched mesh method or the open mesh diagonal method, it would have been more clearly spelled out in the amendment. The record contains competent substantial evidence that the industry-accepted method of measuring open mesh is across the bar and that the bar length is one half the stretched mesh length. We hold that the "maximum length" required to measure the slant height from the net mouth to the tail end refers to the maximum length with the meshes open, measured in the usual way open mesh is measured-across the bar.

We have previously stated that in order for voters to cast an intelligent and informed ballot, the ballot summary must provide fair notice of the content of the proposed amendment. In re Advisory Opinion to the Attorney General-Save Our Everglades, 636 So.2d 1336, 1341 (Fla.1994). Here we find that the voters could not have understood the language provided on the ballot summary to imply the complicated method of measurement the state proposes, nor is it likely that they would have understood it to mean that a net containing less than 500 square feet of raw stock could measure almost twice that amount within the context of the amendment. Voters reading the summary or the entire amendment would most likely understand that a trawl constructed from 500 square feet or less of net mesh would be permitted under the amendment.

FCA contends that the amendment is unambiguous, and that the fourth sentence in subsection (c)(2) trumps previous conflicting provisions because the last expression of the legislative will is the law that prevails. See Johnson v. State, 157 Fla. 685, 697, 27 So.2d 276, 282 (1946), cert. denied, 329 U.S. 799, 67 S.Ct. 491, 91 L.Ed. 683 (1947). This rule of statutory construction is subservient, however, to the overarching rule that where a paragraph contains inconsistent sentences the paragraph should be read so as to be consistent with the apparent policy sought to be implemented. The obvious policy and intent of the amendment is to limit nearshore and inshore net fishing while permitting trawl nets containing up to 500 square feet of netting.

FCA further maintains that specific language requiring "maximum length" governs over language requiring measurements to be "with the meshes open." We reject this interpretation and find that the voters passed the amendment as an entity, thus an attempt to exclude any portion from consideration distorts voter intent. Proposed methods of measurement by the state and FCA reach an absurd result and defy common sense. "An interpretation of a constitutional provision which would lead to an absurd result will not be adopted" when a contra interpretation is more in keeping with the obvious intent and purpose sought to be accomplished. Plante, 372 So.2d at 936. Neither the state nor FCA has demonstrated that the trial court's construction of the amendment is unreasonable, produces an absurd result, or is obviously contrary to voter intent.

Next, the state argues that the trial court erred by relying upon the amount of mesh stock used to construct the net and evidence that the nets proposed by the state and FCA are not commercially viable. The state claims that this evidence is irrelevant and prejudicial. We disagree. "If the purpose of construction is the ascertainment of meaning, nothing that is logically relevant should be excluded." Felix Frankfurter, Some Reflections on the Reading of Statutes, 47 Col.L.Rev. 527, 541 (1947). The amount of net mesh actually contained in the net is directly relevant to the 500 square foot limitation expressed in section (b)(2). We agree with the trial court that in the context of the amendment's stated purpose, which is to limit rather than prohibit shrimp trawl fishing, evidence of the nets' commercial viability is relevant. The record contains competent, substantial evidence that shrimp trawling would be rendered commercially infeasible in the nearshore and inshore waters if either the state's method or FCA's method of measuring slant height is adopted. We hold that both the evidence of the amount of raw stock used to construct the Golden-Crum net and the evidence of commercial viability are relevant and were properly considered by the court.

Accordingly, we affirm the judgment of the circuit court and hold that for purposes of measuring trawl nets under article X, section 16, slant height equals one half the stretched mesh length from the mid-point of the net mouth to the tail end of the net, and that the Golden-Crum net complies with the amendment's specifications.

It is so ordered.

GRIMES, C.J., and OVERTON, KOGAN, HARDING, WELLS and ANSTEAD, JJ., concur.

NOTES AND QUESTIONS

1. Why does the general policy behind the statute trump the rule that the last expression of the legislative will is the law that prevails?

2. What authority does the Court provide for this rule?

3. Why would the FCA's interpretation defeat the policy behind the law?

4. What is the difference between legislative intent, purpose, and policy?

5. If the FCA is correct that the legislature intended for the square footage of nets of this type to be measured in the way it suggests, does this lead to an absurd result? Is it physically possible to make a 953.3 square foot net out of less than 500 square feet of netting (if you are not a god, that is)? Should rather simple mathematics not solve this problem?

6. Do you agree with the Court that, "If the purpose of construction is the ascertainment of meaning, nothing that is logically relevant should be excluded." Quoting Felix Frankfurter, Some Reflections on the Reading of Statutes, 47 Col.L.Rev. 527, 541 (1947).

ABOOD V. CITY OF JACKSONVILLE

80 So.2d 443 (Fla. 1955)

DREW, Chief Justice.

The question presented in this litigation in whether the appellant, who operates a restaurant in Jacksonville, Florida, 'having accommodations for service of 200 or more patrons at tables and occupying more than 4000 square feet of space,' is entitled to a liquor license regardless of the fact that the maximum number of liquor licenses which may be issued in the City of Jacksonville, Florida, pursuant to the provisions of Section 1 of Chapter 25919, Laws of Florida, Special Acts of 1949, have already, and long since, been issued and are outstanding.

The appellant contends that he is entitled to have such license issued to him for the reason that Chapter 25359, Laws of Florida, Acts of 1949, F.S.A. s 561.01 et seq., which was passed in the same session but subsequent to the aforesaid Chapter 25919, supra, contains the controlling provision authorizing the issuance of such a license as an exception to the limitations imposed in Chapter 25919. Appellant further argues that if any doubt exists that the Legislature intended to authorize the issuance of a liquor license to establishments such as that operated by appellant, regardless of the provisions of any local or special act, such doubt is dispelled by a consideration of Chapter 28117, Laws of Florida, Acts of 1953, F.S.A. s 561.20 and note, which is the last expression of the Legislature on the subject and concerning which more will be said later.

It was the judgment of the lower court set forth in an exhaustive decree that the statutes herein mentioned, construed according to the precepts and rules approved by this Court, led him to the conclusion that so far as the City of Jacksonville was concerned the status of appellant was governed by Chapter 25919, supra, and that appellant was not entitled to the issuance of a license. The appeal is from that decree.

In the 1949 session of the Legislature, a local law relating wholly to the City of Jacksonville (Chapter 25919, supra, effective June 3, 1949) was adopted by the Legislature. This law provided that the number of liquor licenses to vendors in the City of Jacksonville was limited to one license for each 4,000 persons in said City but that at least 76 licenses could be issued in any event. The act contained a provision that it should not apply to certain designated types of licenses which were specifically described. Restaurants were not mentioned in the exceptions. Parenthetically, these exceptions, outside the one relating to the larger hotels, were with reference to licenses for establishments dealt with under the general beverage act such as steamships, trains, etc.

The same session of the Legislature enacted a general revision of a substantial portion of the beverage act, which was designated Chapter 25359, supra, and which became effective June 13, 1949, ten days subsequent to the effective date of the foregoing special act. Included in this general act was a Section 7 which provided that liquor licenses (by liquor licenses we refer to hard liquor licenses) under the applicable statutes should be issued so that the number of such licenses within the limits of any incorporated city or town, or in the territory of any county lying outside of any such cities or towns, should not exceed one such license for each 2,500 residents or major fraction thereof within such city or town or within such county outside the limits thereof. The act contained a proviso that in any event any city or town in a 'wet' county would be entitled to two licenses and the territory outside of any such city or town in any county to three licenses. Said Section 7 also contained the provision, 'no such limitation of the number of licenses as herein provided shall be applicable to * * * restaurant(s) * * * having accommodations for service of two hundred or more patrons at tables and occupying more than four thousand square feet of space * * *.' F.S.A. s 561.20. This Section also contained the following paragraph which is the real nub of this controversy: '*The limitations herein prescribed shall be cumulative to and shall not affect or repeal any existing or future local or special act relating to the* <u>*limitation by population*</u> *of such licenses within any incorporated city or town or county that may be in conflict herewith.*' (Italics and emphasis added.)

In the consideration of Chapter 25359, supra, in the determination of the instant problem, we observe that said Section 7 was amended by Chapter 28117, supra, in 1953, primarily, it would seem, for the purpose of restricting further the exception in the 1949 act so far as it concerned restaurants having accommodations for service of 200 or more patrons and more than 4,000 square feet of space by further requiring that these excepted restaurants also be restaurants 'containing all necessary equipment and supplies for, and serving full course meals regularly.' This act also contained the usual provision that all laws in conflict with it are repealed, 'provided that nothing in this act shall be construed to affect or cancel any license heretofore issued pursuant to any special or local law.'

The myriad rules which have been designed by courts for the purpose of construing legislative acts were designed for the purpose of ascertaining, in doubtful cases, the legislative intent because of the law is what the lawmaking body intended it to be. Words are the means of expressing that intention, making a permanent monument of it and are, when clear, the best evidence of what the law is. The search in cases of this kind is to ascertain this intent. Because of the complexities and limitations of language and the difficulty ofttimes experienced in expressing thoughts in printed words, the problems of statutory construction are often difficult. In doubtful cases we must, among other things turn to the language used, the general policy of the law on the subject, the objects which the Legislature had in mind in the enactment of the legislation, the purposes sought to be accomplished by such legislation, and the nature of the subject being legislated upon, in order to determine as near as we can just what the Legislature intended the law to be. We are entitled to, and should, ascribe to the acts of the members of the lawmaking body a purpose to serve the best interest of the people and the general welfare of the State. See 50 Am.Jur. 'Statutes' 279, Sec. 298.

Chapter 25919, supra, (the local law) contained a clear limitation of one license for each 4,000 residents but, in any event, 76 licenses for such city. The act provided that, in determining the number of such licenses certain types of licenses should not be considered in calculating the number authorized. Restaurants were not included in the description. During this same session of the Legislature it had under consideration Chapter 25359, supra, (the General Law) which was a general revision of a substantial portion of the beverage act with particular emphasis on licenses and the various aspects thereof. So it is-and this much we know-both the Jacksonville situation and the situation regarding the State at large were being considered by the Legislature at the same time. A few days after the Jacksonville act was passed, Chapter 25359, supra, became a law. It contained the provisions which we have described above. This general law limited the number of liquor licenses to one in 2,500 population but contained a specific provision with reference to the large hotels and large restaurants of the type specifically noted herein. This act also contained the provision which we have quoted at length above with reference to being cumulative to and not designed to affect or repeal local or special acts. We think the decision in this case turns primarily upon this italicized language that we have quoted. We hold that it was the intention of the Legislature, in inserting this paragraph in Chapter 25359, to preserve the effect of any existing or future local or special act so far as it related to the *limitation by population* of liquor licenses within its territory. That, in fact, is exactly what it says. The exceptions (those licenses issued to designated establishments under the exceptions in the act) were matters to be and were governed by the general law.

We think these two 1949 acts may be construed together and effect be given to both. This can be accomplished by construing the quoted provision as leaving for local determination the number of licenses on a population basis but leaving in the General Law the *exceptions* noted.

To put it another way, the Legislature recognized the propriety and reasonableness of allowing cities and towns, through their representatives in the Legislature, to determine the number of liquor licenses in such communities *according to population* on such reasonable basis as might be in the interest of said cities or towns. But it withheld for general application throughout the State certain specific types of licenses from the operation of such limitations. This is a logical and reasonable result. It is the large number of bars and package stores and the attendant police problems arising therefrom as well as the moral and social issues involved that furnish the basis of legislation limiting the number of such establishments. These limitations are directed to the type of establishments exclusively or primarily engaged in the sale of hard liquors. The *exceptions* mentioned deal exclusively with those types of establishments where the sale of liquor is an incident to the main business and where obviously the police problems are not the same nor the moral or social issues similar. Even the exceptions in the Local Act are of this kind.

Moreover, the type of hotels and restaurants excluded from the operation of the limitation by population provision are ones that would be logically considered by the Legislature, in the interest of the general welfare of the State, to require such licenses for the purpose of effective operation, the payment of their tax obligations and the promotion of the general good. Florida is one of the more rapidly developing states, if not actually the leader in this field. It is only natural that the Legislature would have great regard for large enterprises of this kind. Such are necessary in the great and profitable tourist trade. It would not likely want to leave to local governments the right to determine whether institutions of this kind would be granted licenses which are so essential to their successful operation and without which they would probably not be built or operated. That the State is interested in enterprises of this kind is evident from the passage in recent years of many acts granting tax exemptions and other inducements to new enterprises. Notably among these of recent years was the act of the 1953 Legislature granting tax concessions to certain large insurance organizations. Chapter 27989, Laws of Florida, Acts of 1953, F.S.A. s 205,432 and note. Even our Constitution contains many provisions of this nature. See notably Sections 12 and 14 of Article IX of the Florida Constitution, F.S.A. Moreover, the passage of the 1953 Amendment (Chapter 28117, supra) above alluded to is a clear expression at least that the Legislature intended that large hotels and restaurants of the type described in the act should receive uniform consideration throughout the length and breadth of the State.

We think the construction we have given this act is what the Legislature meant to accomplish and that is what the law is. It its precisely into the historic legislative patters of encouraging new enterprises in this fast growing State. It is recognized that, 'in interpreting an ambiguous statute the courts may among other matters take into consideration the general policy of the law, or the settled policy of the state, in so far as it may throw light on the legislative intention, and that a statute should be interpreted in the light of, and to effectuate, such policy, where it is clearly deducible from consistent acts of the Legislature, or where the statute is a part of other legislation designed as a whole to establish an expressed state policy.' 50 Am.Jur. 280, Sec. 299.

The decree of the lower court must be reversed with directions to enter one in accordance with the views herein expressed.

Reversed.

TERRELL, THOMAS, HOBSON, and ROBERTS, JJ., concur.

SEBRING, J., dissents.

THORNAL, J., not participating

NOTES AND QUESTIONS

1. If the legislature intended for the exceptions for large restaurants from the general state-wide law to apply, why did it not say so in the legislation?

2. Was the general legislation not clear that it did not supersede local special laws? The general legislation states that the general law, "...shall not affect or repeal any existing or future local law or special act relating to the limitation by population of such licenses within any incorporated city, town, or county that might conflict herewith."

3. The Court notes that the local act has exceptions that are of the same kind as the exception in the general law relating to large restaurants. If the list of exceptions in the special law were merely illustrations of the kinds of exceptions allowable, then the noscitur a sociis and ejusdem generis rules should apply. However, if the list is a closed list, then the expressio unius est exclusio alterius maxim should apply. What would be the result of applying these rules?

4. Do you agree with the Court that the result is what is in the best interest of the people and the welfare of the state of Florida? What is the Court's argument that its interpretation is consistent with state policy? Did the legislature intend to take the issue of liquor licenses out of the hands of local government? Are these the kinds of things that are best for the state to decide or for local government to decide? Did the Court take the decision out of the hands of both the state legislature and local government?

5. How did the Court identify the state policy? Did you find its references to tax exemption provisions in the Constitution and in recent legislation persuasive?

6. State policy implies something broader than the specific purpose of a given provision, or even the statute as a whole. Legislative purpose is sometimes clear from the preamble, purpose clauses, or from legislative findings and history (See, e.g. Vanner v. Goldshein 216 So.2d 759 (Fla. Dist. Ct. App. 3rd 1968) above where the statute contained a purpose clause).Sometimes, the purpose of legislation is not explicit but must be gleaned from the broader social context in which a law is passed and the text of the law. How one interprets the conflict of laws in this case depends in large part on whether the purpose behind the law was to allow for local decision making or was to further economic growth by taking decisions regarding large restaurants out of the hands of local government.

C. LEGISLATIVE BACKGROUND/HISTORY

Introduction

Similar to the general rule that one should not look to the substantive tools/canons of statutory construction if the statute is clear, as a general rule, judges do not look to legislative history if a statute is clear.[1] Like the plain meaning rule above, the courts sometimes use language that indicates that this is a pragmatic consideration rather than a legal prohibition. For instance, the Court in Mitchell v. State merely stated, "Legislative history is not needed to determine intent when the language is clear."[2] When statutes are ambiguous (and it is common for it to be ambiguous whether a given statute is ambiguous), it is common for Florida courts to turn to the legislative history for guidance.

While courts are generally receptive to legislative history arguments, there may be some who see it as too unreliable, and perhaps illegitimate. This is the view of what are called "new textualists."[3] There are many pitfalls in looking to the legislative history in order to determine legislative intent. These pitfalls include: many different types of sources, the status of those sources, the fact that the record can be strategically manipulated, and that many of the sources used are only indirect indications of what a majority of the legislature may or may not have intended when passing the law. As Justice Scalia noted In Conroy v. Aniskoff, "Judge Harold Leventhal used to describe the use of legislative history as the equivalent of entering a crowded cocktail party and looking over the heads of the guests for one's friends."[4]

As noted, there is no one single authoritative legislative history for a lawyer to turn to. Rather, there is a whole range of sources including: previous enacted versions of a law, previous drafts of a law, subsequent amendments to the law, legislative journals and records, the public statements and explanatory notes of those who drafted and put forward the original bill (e.g. sometimes a public interest group, sometimes a commission), the staff reports of legislative committees, and even the statements of legislators in the floor debates.[5] There is no clear hierarchy in these sources and

---

[1] See, e.g. Knowles v. Beverly Enters.-Fla., Inc., 898 So. 2d 1, 11 (Fla. 2004) ("In other words, not only do we not need to resort to legislative history, as the dissent does, to understand this plain meaning; we cannot do so.") See also. Nicarry v. Eslinger, 990 So. 2d 661 (Fla. Dist. Ct. App. 5th Dist. 2008).

[2] 911 So. 2d 1211, 1214 (Fla. 2005)(citing Goldenberg v. Sawczak, 791 So.2d 1078, 1083 (Fla.2001).

[3] See, e.g. Antonin Scalia, A Matter of Interpretation: Federal Courts and the Law (1997). See Antonin Scalia, Common-Law Courts in a Civil-Law System: The Role of United States Federal Courts in Interpreting the Constitution and Laws, in A Matter of Interpretation 3, 29-30 (Amy Gutmann ed., 1997) ("My view that the objective indication of the words, rather than the intent of the legislature, is what constitutes the law leads me, of course, to the conclusion that legislative history should not be used as an authoritative indication of a statute's meaning."). Justice Scalia further states "that it is simply incompatible with democratic government, or indeed, even with fair government, to have the meaning of law determined by what the lawgiver meant, rather than by what the lawgiver promulgated." Id. at 17.

[4] Conroy v. Aniskoff, 507 U.S. 511, 519 (1993) (Scalia, J., concurring in judgment).

[5] Note that for laws prior to 1969 there is no archival record of legislative debates or committee reports (staff analysis). The records have been kept in the State Archives since the 1970s. Staff Analyses have been available to libraries from the 1988 legislative session to present. Legislative history materials from 2001 to the present are available through Lexis (FLA library; FLLH file). Westlaw has materials from 1998 to the

lawyers and judges alike will sometimes pick and choose the ones (their friends) that support their argument the most while ignoring or downplaying others (their enemies).

While the statements of those who sponsor bills are often informative about what those individuals/groups intend the law to mean, it does not necessarily follow that those who voted on the law have the same intentions. The same goes for the committee reports (known as "Staff Analysis" in Florida). Committee reports are often very useful because they are fairly detailed and well organized reports that provide a good deal of insight into the committee's views on the bills that they put before the legislature. These reports are important because many of the representatives rely on them when deciding how to vote. Nonetheless, it is important to remember: reports are written by staff and not legislators; the committee report is not voted on or even officially endorsed by the Legislature,[6] and sometimes things may be put in a report for strategic purposes.

Overview of the Legislative Process[7]

Before looking at the cases that address some of these issues concerning the use of legislative history, it is important to have a rough idea of how the legislative process works and how the history is generated and recorded.

The legislative process in Florida is essentially the same as the process for federal law. The legislative process begins when a concerned citizen, an organization, group, or a legislator decides to put forth an idea for a law in a bill. Bills need to be sponsored by a representative in order for the process to begin.[8] Bills can originate in any house; however, the process for the two houses is slightly different. If a bill has a sponsor, the idea or bill is given to the Bill Drafting Service, who either writes or reviews and edits the bill. The bill is then distributed to the Clerk of the House or the Secretary of the Senate for numbering and publication in the Journal (the first reading). The bill is then referred to one or more committees who specialize in the areas related to the bill's

---

present in the FL-BILLS database and the FL-LH database. For information on pending, passed, and rejected House or Senate bills, see Lexis Library: FLA, File: FLTEXT (from 1992 to present) and on Westlaw see FL-BILLS and the FL-BILLS-OLD databases (1991 to present) and at Florida Online Sunshine. The floor debates are available in audio from the State Archive.

[6] In Florida, the "Committee Report" is known as a "Staff Analysis." The committee reports included the following disclaimer at the end: "This Senate staff analysis does not reflect the intent or official position of the bill's sponsor or the Florida Senate." Note, there is also something called a "Committee Report" in Florida, which is merely a short fact sheet letter of transmittal that accompanies the bill. Generally, it is not useful in determining legislative intent or purpose.

[7] For a helpful diagrams of the process, See,
http://www.myfloridahouse.gov/FileStores/Web/HouseContent/Approved/Public%20Guide/Uploads/Documents/How%20Bill%20Become%20A%20Law-2006-2008.pdf.

[8] Florida's Constitution allows for voter initiatives to amend the Constitution. The process allows voters who gather sufficient support to put proposed amendments on the election ballot (limited to a single subject). These voter initiatives do not follow the normal legislative process, therefore, do not need to be sponsored by a representative.

subject. The committee studies the bill, often holding hearings[9], and then either makes a favorable, unfavorable or conditioned favorable decision on the bill. In other words, the committee passes it, fails it, or passes it with amendments (in the House, the committee may decide to vote favorably with a substitute). The committee then has a Staff Analysis, or "Committee Report," prepared, which often summarizes the bill, states the bills purpose(s), addresses the bill's relation to existing legislation and the economic impact of the bill.[10] If passed, the bill moves to any other relevant committees or to the full house. If the bill makes it out of committee, it goes to the full house for debate, and vote. If the bill passes in one house, it goes to the other house for review. The bill then goes through a similar process in the second house, in which it may be amended or rejected. If amended, the bill must go back and forth until a consensus of both houses is reached, or the bill fails. The bill then goes to the Governor who may sign it, veto it, or let it pass into law without action (after 15 days). The legislature can override the veto with a two-thirds vote in each house. If the bill survives all this, it gets a session law number and is sent back to committee for codification in the Florida Statutes.

GELZER V. DIAMOND

920 So.2d 1235 (Fla. Dist. Ct. App. 5th Dist. 2006)

MONACO, J.

This case grows out of the mayoral and city council elections held in March of 2004, in the City of Orlando. Appellants, Lawanna Gelzer and Kenneth Mulvaney (the "Challengers"), contest the order of the trial court granting summary final judgment in favor of the Appellees, Phillip Diamond, Jose Fernandez, and Daisy Lynum, as members of the Elections Canvassing Board of the City of Orlando (Canvassing Board), and John H. "Buddy" Dyer and Ernest Page (the "Incumbents"). Mr. Mulvaney and Mr. Dyer, along with three other persons who are not parties to this suit, were candidates for the position of mayor, and Ms. Gelzer, Mr. Page and one other person were candidates for the position on the Orlando City Council. The Challengers assert that a number of the absentee ballots voted in these elections were mailed to the Supervisor of Elections in violation of a provision within the city election ordinance. Accordingly, they argue that all of the absentee ballots should be disqualified, and the election determined on the basis of the results of the machine votes alone. To do so would require a run-off election between Mr. Mulvaney and Mr. Dyer in the mayor's race, and between Ms. Gelzer and Mr. Page for the City Council seat. The trial court, however, disagreed with the Challengers and granted a summary judgment in favor of the Canvassing Board and the Incumbents. We find no error and affirm.

The essential facts are not controverted. During the course of the election contest, Mr. Dyer hired an election consultant, Ezzie Thomas, to "get out the vote" in African-American communities. Mr. Thomas encouraged voters to request, obtain and submit

[9] The hearings are not published but audio copies may be obtained from the State Archives.

[10] The Staff Analysis is updated throughout the process as the bill is amended. Note that while most laws have committee Staff Analysis reports, not all do.

their absentee ballots, and apparently offered instruction on how to correctly mark and seal the absentee ballots. In addition, he personally witnessed approximately 270 signatures on the return envelopes, and mailed the absentee ballots when voters so requested. Mr. Thomas admitted in one instance to assisting a blind voter in voting his ballot, but swore that he never opened or looked inside any other ballot, never changed or inserted any votes, and never discarded any absentee ballot.

Mr. Thomas was assisted in this enterprise by four volunteer campaign workers. Each of the volunteer workers signed sworn affidavits in which they admitted that they had witnessed the signatures of absentee voters, and mailed the absentee ballots when so requested by the voters. Prior to the date of the election, the Supervisor of Elections published some electoral advertising to the effect that the public had a right to inspect absentee ballots. Appellant Mulvaney attended but protested only one ballot witnessed by Mr. Thomas.

Mr. Dyer and Mr. Page were reelected to the positions of mayor and city council person, respectively...

. . .

Following the election, the Challengers filed separate actions contesting the results based on the mailing of absentee ballots by Mr. Thomas and his associates, which according to their theory, violated section 21.18(B)(2) of the Orlando City Code. That ordinance reads:

> An absentee ballot not cast in person must be mailed or delivered directly to the Supervisor of Elections by the elector or the elector's designee, and not to any other person, group or entity.

After the pleadings were closed, both sides moved for summary judgment. In support of its motion for summary judgment, the Canvassing Board submitted a lengthy appendix with many affidavits and supporting documents. Among the affidavits were those of voters who received assistance from Mr. Thomas in casting their absentee votes. More than 200 voter affidavits indicated that the individual voter marked his or her own absentee ballot, sealed it in the envelope provided, signed it with Mr. Thomas as the witness, and asked Mr. Thomas to mail it for them. The affiants also indicated that Mr. Thomas and his volunteer associates did not try to influence their votes.

The Canvassing Board's appendix also contains a transcript from the October 29, 2001, Orlando City Council meeting at which City Ordinance section 21.18 was adopted. At this meeting, Amy Iennaco, an assistant city attorney and the person responsible for drafting section 21.18, explained that the ordinance authorized three ways for an absentee voter to return the ballot. The ballot could be: mailed; delivered directly by the elector to the Supervisor of Elections; or delivered directly by the elector's designee to the Supervisor of Elections. A person could act as a designee, however, for no more than two ballots. One council member specifically asked whether it would be illegal for someone to pick up and mail a ballot for a senior citizen, and Ms.

Iennaco and Commissioner Lymon, a sitting member of the City Council, both explained that it does not matter who physically puts the absentee ballot in the mail.

The trial court granted summary final judgment in favor of the Canvassing Board and the Incumbents. The court concluded that section 21.18 is plain and clear in its meaning, and that it permits "another individual to mail voters' absentee ballots to supervisors of elections." Citing Quindlen v. Prudential Ins. Co. of Am., 482 F.2d 876 (5th Cir.1973), the trial court explained that statutes employing a disjunctive are generally construed to treat the alternative clauses separately; meaning that the language in a clause following a disjunctive word or phrase is inapplicable to the subject of the preceding clause. Additionally, citing Kirksey v. State, 433 So.2d 1236 (Fla. 1st DCA 1983), petition for review denied, 446 So.2d 100 (Fla.1984), the trial court noted that under the "doctrine of the last antecedent," courts construe qualifying words, phrases, and clauses to apply to the words or phrases immediately preceding them, and not to other words or phrases that are more remote. Finally, the trial court held that even if the provision is ambiguous, the legislative intent behind section 21.18(B)(2) would still lead to the same result: that ballots mailed by people other than the voter are not invalid. The Challengers appeal this judgment.

Summary judgment may only be granted if the pleadings, discovery on file, and any affidavits properly filed by the parties reflect that there is no genuine issue of any material fact and that the moving party is entitled to a judgment as a matter of law. See rule 1.510(c), Fla. R. Civ. P. A party moving for summary judgment must show conclusively that there is no genuine issue of material fact, and the court must draw every possible inference in favor of the nonmoving party. See Kitchen v. Ebonite Recreation Ctrs., Inc., 856 So.2d 1083, 1085 (Fla. 5th DCA 2003). We review the grant of a summary judgment using a de novo standard. Major League Baseball v. Morsani, 790 So.2d 1071 (Fla.2001).

The Challengers urge that section 21.18(B)(2) should be read to prohibit anyone other than the voter from physically mailing an absentee ballot to the Supervisor of Elections. They suggest that the phrase, "and not to any other person, group or entity" should be read in consonance with "mailed." The Incumbents argue conversely that everything after the word, "mailed," applies only to delivery of an absentee ballot to the Supervisor of Elections. Thus, under their theory, anyone can mail a ballot for an absentee voter. Although the parties disagree regarding the interpretation of section 21.18(B)(2), the trial court found that the ordinance is not ambiguous, and that its clear meaning does not require voters to mail the ballots personally.

While the trial court's interpretation of section 21.18(B)(2) is certainly reasonable and logical, we cannot help but observe that the provision is not a model of clarity. It is arguably susceptible to the two interpretations placed on it by the parties. In circumstances in which the meaning of a legislative enactment is ambiguous, we generally look to its legislative history to determine the intention of the legislative body in enacting it. See, e.g., Rollins v. Pizzarelli, 761 So.2d 294 (Fla.2000). As the trial court correctly pointed out, all of the legislative history of the ordinance clearly supports the view that anyone may lawfully put an absentee ballot in the mailbox at the request of a voter. Indeed, even the Challengers appear to agree that if the ordinance is ambiguous, and legislative intention becomes the issue, they lose. Thus, we conclude that under section 21.18(B)(2) the absentee ballots mailed by Mr. Thomas could lawfully be counted, and that the trial court properly granted summary judgment in favor of the Canvassing Board and the Incumbents.

In Boardman v. Esteva, 323 So.2d 259, 269 (Fla.1975), cert. denied, 425 U.S. 967, 96 S.Ct. 2162, 48 L.Ed.2d 791 (1976), the Florida Supreme Court wrote that "the primary consideration of an election contest is whether the will of the people has been effected." Nothing has been brought to our attention which causes us doubt in this regard. Although the Challengers have raised a number of other issues, we find no merit to them. Accordingly, the judgment is affirmed.

AFFIRMED.

PLEUS, C.J., and TORPY, J., concur.

NOTES AND QUESTIONS

1. Is the language of the provisions not relatively clear? It reads: "An absentee ballot not cast in person must be mailed or delivered directly to the Supervisor of Elections by the elector or the elector's designee, and not to any other person, group or entity." Does it not tell us that the elector or elector's designee must mail or deliver it directly? Or, does it tell us that anyone can mail it and only the elector or the elector's designee can deliver it directly?

2. Does the last antecedent rule that "courts construe qualifying words, phrases, and clauses to apply to the words or phrases immediately preceding them, and not to other words or phrases that are more remote" change the meaning of the clause?

3. Is this a case where the legislative history makes an otherwise clear provision ambiguous?

ROLLINS V. PIZZARELLI

761 So.2d 294 (Fla. 2000)

OPINION ON REHEARING

PER CURIAM.

. . .

We have for review Pizzarelli v. Rollins, 704 So.2d 630 (Fla. 4th DCA 1997), in which the district court recognized conflict with the opinion in Kokotis v. DeMarco, 679 So.2d 296 (Fla. 5th DCA 1996), and certified the following question to this Court:

WHETHER THE TERM "PAID OR PAYABLE" IN SECTION 627.736(3), FLORIDA STATUTES (SUPP.1996), SHOULD BE DEFINED AS "THAT WHICH HAS BEEN PAID, OR PRESENTLY EARNED AND CURRENTLY OWING" SO THAT THE STATUTORY LANGUAGE OF SECTION 627.736 WILL NOT BE INTERPRETED TO PERMIT ANY REMAINING PERSONAL INJURY PROTECTION BENEFITS TO BE USED FOR SET-OFFS FOR FUTURE COLLATERAL SOURCES.

704 So.2d at 633. We have jurisdiction pursuant to article V, section 3(b)(4) of the Florida Constitution. For the reasons expressed below, we answer the certified question in the affirmative.

FACTS

The record in this case is silent regarding many of the relevant facts, as it fails to provide a complete transcript of the trial. Additionally, the district court opinion does not provide a factual background. Based on the parties' representations at oral argument and in their briefs, we are able to glean the following facts. Carlene Pizzarelli, the daughter of Michael and Michelle Pizzarelli, was injured in an accident when she was a passenger in a car that was hit by another car driven by Dasha Marie Cates and owned by Jane Rollins. The Pizzarellis sued Rollins and Cates. Medical bills incurred prior to trial by the Pizzarellis in the amount of $13,212.60 were admitted into evidence without objection. Section 627.736(1)(a), Florida Statutes (1991), provides that personal injury protection ("PIP") benefits will cover 80% of medical bills. The Pizzarellis had $10,000 in PIP coverage.

During the trial, the issue arose as to whether the jury should be advised that $524.78 in additional PIP benefits were available to the Pizzarellis to defray the cost of future medical expenses. The defendants, Rollins and Cates, argued that the plain language of section 627.736(3), Florida Statutes (1991),[1] required the court to instruct the jury not to compensate the Pizzarellis for PIP benefits that had been paid or were to be paid in the future. The Pizzarellis argued that section 627.7372, Florida Statutes (1991),[2] applied and entitled Rollins and Cates to a setoff only for those PIP benefits that had been paid up until the time of trial.

---

[1] This statute provides:

> (3) Insured's rights to recovery of special damages in tort claims.—No insurer shall have a lien on any recovery in tort by judgment, settlement, or otherwise for personal injury protection benefits, whether suit has been filed or settlement has been reached without suit. An injured party who is entitled to bring suit under the provisions of ss. 627.730–627.7405, or his legal representative, shall have no right to recover any damages for which personal injury protection benefits are paid or payable. The plaintiff may prove all of his special dam- ages notwithstanding this limitation, but if special damages are introduced in evidence, the trier of facts, whether judge or jury, shall not award damages for personal injury protection benefits paid or payable. In all cases in which a jury is required to fix damages, the court shall instruct the jury that the plaintiff shall not recover such special damages for personal injury protection benefits *paid or payable*.

§ 627.736(3), Fla. Stat. (1991) (emphasis sup- plied).

[2] Specifically, section 627.7372(1), Florida Statutes (1991), provides:

> (1) In any action for personal injury or wrongful death arising out of the owner- ship, operation, use, or maintenance of a motor vehicle, the court shall admit into evidence the total amount of all

The trial judge ruled that because the PIP payments were made a part of the record of the case through the payout ledger, the future PIP benefits issue could be taken up post-trial. The jury awarded the Pizzarellis $5000 in future medical expenses and $48 in lost earnings. The jury also found that the victim suffered permanent injury and awarded the Pizzarellis $20,000 for past and future pain and suffering. After trial, both parties stipulated that there remained $524.78 in available PIP benefits.

Section 627.736(3) provides that "An injured party who is entitled to bring suit under the provisions of §§ 627.730-627.7405, or his legal representative, shall have no right to recover any damages for which personal injury protection benefits are paid or payable." The trial court concluded that the remaining $524.78 in PIP benefits fit the definition of "payable" and therefore set off the $524.78 from the $5000 future medical expense award.

On appeal, the Fourth District Court of Appeal agreed with the trial court that section 627.736(3) applied rather than section 627.7372. However, the Fourth District disagreed with the trial court as to the definition of "payable," reasoning that under the plain language of the statute, "payable" benefits do not include those for future medical expenses that have not yet been incurred. See Pizzarelli, 704 So.2d at 633. The district court reversed and instructed the trial court on remand to reinstate the jury's verdict for the full amount of future damages and to award reasonable costs and attorney's fees under section 768.79, Florida Statutes (1991).[3] See Pizzarelli, 704 So.2d at 633.

ANALYSIS

The question presented by this case is whether the Legislature, by using the term "payable" in section 627.727(3), intended to limit the setoff from damages only to expenses that had been incurred and were due and owing at the time of the judgment or whether the Legislature intended the setoff to be coextensive with the remaining amount of PIP benefits. The Fifth District concluded in Kokotis that " 'payable' as used in this statute includes expenses which have not yet accrued but which will result from the covered injury." 679 So.2d at 297. In contrast, the Fourth District concluded that the term "payable" in section 627.727(3) means only those medical expenses that have been incurred prior to trial but not yet paid or processed by the PIP carrier. See Pizzarelli, 704 So.2d at 632.

> collateral sources *paid to* the claimant, and the court shall instruct the jury to deduct from its verdict the value of all benefits *received by* the claimant from any collateral source.

(Emphasis supplied.) This statute has since been repealed, see ch. 93–245, § 3 at 2439, Laws of Fla., and the general collateral source statute is now found in section 768.76, Florida Statutes (1999).

[3] Because the total verdict in the case was $25,048 ($5000 in future medical expenses, $20,000 in pain and suffering, and $48 in lost earnings), after the trial court set off the remaining $524.78 in available PIP benefits, the total judgment became $24,523.22. The Pizzarellis had made a demand for judgment in the case for $20,000. According to section 768.79, Florida Statutes (1991), if the plaintiff makes a demand which is not accepted by the defendant and the plaintiff recovers a judgment in an amount at least 25% greater than the demand, he or she shall be entitled to recover reasonable costs and attorney's fees incurred from the date of the filing of the demand. Thus, after setting off the available PIP benefits, the judgment was no longer 25% greater than the demand and the trial court found the Pizzarellis were no longer entitled to reasonable costs and attorney's fees under section 768.79.

The Legislature's intent must be determined primarily from the language of the statute. See Aetna Cas. & Sur. Co. v. Huntington Nat'l Bank, 609 So.2d 1315, 1317 (Fla.1992). Accordingly, "[w]hen the language of the statute is clear and unambiguous and conveys a clear and definite meaning, there is no occasion for resorting to the rules of statutory interpretation and construction; the statute must be given its plain and obvious meaning." Modder v. American Nat'l Life Ins. Co., 688 So.2d 330, 333 (Fla.1997) (quoting Holly v. Auld, 450 So.2d 217, 219 (Fla.1984)). "Ambiguity suggests that reasonable persons can find different meanings in the same language." Forsythe v. Longboat Key Beach Erosion Control Dist., 604 So.2d 452, 455 (Fla.1992). We find that because the term "payable," as used by the Legislature in section 627.736(3), is susceptible to more than one reasonable interpretation, it is necessary to resort to principles of statutory construction to ascertain legislative intent. See Forsythe, 604 So.2d at 455; Holly, 450 So.2d at 219.

The term "payable" is not defined by statute. When a term is undefined by statute, "[o]ne of the most fundamental tenets of statutory construction" requires that we give a statutory term "its plain and ordinary meaning." Green v. State, 604 So.2d 471, 473 (Fla.1992). When necessary, the plain and ordinary meaning "can be ascertained by reference to a dictionary." Id. Further, it is a well-settled rule of statutory construction that in the absence of a statutory definition, courts can resort to definitions of the same term found in case law. See State v. Mitro, 700 So.2d 643, 645 (Fla.1997); State v. Hagan, 387 So.2d 943, 945 (Fla.1980); Delgado v. J.W. Courtesy Pontiac GMC-Truck, Inc., 693 So.2d 602 (Fla. 2d DCA 1997).

The term "payable" has been defined in this Court's case law as "meaning 'capable of being paid; suitable to be paid; admitting or demanding payment; justly due; legally enforceable.' " In re Advisory Opinion to the Governor, 74 Fla. 250, 254, 77 So. 102, 103 (1917). Black's Law Dictionary provides this same definition, but with an important amplification that "when used without qualification, [the] term normally means that the debt is payable at once, as opposed to 'owing.' " Black's Law Dictionary 1128 (6th ed.1990).

In accounting parlance, the term "payable," as in "accounts payable," has a similar usage. An "account payable" is defined in Black's Law Dictionary, in part, as a "liability representing an amount *owed* to a creditor, usually arising from purchase of merchandise or materials and supplies; not necessarily due or past due." Id. at 18 (emphasis supplied).

Thus, the most common usage of "payable" strongly suggests a limitation to incurred expenses that have not yet been paid at the time of trial, rather than potential future expenses that have not yet been incurred. Because a plaintiff's future medical expenses have not yet been incurred, these expenses cannot be presented to the PIP carrier for payment and therefore do not represent a liability or a "payable" benefit of the PIP carrier.

This definition is also consistent with the usage given to the term "payable" in the very next subsection of the PIP statute to describe when PIP benefits are "due." §

627.736(4).[4] That subsection provides that PIP benefits are "*due* and *payable* as loss accrues, upon receipt of reasonable proof of such loss." Id. (emphasis supplied). This use of the term "payable" in section 627.736(4) supports the construction of the term as referring to those medical expenses that have been already been incurred. This interpretation is thus consistent with the axioms of statutory construction that statutes must be read together to ascertain their meaning, see Forsythe, 604 So.2d at 455; City of Boca Raton v. Gidman, 440 So.2d 1277, 1282 (Fla.1983), and that the same meaning should be given to the same term within subsections of the same statute. See WFTV, Inc. v. Wilken, 675 So.2d 674, 678 (Fla. 4th DCA 1996).

Further, as the Fourth District's opinion in Rollins points out, "[w]hen the Florida Legislature wishes to provide for set-offs for future benefits it well knows how to express itself." Pizzarelli, 704 So.2d at 633. For example, section 440.39(3)(a), Florida Statutes (Supp.1996), provides workers' compensation carriers with claims against responsible third-party tortfeasors for "future benefits to be paid" to the injured employee. In the context of arbitration of medical malpractice cases, the Legislature has provided that "[d]amages for future economic losses shall be ... offset by future collateral source payments." § 766.207(7)(c), Fla. Stat. (1995). The clear intent of both these sections, expressed by the use of the terms "future benefits" and "future collateral source payments," is to require setoff of future collateral benefits. Neither section uses the more limited term "payable." Just as the legislative use of different terms in different portions of the same statute is evidence that different meanings were intended, see State v. Mark Marks, P.A., 698 So.2d 533, 541 (Fla.1997), the use of the more limited term "payable" in section 627.736(3) is evidence that the Legislature did not intend to set off future benefits.

We recognize that when the statutory language is clear, legislative history cannot be used to alter the plain meaning of the statute. See Aetna, 609 So.2d at 1317. However, when the statutory language is susceptible to more than one meaning, legislative history may be helpful in ascertaining legislative intent. See Magaw v. State, 537 So.2d 564, 566 (Fla.1989); cf. Hawkins v. Ford Motor Co., 748 So.2d 993 (Fla.1999) (using legislative history to support an interpretation of the plain meaning of the statute).

The legislative history in this case is most persuasive. A legislative committee report on the 1976 amendments to the PIP statute states that the changes were intended to replace the "complicated system of equitable distribution of PIP benefits" with a system under which a plaintiff could "plead and prove all of his special damages" but would not be awarded PIP benefits that "have been paid or are currently payable."

---

[4] Section 627.736(4), Florida Statutes (1991), provides in relevant part:
(4) BENEFITS; WHEN DUE.-Benefits due from an insurer under ss. 627.730-627.7405 shall be primary, except that benefits received under any workers' compensation law shall be credited against the benefits provided by subsection (1) and shall be *due and payable as loss accrues*, upon receipt of reasonable proof of such loss and the amount of expenses and loss incurred which are covered by the policy issued under ss. 627.730-627.7405. (Emphasis supplied.)
* SENATE STAFF ANALYSIS AND ECONOMIC IMPACT STATEMENT for BILL: CS/SB 1992 (The Sexual Predators Act 1998) (Bill SPONSOR: Criminal Justice Committee and Senator Burt) 1, available at: http://www.flsenate.gov/data/session/1998/Senate/bills/analysis/pdf/SB1992.cj.pdf

Summary of No-Fault Conference Comm. Rep. on Fla. CS for HB 2825 (June 8, 1976) (available at Fla. Dep't of State, Bureau of Archives & Records Management, Fla. State Archives, ser. 69, carton 319, Tallahassee, Fla.) (emphasis supplied) [hereinafter Summary of Report].

Under the former equitable distribution scheme, the tortfeasor received no offset for PIP benefits. Instead, the PIP carrier received a pro rata share of the plaintiff's recovery based on an equitable distribution formula, but only PIP "payments made" to the insured were subject to reimbursement based on equitable distribution. § 627.736(3)(b), Fla. Stat. (1975); see Williams v. Gateway Ins. Co., 331 So.2d 301, 304-05 (Fla.1976).

There is nothing in the legislative history of the 1976 amendments to indicate that, in replacing the complicated equitable distribution scheme and eliminating the PIP carrier's lien for payments made, the Legislature intended to grant tortfeasors a complete windfall by allowing a setoff against the verdict of all remaining PIP benefits. In fact, the committee report specifically used the modifier "currently" payable, which evidences its intent to limit the setoff to benefits that were owed by the PIP carrier because the expenses had been incurred. Summary of Report, supra. Thus, the legislative history supports the interpretation we give to the term "payable."

...Instead, the PIP carrier has a separate right to contest the reasonableness and necessity of the medical expenses at the time the expenses are incurred in the future. Additionally, the insurer might not even be in business when the plaintiff's medical expenses are incurred.

If we interpreted the term "payable" as the defendants suggest, the injured victim would have no guarantee that the PIP carrier would in fact pay the remaining benefits when the expenses are actually incurred, yet the jury's verdict in the plaintiff's favor would be prematurely reduced by those remaining benefits. There would be no guarantee that the plaintiff would ever be made completely whole for her injuries. See Haugen v. Town of Waltham, 292 N.W.2d 737, 740 (Minn.1980). Under this interpretation, the entity receiving the windfall is the tortfeasor, who obtains a setoff from the jury's verdict by the amount of the remaining benefits, but the insured has no concomitant immediate right to receive those remaining PIP benefits.

. . .

In summary, by examining the dictionary and case law definitions of the term "payable," applying well-recognized principles of statutory construction and examining legislative history, we conclude that the proper interpretation of the term "payable" is that only PIP benefits "currently payable" or owed by the PIP carrier as a result of expenses incurred by the plaintiff should be set off from a verdict that includes an award of future medical expenses. Accordingly, we answer the certified question in the affirmative, approve the decision of the Fourth District, and disapprove Kokotis.

It is so ordered.

ANSTEAD, PARIENTE, LEWIS and QUINCE, JJ., concur.

HARDING, C.J., dissents with an opinion, in which WELLS, J., concurs.

WELLS, J., dissents with an opinion.

SHAW, J., dissents.

HARDING, C.J., dissenting.

I respectfully dissent. The issue presented in this case is whether an award of future medical damages should be set off by the amount of remaining personal injury protection (PIP) benefits, if such benefits remain at the time of judgment. The answer to this question depends on the definition of the term "payable" as found in section 627.736(3), Florida Statutes (Supp.1996). In the decision below, the Fourth District Court of Appeal concluded that future medical expenses that have not been incurred at the time of trial are not included within the meaning of "payable," and therefore a verdict should not be reduced by the amount of remaining PIP benefits. Pizzarelli v. Rollins, 704 So.2d 630, 632-33 (Fla. 4th DCA 1997). In contrast, the Fifth District Court of Appeal in Kokotis v. DeMarco held that "payable" includes "expenses which have not yet accrued but which will result from the covered injury." 679 So.2d 296, 297 (Fla. 5th DCA 1996). This Court originally issued an opinion approving the definition of "payable" announced by the Fifth District in Kokotis. See Rollins v. Pizzarelli, 24 Fla. L. Weekly S69 (Fla. Feb. 4, 1999). However, on rehearing, the majority now adopts the definition of "payable" articulated by the district court below. I disagree with this "judicial U-turn."

The purpose behind the Florida no-fault statutory scheme is to allow each driver to collect certain statutorily required medical, disability, or death benefits regardless of fault. See Mansfield v. Rivero, 620 So.2d 987, 988 (Fla.1993) (citing Lasky v. State Farm Ins. Co., 296 So.2d 9 (Fla.1974)). In essence, the no-fault scheme grants tortfeasors a limited exemption from liability to the extent of the PIP benefits. See Mansfield, 620 So.2d at 988-89. I believe that the definition of "payable" adopted by the Fifth District in Kokotis is more in keeping with the spirit of the no-fault statutory scheme. See also State Farm Mut. Auto. Ins. Co. v. Klinglesmith, 717 So.2d 569, 571-72 (Fla. 5th DCA 1998) (Harris, J., dissenting). If the no-fault scheme immunizes tortfeasors from liability for a victim's medical expenses to the extent of the victim's PIP benefits, then this immunity must extend to all of the victim's PIP benefits, even those that remain at the time of trial. The interpretation of "payable" articulated by the Fourth District and now adopted by the new majority will extinguish a portion of this immunity (the remaining PIP coverage) and potentially permit a victim to collect a double recovery for future medical expenses. This result is contrary to the no-fault statutory scheme. See Purdy v. Gulf Breeze Enters., 403 So.2d 1325, 1329 (Fla.1981) ("To prevent the injured persons from receiving double recovery, the legislature has provided that any PIP benefits they have received from their insurers will be set off from the amount they are entitled to recover from the tortfeasors."). Therefore, I would deny the motion for rehearing and adhere to this Court's previous holding in this case.

WELLS, J., concurs.

[the dissenting opinion of Wells, J. is omitted]

NOTES AND QUESTIONS

1. Note that in addition to the legislative history argument found above, the Court also used dictionary and case law definitions of the term "payable," and "well-recognized principles of statutory construction" to make its argument that the term "payable" only refers to PIP benefits that are "currently payable."

2. Do you find the dissents reference to the "spirit" of the law persuasive? Is the spirit of the law a better indication of what the legislature intended the language to mean than the legislative history?

3. Is the spirit of the law, as argued by the dissent, a more rational and coherent purpose? Is it the intent the legislature would have if it had thought about its statutory scheme more thoroughly, or is it simply the dissent's view of the "best policy"?

4. Although the majority states that "[a]n interpretation of a statutory term cannot be based on this Court's own view of the best policy" it argues that its opinion supports the best policy.

5. Who has the better policy argument, the majority or dissent?

MARVIN V. HOUS. AUTH. OF JACKSONVILLE

183 So. 145 (Fla. 1938)

CHAPMAN, Justice.

On June 15, 1938, plaintiff, as a tax payer, filed in the Circuit Court of Duval County, Florida, his bill of complaint alleging, among other things, that The Housing Authority of Jacksonville, Florida, was organized pursuant to Chapter 17981, Laws of Florida, Acts of 1937; that the Housing Authority selected a site for a municipal low cost housing project and authorized the acquisition of land and a survey of slum conditions in the City of Jacksonville; that for the purpose of obtaining capital the Housing Authority entered into a loan contract with the United States Housing Authority whereby it was provided that a loan would be made by it to the Housing Authority of Jacksonville, Florida, in the sum of $1,027,000, being 90% of the estimated cost of the project; that the Housing Authority of Jacksonville agreed to issue debentures or bonds for said amount purchasable by the United States Housing Authority for the purpose of retiring the indebtness represented by the loan. The bill of complaint also described the lands by metes and bonds and alleged that it is situated within the City of Jacksonville and commonly known as Brentwood Park Housing Project, and that the plaintiff's decedent owned an interest, in part, in and to the lands therein described.

. . .

The Housing Authority of the City of Jacksonville entered into a contract with the City of Jacksonville providing for the elimination of unsafe and unsanitary dwelling units of said City and other services were pledged by the City of Jacksonville to the Housing Authority of said City.

. . .

The bill of complaint ... alleged that the proposed 'low cost housing project' is not for a public purpose, as contemplated by law, and that the power of eminent domain should not be exercised by said Authority to acquire property, because it is not for a public purpose and that to permit it so to do would be in contravention with the Constitution of Florida.

The prayer of the bill of complaint is for a temporary and permanent injunction against the City of Jacksonville ... (c) that it be temporarily and permanently enjoined from acquiring title to lands and property within the City of Jacksonville for a slum clearance low cost housing project; (d) that the power of taking over property under Chapter 17981 is not a public purpose; (e) that the proposed bonds are obligations of the City of Jacksonville within the meaning of Amended Section 6 of Article 9 of the Constitution of Florida.

. . .

On June 15, 1938, the Housing Authority of Jacksonville filed a motion to dismiss the bill of complaint on the grounds, (a) that there is no equity in the bill; (b) that it affirmatively appears from the bill of complaint that the purposes of Chapter 17981, Acts of 1937, are public purposes; [and] (c) that Chapter 17981, Acts of 1937, Laws of Florida, providing for the exercise of the power of eminent domain, will not violate the Declaration of Rights of the Constitution of Florida.

. . .

Upon a hearing on the part of counsel for the respective parties, the court below made and entered an order sustaining the motions to dismiss and did dismiss the bill of complaint on June 16, 1938, and an appeal was perfected from said order of dismissal and the cause is here for review on a number of assignments of error. The parties will be referred to in this opinion as they appeared in the court below as plaintiff and defendants.

1. It is contended that Chapter 17981, Laws of Florida, Acts of 1937, is invalid because the low cost housing and slum clearance is not a public purpose within the meaning of the law. In construing a statute, resort may be had, if necessary, to the history of the legislation and to public history of the times in which it was passed in

order to determine its purpose, meaning and effect, as an aid in determining its validity. See Sheip & Co. v. Amos, 100 Fla. 863, 130 So. 699. The 1937 Legislature made a finding and declaration of necessity when enacting Chapter 17981, and in so doing employed the following language:

'Section 2. *Finding and Declaration of Necessity*.-It is hereby declared:

"(a) that there exist in the State insanitary or unsafe dwelling accommodations and that persons of low income are forced to reside in such insanitary or unsafe accommodations; that within the State there is a shortage of safe or sanitary dwelling accommodations available at rents which persons of low income can afford and that such persons are forced to occupy overcrowded and congested dwelling accommodations; that the aforesaid conditions cause an increase and spread of disease and crime and constitute a menace to the health, safety, morals and welfare of the residents of the State and impair economic values; that these conditions necessitate excessive and disproportionate expenditures of public funds for crime prevention and punishment, public health, welfare and safety, fire and accident protection, and other public services and facilities; (b) that slum areas in the State cannot be cleared, nor can the shortage of safe and sanitary dwellings for persons of low income be relieved, through the operation of private enterprise, and that the construction of housing projects for persons of low income (as herein defined) would therefore not be competitive with private enterprise; (c) that the clearance, replanning and reconstruction of the areas in which insanitary or unsafe housing conditions exist and the providing of safe and sanitary dwelling accommodations for persons of low income (including the acquisition by a housing authority of property to be used for or in connection with housing projects or appurtenant thereto) are exclusively public uses and purposes for which public money may be spent and private property acquired and are governmental functions of public concern; (d) that it is in the public interest that work on projects for such purposes be commenced as soon as possible in order to relieve unemployment which now constitutes an emergency; and the necessity in the public interest for the provisions hereinafter enacted, is hereby declared as a matter of legislative determination."

The objective here is clearly shown by the above finding and declaration of the Legislature.

Section 12 of the Declaration of Rights of the Constitution of Florida provides:

"Sec. 12. No person shall be subject to be twice put in jeopardy for the same offence, nor compelled in any criminal case to be a witness against himself, nor be deprived of life, liberty, or property without due process of law; nor shall private property be taken without just compensation."

Likewise Section 29 of Article 16 of the Constitution of Florida provides:

"Section 29. No private property nor right of way shall be appropriated to the use of any corporation or individual until full compensation therefor shall be first made to the owner, or first secured to him by deposit of money; which compensation, irrespective of any benefit from any improvement proposed by such corporation or individual, shall be ascertained by a jury of twelve men in a court of competent jurisdiction, as shall be prescribed by law."

Section 6042, C.G.L., read in connection with the above quoted provisions, means that when private property is sought to be taken it must be taken for a public use or purpose and not a private use or purpose, but when taken as provided by law, it must be fully compensated for. See Demeter Land Co. v. Florida Public Service Co., 99 Fla. 954, 128 So. 402; State ex rel. Moody v. Baker and Jacksonville, T. & K. W. R. Co., 20 Fla. 616; Wilton v. County of St. Johns, 98 Fla. 26, 123 So. 527, 65 A.L.R. 488; Isleworth Grove Co. v. County of Orange, 79 Fla. 208, 84 So. 83; Spafford v. Brevard County, 92 Fla. 617, 110 So. 451.

...

It is next contended that Section 12 of Chapter 17981, Acts of 1937, Laws of Florida, violates Section 12 of the Declaration of Rights of the Constitution of Florida and Section 29 of Article 16 of the Constitution of Florida. Section 12 of Chapter 17981, supra, provides:

"Section 12. *Eminent Domain.*-An authority shall have the right to acquire by the exercise of the power of eminent domain any real property which it may deem necessary for its purposes under this Act after the adoption by it of a resolution declaring that the acquisition of the real property described therein is necessary for such purposes. An authority may exercise the power of eminent domain in the manner provided in Sections 3276 to 3295, both inclusive, Revised General Statutes of Florida, 1920, as amended by Chapters 15927 and 15928, Laws of Florida, Acts of 1933, and Acts amendatory thereof or supplementary thereto; or it may exercise the power of eminent domain in the manner provided by any other applicable statutory provisions for the exercise of the power of eminent domain. Property already devoted to a public use may be acquired in like manner, provided that no real property belonging to the city, the county, the State or any political sub-division thereof may be acquired without its consent."

The right to appropriate private property for public use lies dormant in the State until legislative action is had pointing out the occasion, modes, conditions and agencies for its appropriation. Private property can be taken only pursuant to law; but a legislative act declaring the necessity, being the customary mode in which that fact is determined, must be held to be for this purpose 'the law of the land', and no other finding or adjudication can be essential, unless the Constitution of the State has expressly required it.

...

The order made and entered by the Chancellor below sustaining the separate motions of the defendants to dismiss the bill of complaint was proper and free from error. The order of dismissal appealed from is hereby affirmed. It is so ordered.

ELLIS, C. J., and WHITFIELD and BUFORD, JJ., concur.

BROWN, J., concurs in part and dissents in part.

[The partial dissent of Justice Brown is omitted]

NOTES AND QUESTIONS

1. What are the two kinds of history the Court turns to in order to find the purpose, meaning, and effect of the statute in this case?

2. Are both types of history equally legitimate?

BURGOS V. STATE

765 So. 2d 967 (Fla. Dist. Ct. App. 4th Dist. 2000)

GROSS, J.

Appellant Christian Burgos pled no contest to three felonies in 1996. He was sentenced as a youthful offender to concurrent terms of community control followed by concurrent terms of probation.

Burgos appeals a 1999 order requiring him to register as a felon pursuant to section 775.13(1), Florida Statutes (1995). That statute provides that:

> [a]ny person who has been convicted of a felony in any court of this state shall, within 48 hours after entering any county in this state, register with the sheriff of said county, be fingerprinted and photographed, and list the crime for which convicted, place of conviction, sentence imposed, if any, name, aliases, if any, address, and occupation.

In the 1998 supplement to the 1997 Florida Statutes, the former section 775.13(1) became section 775.13(2). A new section (1) was added to explain:

> As used in this section, the term "convicted" means, with respect to a person's felony offense, a determination of guilt which is the result of a trial or the entry of a plea of guilty or nolo contendere, regardless of whether adjudication is withheld.

The section 775.13(1) registration requirement in place at the time of defendant's sentencing was thus clarified two years later. The 1998 amendment to the statute clears up the meaning of the term "convicted." The supreme court has recognized that "the term 'conviction' as used in Florida law has been a 'chameleon-like' term that has drawn its meaning from the particular statutory context in which the term is used." Raulerson v. State, 763 So.2d 285, 291 (Fla. 2000) (quoting State v. Keirn, 720 So.2d

1085, 1086 (Fla. 4th DCA 1998)). The legislature's subsequent amendment of a statute may properly be used to ascertain the legislative intent behind an earlier version of the statute. See Palma Del Mar Condominium Ass'n No. 5 of St. Petersburg, Inc. v. Commercial Laundries of West Florida, Inc., 586 So.2d 315, 317 (Fla.1991) (noting "courts may consider subsequent legislation to determine the intended result of a previously enacted statute"); Lowry v. Parole & Probation Comm'n, 473 So.2d 1248, 1250 (Fla.1985); Gamble v. State, 723 So.2d 905, 907 (Fla. 5th DCA 1999) (stating "our courts have a duty to consider subsequent legislation in arriving at a correct interpretation of a prior statute").

We reject appellant's contention that the trial court's order that he register as a convicted felon violates his constitutional right against ex post facto laws under Article I, Section 10, Clause 1 of the United States Constitution and Article I, Section 10 of the Florida Constitution.

The case at bar is analogous to cases where this court has held the registration provisions in sexual predator statutes to be regulatory, not punitive, and thus not ex post facto violations. For example, in Simmons v. State, 753 So.2d 762, 763 (Fla. 4th DCA 2000), the defendant pled guilty to one count of armed kidnapping, three counts of sexual battery, and three counts of armed sexual battery. He was sentenced to six-years incarceration followed by ten years probation. See id. After the defendant's release from prison, the legislature enacted legislation requiring sex offenders to submit to a digital photograph which could be disseminated on the Internet. See id. The defendant refused to comply and filed motions for relief from this requirement. See id. The trial court denied relief and the defendant appealed. See id.

On appeal, the defendant in Simmons argued that section 943.0435, Florida Statutes (1997), violated the ex post facto clause as applied to him. See id. We explained:

> "In evaluating whether a law violates the ex post facto clause, a two-prong test must be applied: (1) whether the law is retrospective in its effect; and (2) whether the law alters the definition of criminal conduct or increases the penalty by which a crime is punishable."

Id. (quoting Arnold v. State, 755 So.2d 696, 699 (Fla. 4th DCA 1999)); Gwong v. Singletary, 683 So.2d 109, 112 (Fla.1996). In affirming the trial court, the Simmons court found that the first prong was clearly met. See 753 So.2d at 763. However, the second prong was not met because "the statute does not alter the definition of criminal conduct and does not constitute punishment." Id. We noted that we had previously found section 943.0435 to be regulatory and "[r]egulatory statutes do not constitute punishment." Id. (citation omitted). See Walker v. State, 718 So.2d 217, 218 (Fla. 4th DCA 1998) ("The sexual predator designation 'is neither a sentence nor a punishment but simply a status resulting from the conviction of certain crimes.' ") (quoting Fletcher v. State, 699 So.2d 346, 347 (Fla. 5th DCA 1997)); Ortega v. State, 712 So.2d 833, 834 (Fla. 4th DCA 1998) (holding application of successor statute regarding registration of sexual predator was regulatory and not an ex post facto violation); State, Dep't of Corrections v. Goad, 754 So.2d 95, 97 (Fla. 1st DCA 2000) (discussing standard for determining whether a statute violates the ex post facto clause and holding statutes authorizing initiation of civil action against prison inmate to recover cost of incarceration were not ex post facto).

Unlike the statute at issue in Simmons, the registration requirement in this case was in place at the time of appellant's sentencing and was clarified two years later. This case does not involve a law "retrospective in its effect," the first prong of the test described in Simmons. 753 So.2d at 763. Moreover, like the statute in Simmons, the registration requirement in this case is regulatory, such that it does not constitute punishment. See id. Thus, there was no constitutional violation.

. . .

We therefore affirm the order requiring appellant to register as a convicted felon and dismiss that portion of the appeal directed at the trial court's refusal to terminate probation.

KLEIN, J., and FINE, EDWARD H., Associate Judge, concur.

NOTES AND QUESTIONS

1. Is it logical for the Court to use the 1998 amendment as a means to clarify the legislative intent behind section 775.13(1), Florida Statutes (1995)?

2. Should one not imply from the fact that the legislature amended the act in 1998, that the amendment changed the existing law rather than clarified previous law?

3. The Court states that "The Supreme Court has recognized that "the term 'conviction' as used in Florida law has been a 'chameleon-like' term that has drawn its meaning from the particular statutory context in which the term is used." Would an analysis of the context and legislative history behind the clarification not be helpful here?

4. The amendment to §775.13 in 1998 was in fact a small piece of a rather comprehensive treatment of sexual offenders. As the staff report states in its summary:

    > The CS for SB 1992 is intended to conform Florida's laws relating to registration of sexual predators and sexual offenders with federal standards to preserve all of the federal Byrne formula funding the state receives; correct deficiencies in the current sexual predator and sexual offender registration system and the reporting of public records information relating to these offenders; provide for the sharing of criminal history information for the purpose of child protective investigations; enhance collection of DNA samples from criminal offenders; and prohibit offenders convicted of certain offenses, primarily sex offenses, from being placed on administrative probation; providing that certain probation and community control conditions

relating to specified sex offenders are standard conditions that do not require oral pronouncement at sentencing.

> This CS substantially amends or creates the following sections of the Florida Statutes: 415.5018, 775.13, 775.21, 775.24, 775.25, 943.043, 943.0435, 943.325, 944.605, 944.606, 944.607,947.177, 948.01, and 948.03.*

In the section dealing specifically with §775.13 the staff report implies that the amendment was designed to bring the definition of "conviction" in line with the definition used in other sections related to sexual predators and sexual offenders, as it states:

> Section 2 of CS/SB 1992 amends s. 775.13, F.S., relates to the registration of convicted felons, exemptions from the registration requirements and penalties for failure to comply with the registration requirements. The CS provides a definition of the term "conviction" that is consistent with the definitions of this term in the other sections relating to registration of sexual predators and sexual offenders.**

Is there any indication that the amendment was designed to clarify the existing law, rather than to change the law so as to harmonize the provisions of that section with other provisions related to sex offenders?

5. Without the clarification, is it clear that a juvenile offender who is sentenced to community control and probation as a youth offender, after pleading no contest, was convicted of the three felonies?

6. Should the rule of lenity, i.e. that penal statutes be interpreted strictly, not be applied here?

7. Does the "fact" that this is not legally "a punishment" change anything in this case?

8. Do you agree that such "regulatory" laws are not punishments and that this was not an ex-post facto punishment of the appellant?

9. Note that Florida courts have held that it is not necessary for trial courts or counsel to advise defendants of the convicted felon registration requirement

---

* Id at 8.

** The Commission on Human Relations was created in part to "promote and encourage fair treatment and equal opportunity for all persons regardless of race, color, religion, sex, national origin, age, handicap, or marital status." § 760.05, Fla. Stat. (1997). Any person alleging discriminatory practices may file a complaint with the Commission. See id. § 760.11(1). If the Commission finds reasonable grounds to believe that a discriminatory act has occurred, the aggrieved party may file suit in circuit court or request an administrative hearing. See id. § 760.11(4). If the party requests an administrative hearing, the Commission may hear the case or request that the case be heard by an administrative law judge. See id. § 760.11(6).

prior to accepting a nolo contendere plea, because registration is viewed as merely a collateral consequence of the plea, not a direct consequence. Cella v. State, 831 So.2d 716 (Fla. Dist. Ct. App. 5th Dist. 2002), rehearing denied.

D. Agency Interpretation

Introduction

From the 1930s to the present, our country has seen an explosion of administrative agencies. The State of Florida has approximately forty administrative agencies.[1] Those agencies are often tasked with performing quasi legislative (rule and regulation making) and quasi judicial functions (administrative hearings) in addition to its executive (regulatory or enforcement) functions. Agencies are given their powers by the legislative branch, but once constituted, they function under the executive branch. Agencies often oversee the implementation and enforcement of legislative schemes. Thus, agencies have a "boots on the ground" expertise that is worthy of some level of deference when it comes to interpreting the legislation that they oversee.[2] Further, if the legislature delegates authority to an agency to fill in the gaps of the law through regulations, courts should defer to that agency out of respect for the co-equal branches of government.

Nonetheless, as with the other tools of construction, the courts of Florida generally do not rely on, or defer to, the interpretation of agencies if the legislation is clear.[3] What if the court and the agency disagree over the "plain" or clear meaning of a statute? Sometimes the courts state the rule in terms of giving "great deference" to the agency's contemporaneous construction of a statute,[4] such that the court should not overturn or depart from that interpretation unless the agency's construction is clearly erroneous, or is clearly unauthorized.[5] It probably goes without saying that if the issue is not one that requires the special expertise of the agency or is unrelated to its regulatory functions then there is no need for deference.[6]

Should the courts give more deference when the legislature has delegated rule making functions than when it merely empowers the agency to perform enforcement and adjudicatory functions? Should the amount of deference depend on whether the

---

[1] See, http://dlis.dos.state.fl.us/fgils/agencies.html for a list of Florida Agencies with links to the agencies websites.

[2] Rizov v. State, Bd. of Prof'l Eng'rs, 979 So. 2d 979 (Fla. Dist. Ct. App. 3rd Dist. 2008)

[3] See, e.g. Florida Pub. Employees Council 79, AFSCME, AFL-CIO v. State, 921 So. 2d 676 (Fla. Dist. Ct. App. 1st Dist. 2006); Diagnostic Servs. of S. Fla. v. State Farm Mut. Auto. Ins. Co., 877 So. 2d 1 (Fla. Dist. Ct. App. 3rd Dist. 2004); Doyle v. Dep't of Bus. Regulation, 794 So. 2d 686 (Fla. Dist. Ct. App. 1st Dist. 2001).

[4] Creative Choice XXV, Ltd. v. Florida Hous. Fin. Corp., 991 So. 2d 899 (Fla. Dist. Ct. App. 1st Dist. 2008).

[5] GTC, Inc. v. Edgar, 967 So. 2d 781 (Fla. 2007); Carter v. Health Mgmt. Assoc., 989 So. 2d 1258 (Fla. Dist. Ct. App. 2d Dist. 2008); Level 3 Commc'ns, LLC v. Jacobs, 841 So. 2d 447 (Fla. 2003). Cheveron v. Natural Res. Def. Council, 467 U.S. 837, 842-844 (1984) articulates the Federal rule in a similar fashion.

[6] See, e.g. Health Options, Inc. v. Agency for Health Care Admin., 889 So. 2d 849 (Fla. Dist. Ct. App. 1st Dist. 2004), review denied, 903 So. 2d 189 (Fla. 2005); Arza v. Florida Elections Comm'n, 907 So. 2d 604 (Fla. Dist. Ct. App. 3d Dist. 2005).

agency has received political directives from the executive branch with regards to its interpretation/enforcement of legislation (in other words, if the interpretation is shaded by politics rather than technical expertise)? Are some agencies, by their nature, or due to external influence (e.g. funding, staffing, etc.) more or less likely to render broad or liberal interpretations, or narrow and restrict interpretations? E.g. would one expect a Human Rights Commission to give a narrow or restrictive interpretation of the rights it is expected to protect? Might strict or narrow interpretations lighten some agencies workloads? Should a change in interpretation following budget cuts be treated with skepticism or deference?

DONATO V. AM. TEL. & TEL. CO.

767 So.2d 1146 (Fla. 2000)

ANSTEAD, J.

We have for review a question of Florida law certified by the Eleventh Circuit Court of Appeals that is determinative of a cause pending in that court and for which there appears to be no controlling precedent:

> CAN AN INDIVIDUAL PROCEED UNDER THE FLORIDA CIVIL RIGHTS ACT BY ALLEGING THAT HE WAS DISCHARGED, IN VIOLATION OF THE PROHIBITION ON MARITAL STATUS DISCRIMINATION, BECAUSE HE IS MARRIED TO AN INDIVIDUAL WHO FILED SUIT AGAINST HIS EMPLOYER?

We have jurisdiction. Art. V, § 3(b)(6), Fla. Const. We answer the certified question in the negative and hold that the Florida Civil Rights Act does not recognize a cause of action for marital status discrimination where the discrimination is allegedly based on the actions of the claimant's spouse, rather than on the marital status of the claimant.

MATERIAL FACTS

The facts in this case are taken from the circuit court's opinion in Donato v. American Telephone & Telegraph Co., 146 F.3d 1329 (11th Cir.1998):

> This case is brought by Rosario Donato, alleging that he was the victim of marital status discrimination when AT & T terminated his employment shortly after Mr. Donato's wife, a former AT & T employee, sued AT & T. Mr. Donato filed his complaint in 1996 under the Florida Civil Rights Act, which, inter alia, protects employees from discrimination based on marital status.
>
> In March 1992, Mrs. Lynda Donato filed a claim against AT & T. On October 21, 1993, the Florida Commission on Human Relations concluded that there was reasonable cause to support Mrs. Donato's initial allegations of sex discrimination and retaliation by AT & T. She was discharged from her position with AT & T in February 1994, and filed a federal action in August 1994, alleging sex discrimination and retaliatory discharge. In October 1994, Mrs. Donato applied for a temporary clerical position in the division of AT & T which employed her

husband. During a meeting with manager Al Facini, she disclosed her lawsuit against AT & T and was told that she was "over-qualified" for the open position.

In November 1994, Mr. Donato was informed that his position as a Systems Analyst was placed "at risk", allegedly due to Mr. Donato's poor performance. He also was told by his supervisor, Frank Minardi, that his position was being eliminated (although Mr. Donato alleges that another employee subsequently was assigned to perform all of his duties). On November 15, 1994, just two days before his thirtieth-year anniversary with AT & T, Mr. Donato was discharged.

Mr. Donato filed a charge of discrimination on July 17, 1995, which the EEOC did not timely resolve. He then filed a single-count complaint in state court on July 3, 1996, seeking reinstatement, compensation, and punitive damages up to $100,000. AT & T removed the case to federal court on the basis of diversity and then moved to dismiss the case, arguing that the Act only protects marriage status in general and does not prohibit discrimination against a person because he or she is married to a particular person, e.g., a foreign citizen, a disabled person, or a troublemaker. The District Court granted AT & T's motion in a brief order issued February 21, 1997, and upon Mr. Donato's failure to amend his complaint, the case was dismissed with prejudice on March 11, 1997.

Id. at 1330. Petitioner appealed to the Eleventh Circuit Court of Appeals, which, after hearing oral argument, certified the above question to this Court. Id. at 1332. In doing so, the circuit court noted that this Court has not yet addressed whether a discharged employee can assert a claim based on marital status discrimination under section 760.10 of the Florida Statutes "where the employee allegedly was discharged in retaliation for actions of his spouse." Id. at 1330.

LEGAL ANALYSIS

Donato argues that the term "marital status" should be broadly defined, as it has been by the Florida Commission on Human Relations[1], to include the identity and actions of one's spouse as well as whether one is married, single, divorced, separated or widowed. AT & T, on the other hand, argues that the term "marital status" must be construed in accordance with its common and ordinary meaning and may not be extended to encompass situations not intended by the legislature. Under its plain and ordinary meaning, AT & T contends, "marital status" means simply an individual's legal status with respect to marriage-i.e., married, single, widowed, divorced, or separated.

---

[1] The commission on Human Relations was created in part to "promote and encourage fair treatment and equal opportunity for all persons regardless of race, color, religion, sex, national origin, age, handicap, or marital status." § 760.05, Fla. Stat. (1997). Any person alleging discriminatory practices may file a complaint with the Commission. *See id.* § 760.11(1). If the Commission finds reasonable grounds to believe that a discriminatory act has occurred, the aggrieved party may file suit in circuit court or request an administrative hearing, the Commission may hear the case or request that the case be heard by an administrative law judge. *See id.* § 760.11(6).

During the 1970s, many states amended their anti-discrimination statutes by adding the term "marital status" to the list of protected classes. See John C. Beattie, Prohibiting Marital Status Discrimination: A Proposal for the Protection of Unmarried Couples, 42 Hastings L.J. 1415, 1417 (1991). In 1977, the Florida Legislature expanded its Civil Rights Act ("Act") (formerly known as the Florida Human Relations Act) to include age, handicap, and marital status among the list of proscribed forms of discrimination. See ch. 77-34a, § 1, Laws of Florida. Importantly, this legislation provided greater protection to Florida citizens than is provided under the federal Civil Rights Act, which, for example, does not include protection for marital status.

The general purpose of Florida's Act is to "secure for all individuals within the state freedom from discrimination" and "to protect their interest in personal dignity, to make available to the state their full productive capacities, to secure the state against the domestic strife and unrest, to preserve the public safety, health and general welfare, and to promote the interests, rights and privileges of individual's within the state." Ch. 77-341, § 1, at 1462 (codified at § 13.201, Fla. Stat. (1977)) (current version at § 760.01(2), Fla. Stat. (1997) (Civil Rights Act of 1992)). The Legislature has further noted that the act is to be construed in accord with the fair import of its terms and shall be liberally construed to further the general purposes stated therein. See § 760.01(3). Within the same piece of legislation, the Legislature created a provision enumerating unlawful employment practices. See ch. 77-341, § 6 (codified at § 13.261, Fla. Stat. (1977)). That provision is now codified at section 760.10, Florida Statutes (1997), and states in pertinent part:

> (1) It is an unlawful employment practice for an employer:
>
> (a) To discharge or to fail or refuse to hire any individual, or otherwise to discriminate against any individual with respect to compensation, terms, conditions, or privileges of employment, because of such individual's race, color, religion, sex, national origin, age, handicap, or marital status.

§ 760.10(1)(a), Fla. Stat. (1997). Unfortunately, the Civil Rights Act fails to define the term "marital status".

Indeed, our research reflects that most of the jurisdictions which have included "marital status" within their antidiscrimination statutes have failed to provide any definition of the term. However, most of the states that define the term do so narrowly. See, e.g., D.C.Code Ann. § 1-2502(17) (1981) ("the state of being married, single, divorced, separated, or widowed and the usual conditions associated therewith, including pregnancy or parenthood"); 775 Ill. Comp. Stat. Ann. 5/1-103(J) (West Supp.1999) ("the legal status of being married, single, separated, divorced or widowed"); Md. Ann.Code art. 49B, § 20 (Supp.1999) ("the state of being single, married, separated, divorced, or widowed" in context of housing discrimination only); Wash. Rev.Code. § 49.60.040(7) (1998) ("the legal status of being married, single, separated, divorced, or widowed"); Wis. Stat. Ann. § 111.32(12) (West Supp.1998) ("the status of being married, single, divorced, separated or widowed"); but see, e.g.,

Minn.Stat. Ann. § 363.01 subd. 24 (West Supp.2000) ("whether a person is single, married, remarried, divorced, separated, or a surviving spouse and, in employment cases, includes protection against discrimination on the basis of the identity, situation, actions, or beliefs of a spouse or former spouse").

We also note that there is little to no documented legislative history on the subject in Florida or elsewhere. As one commentator notes:

> Significantly, however, not one marital status discrimination case has cited the legislative history and debate surrounding the addition of the term "marital status" to existing antidiscrimination statutes. In fact, such documented history appears to be largely unavailable. Thus, the court's only guide in discerning the legislative purpose behind the prohibition of marital status discrimination is the language of the statute itself.

Beattie, supra, at 1428. We are also hindered by the lack of judicial treatment of the term "marital status" in Florida. Only one district court has analyzed a claim based on marital status discrimination, and it did not decide the issue. In National Industries, Inc. v. Commission on Human Relations, 527 So.2d 894 (Fla. 5th DCA 1988), Sharon Morand filed a complaint with the Commission based on marital status discrimination after she was fired by her employer, National Industries, because of actions by her spouse, Robert Morand, a former employee of the same employer. The Commission found that Sharon had stated a cause of action for marital status discrimination. In doing so, it relied on its decision in Owens v. Upper Pinellas Association for Retarded Citizens, 8 F.A.L.R. 438 (Fla. Comm'n. on Human Relations 1985), which broadly interpreted the term "marital status" to include the identity of the individual's spouse. The Fifth District, however, reversed the ruling, holding that the Commission's interpretation of section 760.10 was erroneous. National Industries, 527 So.2d at 897. The district court noted that Owens involved a dispute over an antinepotism policy, which was distinguishable from the situation involving Sharon Morand, who was fired not because of her marital status, but because the employer wanted to keep her husband off the premises. Id. In a footnote, but without deciding the issue, the district court recognized the Commission's adherence to a broad definition of the term "marital status," but noted that even under a broad definition of the term, the case did not fall within the scope of "marital status" discrimination. See National Industries, Inc., 527 So.2d at 897 n. 1 (relying on Cybyske v. Independent School District No. 196, 347 N.W.2d 256 (Minn.1984) (holding that identity of spouse is factor to consider but dismissing cause of action based on marital status discrimination where institution of marriage not directly affected by employer's action)). Consequently, the district court did not determine in National Industries whether the term "marital status" includes the identity of one's spouse or merely the state of being married or unmarried.

In essence, then, we are left with the task of interpreting the Legislature's intent based solely on the words utilized in the statute without any instruction or indication from the Legislature as to whether "marital status" refers only to the status of being married, single, divorced, etc., or whether the term includes a much broader scope by including the identity of one's spouse as advocated by Donato.

Absent an explicit statutory definition or helpful legislative history, we must rely on other means to resolve the issue before us. We begin our analysis with the fundamental premise that legislative intent is the polestar that guides us in our inquiry. See McLaughlin v. State, 721 So.2d 1170, 1172 (Fla.1998). In turn, of course, the primary source for determining legislative intent is the language chosen by the Legislature to express its intent. As we stated in Holly v. Auld, 450 So.2d 217 (Fla.1984),

> [w]hen the language of the statute is clear and unambiguous and conveys a clear and definite meaning, there is no occasion for resorting to the rules of statutory interpretation and construction; the statute must be given its plain and obvious meaning.

Id. at 219 (quoting A.R. Douglass, Inc. v. McRainey, 102 Fla. 1141, 1144, 137 So. 157, 159 (1931)). More importantly, we are precluded from construing

> an unambiguous statute in a way which would extend, modify, or limit, its express terms or its reasonable and obvious implications. To do so would be an abrogation of legislative power.

Id. (quoting American Bankers Life Assurance Co. v. Williams, 212 So.2d 777, 778 (Fla. 1st DCA 1968)).

In the majority of states that have construed the term "marital status," most have done so in the context of an antinepotism or no-spouse employment rule. In declaring such employment policies discriminatory, several states have construed the term "marital status" broadly to include the identity of one's spouse in addition to whether one is simply married or unmarried. The Minnesota Supreme Court in Kraft, Inc. v. State, 284 N.W.2d 386 (Minn.1979), explained its reasoning:

> We reject the view that "marital status", while it denotes the fact that one is or is not married, does not embrace the identity or situation of one's spouse. Since respondent does employ married, single and divorced individuals, to hold otherwise would condone discrimination against a portion of a protected class, i.e., job applicants already married to full-time Kraft employees. To do so would ignore the broad prohibition against arbitrary classifications embodied in the Human Rights Act and would elevate form over substance.

Id. at 388 (citations omitted); see also Ross v. Stouffer Hotel Co., 76 Hawai'i 454, 879 P.2d 1037 (1994); Thompson v. Board of Trustees, 192 Mont. 266, 627 P.2d 1229 (1981); Washington Water Power Co. v. Washington State Human Rights Comm'n, 91 Wash.2d 62, 586 P.2d 1149 (1978).

In contrast, a number of states have interpreted the term "marital status" narrowly by limiting it to the state of being married, single, divorced, widowed or separated. Indeed, the New York Court of Appeals in Manhattan Pizza Hut, Inc. v. New York State Human Rights Appeal Board, 51 N.Y.2d 506, 434 N.Y.S.2d 961, 415 N.E.2d 950 (1980), after noting the fundamental rule that words of common usage should be given their ordinary meaning, stated its view that:

> [T]he plain and ordinary meaning of "marital status" is the social condition enjoyed by an individual by reason of his or her having participated or failed to participate in a marriage. Illuminated another way, when one is queried about one's "marital status", the usual and complete answer would be expected to be a choice among "married", "single", etc., but would not be expected to include an identification of one's present former spouse and certainly not the spouse's occupation.

Id. at 953; see also Muller v. BP Exploration, Inc., 923 P.2d 783, 788 (Alaska 1996) (defining marital status as "condition of being married or unmarried"); Blackwell v. Danbury Hosp., No. 321561, 1996 WL 409370 (Conn.Super.Ct. June 26, 1996) (holding that legislative history clearly contemplates that "marital status" only refers to condition of being single, married, separated, divorced, or widowed); Boaden v. Department of Law Enforcement, 171 Ill.2d 230, 215 Ill.Dec. 664, 664 N.E.2d 61, 65 (1996) (defining "marital status" narrowly based on statutory definition-"the legal status of being married, single, separated, divorced, or widowed"); Whirlpool Corp. v. Civil Rights Comm'n, 425 Mich. 527, 390 N.W.2d 625 (1986) (defining marital status as state of being married or unmarried); Miller v. C.A. Muer Corp., 420 Mich. 355, 362 N.W.2d 650, 653 (1984) (holding that the relevant inquiry is "if one is married rather than to whom one is married"); Townshend v. Board of Education, 183 W.Va. 418, 396 S.E.2d 185 (1990) (defining marital status as state of being married or single).

The same narrow construction of the term "marital status" as applied by the New York Court of Appeals appears to have been applied in cases not involving antinepotism policies, but centered on the actions of an individual's spouse. See, e.g., Coyle v. Health Care & Retirement Corp., No. 1:93-CV-664, 1994 WL 928880 (W.D.Mich. June 1, 1994) (holding no marital status discrimination where plaintiff was discharged because supervisor disliked plaintiff's fiancé); Cybyske v. Independent Sch. Dist. No. 196, 347 N.W.2d 256 (Minn.1984) (holding no marital status discrimination where plaintiff discharged because of husband's educational views); State Div. of Human Rights v. Village of Spencerport, 78 A.D.2d 50, 434 N.Y.S.2d 52 (N.Y.App.Div.1980) (holding no marital status discrimination where plaintiff-wife discharged because of husband's position as local property tax assessor).

Donato, however, argues that the term "marital status" is ambiguous when that term is considered in conjunction with other provisions within section 760.10. He maintains that the term "marital status" is sufficiently broad on its face to include "the status of marriage or non-marriage in general" as well as "the status of marriage or non-marriage to a particular individual." Appellant's Initial Brief at 13. The ambiguity arises, he claims, when this definition is read in conjunction with the subsection within section 760.10 which exempts actions based on an antinepotism policy. See § 760.10(8)(d) (stating that it shall not be "an unlawful employment practice ... for an employer ... to ... (d) [t]ake or fail to take any action on the basis of marital status if that status is prohibited under its antinepotism policy"). The argument follows, therefore, that because the nature of an antinepotism policy necessarily considers the marital relationship of two employees, the statutory exclusion for such policies would be unnecessary if the term "marital status" only encompassed the state of being married or unmarried in general. Contrary to Donato's assertion, we do not believe that the legislative enactment of the antinepotism exclusion renders the term "marital status" ambiguous.

In 1992, the Legislature amended section 760.10 by adding several exceptions to the types of unlawful employment practices. The amended version of the statute provides in pertinent part:

> (8) Notwithstanding any other provision of this section, it is not an unlawful employment practice ... for an employer ... to:
>
> . . .
>
> (d) Take or fail to take any action on the basis of marital status if that status is prohibited under its anti-nepotism policy.

§ 760.10(8)(d), Fla. Stat. (1993). Clearly, this section was intended to protect employers who utilize such policies from any liability for terminating or refusing to hire a person because that person is married to another employee. There is nothing within the language of the amended statute itself or the legislative history of the amendment that suggests the Legislature intended to include the *identity* or *actions* of an individual's spouse within the meaning of "marital status."

Moreover, by excluding antinepotism policies from actionable unlawful employment practices, we believe the Legislature intended to limit the scope of the term "marital status" instead of broaden it. In other words, so long as the employer acts in accordance with an antinepotism policy and does not terminate an individual based solely on whether that person is married or unmarried, the employer is not liable for "marital status" discrimination. See Beattie, Prohibiting Marital Status Discrimination: A Proposal for the Protection of Unmarried Couples, supra, at 1422. Beattie notes that:

> The "narrow view" approach emphasizes that discrimination occurs only when marital status is the sole basis for the adverse employment decision. In the context of the antinepotism policy, it is clear that marital status is not the sole reason for the decision because, if it were, every married person would be affected. Instead, an antinepotism policy only disadvantages a subclass of married applicants: those who have spouses already working for the employer. Implicit in this "narrow view" approach, therefore, is the notion that if the challenged policy does not disadvantage all married people, none may invoke the state prohibition against marital status discrimination to challenge it.

Id. Thus, by legislatively upholding antinepotism policies, the Legislature apparently intended to narrow the scope of "marital status" by limiting actions filed on that basis to situations in which an employer discriminates solely on an individual's status relating to marriage.

We likewise reject Donato's contention that we must strictly defer to the Florida Commission on Human Relations' interpretation of the statute. The Commission is the administrative body created by the Legislature to administer the Florida Civil Rights Act. See § 760.03, .05, Fla. Stat. (1997); see supra note 1. As part of its duties, the Commission is permitted by the Legislature to hold hearings and render decisions on claims alleging discrimination. In administering this quasi-judicial function, the Commission has given meaning to the term "marital status" by defining it broadly

> to include one's relationship to one's spouse, rather than narrowly to include only the fact that one is married, single, divorced, or widowed.

Owens v. Upper Pinellas Ass'n for Retarded Citizens, 8 F.A.L.R. 438 (Fla. Comm'n on Human Relations 1985);[3] accord Smith v. Food Lion, Inc., 17 F.A.L.R. 3040 (Fla. Comm'n on Human Relations 1994); Brown v. Viking Fire Protection, Inc., 15 F.A.L.R. 1625 (Fla. Comm'n on Human Relations 1992).

We recognize the general rule that the interpretation of a statute by the administrative agency or body "charged with its enforcement is entitled to great deference and should not be overturned unless clearly erroneous or in conflict with the legislative intent of the statute." See Mayo Clinic Jacksonville v. Department of Prof'l Regulation, 625 So.2d 918, 919 (Fla. 1st DCA 1993) (citing PW Ventures, Inc. v. Nichols, 533 So.2d 281 (Fla.1988)). However, because we conclude that the term "marital status" is not ambiguous, either by itself or in conjunction with the other provisions within the Civil Rights Act, we are less constrained to accept the Commission's interpretation of the statute.

> Administrative construction of a statute, the legislative history of its enactment and other extraneous matters are properly considered only in the construction of a statute of doubtful meaning.

Florida State Racing Comm'n v. McLaughlin, 102 So.2d 574, 576-77 (Fla.1958) (emphasis added); see also Mayo Clinic Jacksonville, 625 So.2d at 919. Indeed, the

---

[3] In Owens, the petitioner was terminated from his position with the Upper Pinellas Association for Retarded Citizens (UPARC), following his marriage to another UPARC employee. Apparently, UPARC had an antinepotism policy which precluded related persons from working together. Owens then filed a petition with the Commission alleging that UPARC unlawfully discharged him based on his marital status. The Commission ruled that the term "marital status" must be construed broadly "to include one's relationship to one's spouse, rather than narrowly to include only the fact that one is married, single, divorced, or widowed." Id. at 440-41 (relying on Kraft, Inc. v. Minnesota, 284 N.W.2d 386 (Minn.1979) (holding that anti-nepotism policy discriminates on basis of marital status, the definition of which includes identity or situation of one's spouse)). It further concluded that absent legislative intent to the contrary, a broad interpretation was consistent with the Legislature's overall purpose in enacting the Civil Rights Act and with the Legislature's stated intent to construe such provisions liberally. Accordingly, it concluded that UPARC violated section 760.10(1)(a) by discharging Owens on the basis of his marital status. Id. at 445. It appears, however, that in enacting the antinepotism exclusion to the list of proscribed employment practices under Florida's Civil Rights Act, the Legislature may well have intended to reverse the Commission's ruling in Owens. See Fla. S. Comm. on Com., S.B. 18H (1992) Staff Analysis 1 (May 27, 1992) (on file with comm.) ("The effect of the amendment would be to reverse the Commission's ruling.")

Legislature itself appears to have rejected the Commission's reasoning in Owens. Thus, we reject the Commission's construction and rely instead on the plain meaning of the words used by the Legislature.

Statutory Exclusions

Finally, Donato contends that the addition of an antinepotism exclusion suggests that the Legislature intended to exclude from the list of discriminatory practices only those cases in which a person is discharged based on the existence of antinepotism policy and not cases in which a person is terminated in retaliation for actions by that person's spouse, as is the case herein. Thus, he argues that the Legislature should be presumed to have included other forms of marital status discrimination, such as termination due to the identity or actions of an individual's spouse, as an unlawful employment practice. We disagree with Donato's contention for reasons similar to those stated above.

The basis of Donato's argument presumes that the Legislature intended to define the term "marital status" broadly. However, without more explicit guidance from the Legislature, we are unable to presume or otherwise conclude that the Legislature intended to include within the scope of the term "marital status" such factors as the identity or actions of one's spouse. As we explained above, the anti-nepotism exclusion listed in section 760.10 merely suggests that the Legislature intended to limit the types of claims for which an employer may be held liable. There is simply no indication or language within the text of the act to suggest that the Legislature intended to exclude employers from liability if the allegedly discriminatory practice is based on an antinepotism policy, but hold employers liable for terminating or refusing to hire an individual on the basis of the identity or actions of an individual's spouse. Under the plain meaning of the statute in this case, "marital status" discrimination arises only when one either is terminated or not hired on the sole basis of that person's status with respect to marriage, which in this case means married, single, divorced, widowed, or separated. To construe the term "marital status" broadly to include the identity or actions of an individual's spouse would expand its meaning beyond that in which it is commonly and ordinarily used.

Plain Meaning

We agree with both the reasoning and logic of those judicial opinions applying a narrow construction of the term "marital status," and, in the absence of legislative intent to the contrary, we conclude that the meaning of the phrase "marital status" without more is limited to one's status as married or not married. As noted, we have consistently held that words or phrases in a statute must be construed in accordance with their common and ordinary meaning. In applying that rule to the phrase "marital status" we agree with the observations of the New York Court of Appeals quoted above from Manhattan Pizza Hut. Typically, for example, we believe that when one is asked for his or her marital status, the answer usually sought is whether that person is married, single, divorced, widowed, or separated. See, e.g., Fla. R. Civ. P. Form 1.984 (Juror Voir Dire Questionnaire) ("5. Marital Status: (married, single, divorced, widow, or widower) ________"). Thus, under the common usage of the term, marital status refers only to the state of being married or not married. If we were to give the term a broader definition by requiring courts to consider the specific person to whom someone is married, we would be expanding the term beyond its common, ordinary use and would give meaning to the term that was not intended by the Legislature. This would be an abrogation of legislative power. Holly.

We also note the difficulty courts have had in applying a broader definition. The court in Village of Spencerport, for example, held that a plaintiff who worked for the mayor of the Village had not stated a claim for marital status discrimination, even though she had been fired because of the actions of her husband:

> The complainant's status must be the cause of the unlawful act, either because of the condition of marriage, singleness or whatever, or because the party charged is motivated by some proscribed bias toward the spouse.
>
> Neither of these considerations motivated the Village. Complainant was not discharged because of her marital status or because of the race, creed or other prohibited consideration related to her husband. She was discharged because of her husband's actions as assessor. *Her discharge was not based upon marital status because discharge was just as certain whether the assessor was her husband, or her brother, father or some other relative.* ... [S]ince the statute does not expressly or by necessary implication grant [the Division of Human Rights] jurisdiction to sanction the Village for discharging complainant as an act of political retaliation against her husband, the petition must be dismissed.

434 N.Y.S.2d at 55 (citations omitted) (footnote omitted) (emphasis supplied); see also National Industries. Had the Legislature intended to include the identity of an individual's spouse or bias against a spouse within the meaning of marital status for the purpose of expanding the scope of discriminatory practices, it certainly could have done so, and, of course, is free to do so after this decision.

CONCLUSION

Accordingly, we hold that the term "marital status" as used in section 760.10 of the Florida Statutes means the state of being married, single, divorced, widowed or separated, and does not include the specific identity or actions of an individual's spouse. We answer the certified question in the negative, holding that Florida does not recognize a cause of action for "marital status" discrimination where the basis of the claim rests on the allegedly unlawful discharge of an employee for actions by the employee's spouse. Having answered the certified question, we return this case to the United States Court of Appeals for the Eleventh Circuit for further proceedings.

It is so ordered.

HARDING, C.J., and SHAW, WELLS and LEWIS, JJ., concur.

PARIENTE, J., dissents with an opinion, in which QUINCE, J., concurs.

PARIENTE, J. dissenting.

I respectfully dissent. The majority correctly observes that the term "marital status" is not defined by statute. Then, after conceding that there could be a "broad" or "narrow" view of the term marital status and reviewing principles of statutory construction, the majority opinion gives the term a "narrow" meaning, which it asserts is unambiguous. I find the majority's analysis strained and inconsistent with principles of statutory construction.

In 1977, the Florida Legislature expanded its Civil Rights Act to prohibit discrimination in employment based on marital status. See ch. 77-341, § 1, Laws of Fla. The purpose of the Civil Rights Act is remedial. See Green v. Burger King Corp., 728 So.2d 369 (Fla. 3d DCA 1999). Remedial statutes should be liberally construed in favor of granting access to the remedy provided by the Legislature. See, e.g., Arrow Air, Inc. v. Walsh, 645 So.2d 422, 424 (Fla.1994); Martin County v. Edenfield, 609 So.2d 27, 29 (Fla.1992). Further, the express terms of the Act provide that it "shall be liberally construed to further the general purposes stated in this section and the special purposes of the particular provision involved." § 760.01(3), Fla. Stat. (1999).

I also disagree with the majority's failure to give deference to the interpretation of this undefined statutory term given by the administrative agency charged with administering the Civil Rights Act. The majority acknowledges the general and important rule of statutory construction that an agency's interpretation of a statute is entitled to great deference and should not be overturned unless clearly erroneous or it is in conflict with the legislative intent of the statute. See BellSouth Telecommunications, Inc. v. Johnson, 708 So.2d 594, 596 (Fla.1998). The majority further acknowledges that the Commission on Human Relations is the administrative body created by the Legislature to administer the Florida Civil Rights Act.

The majority also acknowledges that since at least 1985, the Commission has recognized that the term "marital status" must be construed broadly, and has interpreted it "to include one's relationship to one's spouse, rather than narrowly to include only the fact that one is married, single, divorced or widowed." Owens v. Upper Pinellas Ass'n for Retarded Citizens, 8 F.A.L.R. 438, 440-41 (Fla. Comm'n on Human Relations 1985); see Smith v. Food Lion, Inc., 17 F.A.L.R. 3040 (Fla. Comm'n on Human Relations 1994). However, the majority discards the principle of construction that would accord great deference to the Commission's interpretation by asserting that the principle only applies in cases of "doubtful meaning." Florida State Racing Comm's v. McLaughlin, 102 So.2d 574, 576 (Fla.1958). I disagree.

Finally, I disagree with the majority's failure to read the provisions of this statute together to ascertain the legislative intent. "It is axiomatic that all parts of a statute must be read together to achieve a consistent whole." Forsythe v. Longboat Key Beach Erosion Control Dist., 604 So.2d 452, 455 (Fla.1992). Further, "statutory phrases are not to be read in isolation, but rather within the context of the entire section." Acosta v. Richter, 671 So.2d 149, 154 (Fla.1996). When the Legislature amended section 760.10, it excepted employers with antinepotism policies from the prohibition against discriminating on the basis of marital status. In creating this exception, the Legislature apparently recognized that while an antinepotism policy is potentially discriminatory, it could advance legitimate business interests.

However, the wording of that exception is important. It states:

> (8) Notwithstanding any other provision of this section, it is not an unlawful employment practice ... to:
>
> (d) Take or fail to take any action on the basis of marital status if that status is prohibited under [the employer's] antinepotism policy.

§ 760.10(8)(d). Contrary to the majority's view, in my opinion, by excluding anti-nepotism policies from "marital status" claims, the Legislature clearly indicated its intent to embrace the broad meaning of marital status adopted by the Commission on Human Relations.

For these reasons, I dissent from the majority opinion.. . .

QUINCE, J., concurs.

NOTES AND QUESTIONS

1. If discrimination based on marital status, in general, is inappropriate, then why does the Court think that discrimination based on marital status, in the particular, is appropriate? Put another way, if one's marital status (single, married, divorced) is off limits, then why is it not off limits to consider who one is married to? When a form asks a question about your marital status, it often will only have the three boxes to check: married, single, or divorced. However, when the normal, or average, person asks you about your marital status, are they generally satisfied with the one word response? Or, do they want to know more about who you are married to, or divorced from, or who you are seeing now (and perhaps whether or not you are happy with your current situation)? In the employment context, are these further questions about your marital status more or less appropriate than the tick the box question?

2. If the meaning of the term is clear, then why has Minnesota and the Florida Human Rights Commission misinterpreted it (is it 80% clear and 20% ambiguous)? Are they simply imposing their own policy? Did the Minnesota Supreme Court sound like it was twisting the meaning of the term in Kraft v. State? Was the Human Rights Commission wrong to think that the broad reading was the reading most consistent with the legislators' purpose in enacting the Civil Rights Act?

3. In footnote 3, the Court implies that the inclusion of the anti-nepotism exception may have been intended as a way of overturning the decision of the Human Rights Commission. Is Donato not correct, however, that there can be no exception without the rule? In other words, there would be no need for an

anti-nepotism exception if there was not a rule prohibiting discrimination on the basis of who one is married to. If the rule was truly the narrow rule of only prohibiting discrimination based on whether one is married, divorced or single, then anti-nepotism policies would not violate the rule.

4. If between strict (narrow) interpretation and liberal (broad) interpretation, the legislature itself directed the courts, in the legislation, to give a liberal interpretation, then why is the Court choosing the strict (narrow) interpretation?

5. Do you agree with the majority that the language is so clear that it should not give any deference to the Human Rights Committee? Is its interpretation clearly erroneous or in conflict with the legislative intent?

CAGLE V. ST. JOHNS COUNTY SCH. DIST.

939 So.2d 1085 (Fla. Dist. Ct. App. 5th Dist. 2006)

ORGINGER, J.

Andrea J.B. Cagle timely appeals an order of the Public Employees Relations Commission ("PERC") dismissing her amended unfair labor practices charge against the St. John's County School District ("School District"). On appeal, Ms. Cagle argues that PERC erred by summarily dismissing her unfair labor practices charge and not providing her with an evidentiary hearing on these charges. For the reasons explained hereafter, we affirm.

Ms. Cagle is the wife of a disabled veteran who qualifies for a veterans' preference in hiring pursuant to section 295.07(1)(b), Florida Statutes (2004).[1] After the School District did not hire Ms. Cagle for employment in 2001, she filed an administrative complaint with PERC against the School District based on her veterans' preference. During the hearing, a no trespass order was issued against Ms. Cagle's husband for threatening the well-being of those at the hearing.

Notwithstanding, Ms. Cagle prevailed at the hearing. The School District appealed the decision, but, ultimately, the parties entered into a settlement agreement. As a result of the settlement agreement, Ms. Cagle signed a one-year contract with the School District and was employed at R.B. Hunt Elementary School for the 2003-2004 school year as a fourth grade teacher.

---

[1] In relevant part, section 295.07(1)(b), Florida Statutes (2004), provides:

> (1) The state and political subdivisions in the state shall give preference in appointment and retention in positions of employment to:
>
> . . .
>
> (b) The spouse of any person who has a total disability, permanent in nature, resulting from a service-connected disability and who, because of this disability, cannot quality for employment...

Ms. Cagle entered into service at R.B. Hunt Elementary as agreed upon. In the fall of 2003, the vice-principal of R.B. Hunt assessed Ms. Cagle's skills in the classroom, giving Ms. Cagle overall good marks, with several suggestions for improvement. However, in March 2004, Principal Barbara Stevens conducted an unannounced observation of Ms. Cagle's classroom, or classroom "snap shot," which was not favorable to her.

In response to the unflattering evaluation, Ms. Cagle provided Principal Stevens with a 146-page packet of documents. The packet included a copy of the transcript from the 2002 hearing at which Ms. Cagle testified regarding her veterans' preference. Shortly thereafter, Principal Stevens sent a copy of the documents to James Springfield, the Executive Director of Human Resources at the School District. She explained to Mr. Springfield via e-mail that she needed his "input and support in this recommendation issue" because if she does not recommend Ms. Cagle for re-appointment for the following school year, "it will bring litigation."

In late April 2004, Principal Stevens met with Ms. Cagle for her year-end evaluation. At the meeting, Principal Stevens told Ms. Cagle that she was recommending that Ms. Cagle not be rehired. Ms. Cagle left the meeting without signing her evaluation. The following day, Ms. Cagle called in sick. Later that day, Ms. Cagle's grandson entered her classroom under the guise of giving a chorus announcement, but, instead, informed the class that Principal Stevens was trying to fire his grandmother and the students should tell their parents. After Ms. Cagle refused to answer six investigative questions asked by the School District, she was placed on administrative leave until the end of her contract term. Ms. Cagle's annual contract expired May 25, 2005, and she was not rehired for the following school year.

Ms. Cagle then filed a pre-hearing statement with PERC in a new veterans' preference case. In the statement, Ms. Cagle alleged, among other things, that the School District had retaliated against her, in violation of section 447.501(1)(d), Florida Statutes (2004), by discharging or otherwise discriminating against her through a series of unfair labor practices, including an unlawful suspension and violations of personnel laws. PERC transferred and docketed Ms. Cagle's retaliation claim as an unfair labor practice charge.

Ms. Cagle subsequently filed a separate unfair labor practice charge against the School District. In addition to alleging violations of section 447.501(1)(d), Ms. Cagle also alleged that the School District violated section 447.501(1)(a), which prohibits an employer from interfering with, restraining, or coercing a public employee in the exercise of any rights guaranteed by chapter 447 of the Florida Statutes. Ms. Cagle's charges were consolidated to determine whether the allegations established a prima facie violation of the unfair labor practice laws.

In Ms. Cagle's consolidated charges, she alleged that the School District discriminated against her due to her status as the wife of a disabled veteran and because she had previously filed a veterans' preference case against the School

District in 2001. Specifically, Ms. Cagle asserted that the School District acted adversely to her in the following ways: issued a no trespass order against her husband in 2002 at the previous veterans' preference hearing, did not comply with PERC's 2002 final order or the subsequent settlement agreement between the parties, treated Ms. Cagle disparately during the 2003-2004 school year, charged Ms. Cagle with "unprofessionalism" and sent untruthful letters to the parents of the students in her class, suspended Ms. Cagle and placed her on administrative leave, discharged Ms. Cagle from her teaching position under the guise of a "non-renewal of an annual contract," and subjected her to a hate crime.[2]

PERC's General Counsel summarily dismissed both unfair labor practice cases, finding that they failed to provide facts that demonstrated that Ms. Cagle's prior veterans' preference complaint and testimony were substantial or motivating factors in the alleged retaliation by the School District. However, the General Counsel noted that that if Ms. Cagle felt that the School District had not complied with the settlement agreement, she should seek enforcement of that settlement agreement in the circuit court.

Ms. Cagle appealed to PERC, amending her charge and alleging eleven incidents that constituted violations of section 447.501(1)(d). Because the appeal alleged additional facts and included supporting documents that were not previously considered, the appeal was remanded as an amended charge for the General Counsel to determine the sufficiency of Ms. Cagle's allegations. On remand, PERC's General Counsel determined that Ms. Cagle's amended charge failed to establish a prima facie violation of the unfair labor practice laws and summarily dismissed it. According to the General Counsel, some of the allegations were untimely and others did not constitute adverse actions because there were no tangible punitive impacts as a result of their occurrence. Additionally, the General Counsel found that there were facially valid reasons for the School District to take certain actions against Ms. Cagle but not against other employees, and that there was no objective evidence linking Ms. Cagle's protected activity to the School District's actions.

Ms. Cagle again appealed to PERC, alleging ten "exceptions" to the General Counsel's summary dismissal of the amended charge, which she claimed were sufficient to establish a prima facie violation of section 447.501(1)(d). Ms. Cagle objected to the conclusions of the General Counsel, and also included new factual allegations and supporting documents that had not previously been provided to the General Counsel.

PERC subsequently issued a final order, affirming the General Counsel's summary dismissal of the amended charge. In its final order, PERC incorporated the additional evidence that Ms. Cagle provided in her exceptions, and found that this new allegation would have been dismissed by the General Counsel as untimely. Thereafter, incorporating the new allegation, PERC considered all of Ms. Cagle's

---

[2] The alleged hate crime was requiring Ms. Cagle to attend a ceremony honoring a teacher from her school as teacher of the year. Ms. Cagle asserts this was a "hate crime" because the teacher of the year had been hired instead of Ms. Cagle in 2001.

arguments, and dismissed the unfair labor practice charge in its entirety. This appeal followed.

This Court reviews the record to determine whether the administrative action is supported by competent, substantial evidence. § 120.68, Fla. Stat. (2005); Laney v. Bd. of Pub. Instruction for Orange County, 153 Fla. 728, 15 So.2d 748, 753 (1943); Braddock v. Sch. Bd. of Nassau County, 455 So.2d 394, 396 (Fla. 1st DCA 1984). Review of an agency's statutory interpretation is de novo. See Sullivan v. Fla. Dep't of Envtl. Prot., 890 So.2d 417, 420 (Fla. 1st DCA 2004). However, administrative agencies are "afforded wide discretion in the interpretation of a statute which it is given the power and duty to administer." Republic Media, Inc. v. Dep't of Transp., 714 So.2d 1203, 1205 (Fla. 5th DCA 1998). As a result, "a reviewing court must defer to an agency's interpretation of an operable statute as long as that interpretation is consistent with legislative intent and is supported by substantial, competent evidence." Pub. Employees Relations Comm'n v. Dade County Police Benevolent Ass'n, 467 So.2d 987, 989 (Fla.1985). If the agency's interpretation is within the range of possible and reasonable interpretations, it is not clearly erroneous and should be affirmed. See Novick v. Dep't of Health, Bd. of Med., 816 So.2d 1237, 1240 (Fla. 5th DCA 2002); Republic Media, Inc., 714 So.2d at 1205.

The courts have recognized that PERC has developed special expertise in addressing labor issues and is uniquely qualified to interpret and apply the policies enunciated in chapter 447. See Laborers' Int'l Union of N. Am. v. Greater Orlando Aviation Auth., 869 So.2d 608, 610 (Fla. 5th DCA 2004); Sch. Bd. of Dade County v. Dade Teachers Ass'n, 421 So.2d 645, 647 (Fla. 3d DCA 1982). Thus, its decisions on this area of law are entitled to considerable deference by this Court. See Laborers' Int'l Union of N. Am.; Sch. Bd. of Dade County.

Ms. Cagle asserts that she presented a prima facie case to PERC, and that PERC erred in summarily dismissing the amended complaint. The School District disagrees, arguing that Ms. Cagle did not establish a prima facie violation of the unfair labor practices laws. As a result, the School District contends that PERC properly dismissed the amended charge.

In order to sustain an unfair labor practice charge, the law requires that the charge and supporting documents provide evidence to support a prima facie violation of the unfair labor practice alleged. § 447.503(1), Fla. Stat. (2004). As set forth in PERC's final order, the applicable standard is found in Pasco County School Board v. Florida Public Employees Relations Commission, 353 So.2d 108, 117 (Fla. 1st DCA 1977), in which the court held:

> In order to determine whether the evidence sustains a charge alleging an unfair labor practice, when it is grounded upon an asserted violation of protected activity, the following general principles should be considered by the hearing officer and by PERC:

> (1) In any such proceeding the burden is upon the claimant to present proof by a preponderance of the evidence that (a) his conduct was protected and (b) his conduct was a substantial or motivating factor in the decision taken against him by the employer.
>
> (2) If the hearing officer determines the decision of the employer was motivated by a non-permissible reason, the burden shifts to the employer to show by a preponderance of the evidence that notwithstanding the existence of factors relating to protected activity, it would have made the same decision affecting the employee anyway. In considering the employer's explanation, the examiner should attempt to strike an equitable balance between the rights of an employer whose duty, as here, is to promote the efficiency of public services through its public employees, and the rights of a nontenured public school teacher to be secure in his employment, free from discrimination due to his union activity.

(Footnotes omitted); see Gibbons v. State Pub. Employees Relations Comm'n, 702 So.2d 536, 537 (Fla. 2d DCA 1997). In its final order, PERC addressed each of Ms. Cagle's exceptions to the General Counsel's summary dismissal. PERC cogently articulated its reasoning and conclusions in support of dismissing Ms. Cagle's charges. The record supports PERC's conclusions. Ms. Cagle's allegations do not establish a prima facie case of retaliation.

Lastly, Ms. Cagle argues that PERC erred by summarily dismissing her claim without holding a hearing. She further alleges that the record shows that PERC did not provide her time to finish drafting her appeal before it was denied. We disagree. A claimant is only entitled to an evidentiary hearing when the claimant can show a nexus between the protected activity and the alleged adverse action. Gibbons, 702 So.2d at 537; Pasco County, 353 So.2d at 119. Here, there is competent, substantial evidence in the record to support PERC's finding that Ms. Cagle failed to show a sufficient nexus between the protected activity and the adverse action. Ms. Cagle did not meet her burden of showing that the School District's reasons for placing her on administrative leave were pretextual. In the absence of such evidence, Ms. Cagle did not demonstrate that her prior protected activity was a substantial or motivating factor in either the School District's decision to place her on administrative leave or to not renew her contract. As a result, Ms. Cagle was not entitled to an evidentiary hearing on her unfair labor practices claim.

For these reasons, we affirm PERC's final order.

AFFIRMED.

SAWAYA and TORPY, JJ., concur.

NOTES AND QUESTIONS

1. Does this Court treat PERC differently than the Donato Court treated the Human Rights Commission?

2. The Court tells us that:

   > Ms. Cagle appealed to PERC, amending her charge and alleging eleven incidents that constituted violations of section 447.501(1)(d). Because the appeal alleged additional facts and included supporting documents that were not previously considered, the appeal was remanded as an amended charge for the General Counsel to determine the sufficiency of Ms. Cagle's allegations. On remand, PERC's General Counsel determined that Ms. Cagle's amended charge failed to establish a prima facie violation of the unfair labor practice laws and summarily dismissed it...
   >
   > Ms. Cagle again appealed to PERC, alleging ten "exceptions" to the General Counsel's summary dismissal of the amended charge, which she claimed were sufficient to establish a prima facie violation of section 447.501(1)(d). Ms. Cagle objected to the conclusions of the General Counsel, and also included new factual allegations and supporting documents that had not previously been provided to the General Counsel.
   >
   > PERC subsequently issued a final order, affirming the General Counsel's summary dismissal of the amended charge. In its final order, PERC incorporated the additional evidence that Ms. Cagle provided in her exceptions, and found that this new allegation would have been dismissed by the General Counsel as untimely. Thereafter, incorporating the new allegation, PERC considered all of Ms. Cagle's arguments, and dismissed the unfair labor practice charge in its entirety. This appeal followed.

   After stating the law, the Court deferred to these findings and conclusions. As a reader of the case, is it possible to tell if she did or did not make out a prima facie case? Why does the Court not actually describe the evidence she put forward and tell us why exactly PERC found it insufficient to establish a prima facie case?